THE AMERICAN JOURNEY

United States History Through Letters and Diaries

THE AMERICAN JOURNEY

United States History Through Letters and Diaries

Volume I

Edited by

Marsha C. Markman   Jonathan Boe
and Susan Corey

California Lutheran University

BRANDYWINE PRESS • **St. James, New York**

ISBN: 1-881089-50-9

2nd Printing 1998

Telephone Orders: 1-800-345-1776

Printed in the United States of America

TABLE OF CONTENTS

PART 3
THE NEW NATION

PART 4
SLAVERY, CIVIL WAR, AND RECONSTRUCTION

PREFACE

"There is properly no history; only biography," wrote Ralph Waldo Emerson. *The American Journey: United States History Through Letters and Diaries* rests on this idea. Its focus on diaries and letters provides observations, experiences, and sentiments of both prominent and obscure men and women. Together they forge a collective testimony to the country's evolution, its diverse and multicultural society, and the issues that permeate and affect America today.

Diaries and letters are firsthand accounts in ways unequaled in autobiographies and interviews. Like the excerpts in this volume, they transport the reader to a moment in history through the immediate, eyewitness record of events and reflections. Those moments are benchmarks in American history, depicting the unfolding of both human experience and the experience of a nation.

Included in this volume are diaries and letters of the earliest colonial settlers; the Native Americans they encountered; slave traders, plantation owners, and slaves; indentured servants; military officers and footsoldiers; women on the home front; immigrants; and westward migrants. The accounts reveal much about the impact of war, racism, and the expansion and modernization of the country—subjects that traverse the generations.

EDITORIAL COMMENTS

We have endeavored to remain faithful to each of the diaries and letters excerpted here, in most cases adopting the editorial practices of our published sources. Aside from hash marks, which indicate omitted entries, major textual changes (usually to regularize spelling) are noted in the introductory remarks of relevant selections.

ACKNOWLEDGMENTS

The editors wish to acknowledge the William and Flora Hewlett Foundation for its grant support and California Lutheran University's Pearson Library for its invaluable assistance in obtaining materials for this publication.

Part 1

The Colonial Period

Permanent European colonization of what would become the thirteen original states began with the arrival of the English in Virginia in 1607. Two different types of colonial society soon developed: the Northern, most prominently in Massachusetts, and the Southern, with its most advanced form in Virginia.

The early settlers of Massachusetts arrived with a strong religious mission. The first selection in this anthology of letters and diaries illustrates the religious commitment of the Pilgrim founders of the small Plymouth colony in 1620; the second, the faith of John Winthrop, an organizer of the Puritan emigration to Massachusetts Bay in 1630. The Pilgrims were separatists, regarding themselves as entirely apart from the Church of England. The Puritans, on the other hand, saw themselves as the true members of the English Church, and desired to make Massachusetts, as Winthrop put it, a "Citty upon a Hill," a model for religious reform in England and eventually the world.The journal of Sarah Kemble Knight gives us a glimpse of Puritan society several generations after its founding, contrasting it with the more secular life developing elsewhere in America.

Though the hope of gain or, more modestly, the hope of survival was probably the main motive in the settlement of both Massachusetts and Virginia, the Northern colony had a religious leadership that gave her a character lacking to her Southern sister. While Virginia's early years were difficult, by the mid-seventeenth century an aristocracy had emerged whose wealth was based on a tobacco plantation economy. The diary of William Byrd gives an insight into the life and values of a prominent member of this aristocracy. John Harrower, however, was a member of a very different level of Virginia society from that of Byrd. Many thousands like Harrower were driven to America by economic desperation and arrived as indentured servants, bound to serve their purchaser for several years in order to earn their freedom.

Indentured servants like Harrower at least had a chance at success. The same was not true of the Africans brought to America as slaves. One of the consequences of a tobacco economy was a need for more labor than voluntary immigration could provide. As early as 1619 Virginians had purchased Africans from a Dutch ship that called at Jamestown. The diary of the slave ship *St. John* provides a glimpse of some of the horrors of the slave trade that provided Virginia's plantations with labor. The letters between Peter Stuyvesant and Dutch slave traders are a reminder that while slavery was strongest in the South, it was not unknown in the North.

1.
Mourt's Relation
The Landing at Plymouth, 1620–1621

On August 5, 1620, the Pilgrims set sail from England to the New World, benefactors of a commercial undertaking sponsored by London merchants. One of the two ships that landed at Plymouth in December of that year was the Mayflower. *"Mourt's Relation" is the earliest published account of that landing and the establishment of Plymouth Plantation. While the title and authors are largely a mystery, it is assumed that all were participants in the Plymouth enterprise, the principal contributors being William Bradford, second governor of Plymouth, and Edward Winslow, who sent the journal to England to George Morton for publication in 1622.*

These excerpts describe the landing of the Mayflower *at Plymouth, the search for a suitable place to settle, and the relationship between the Pilgrims and the Native Americans they encountered.*

December, 1620 On the 15th day we weighed anchor, to go to the place we had discovered and coming within two leagues of the land, we could not fetch the harbor but were fain to put room again towards Cape Cod, our course lying west, and the wind was at northwest. But it pleased

Dwight B. Heath, ed. *A Journal of the Pilgrims at Plymouth: Mourt's Relation, A Relation or Journal of the English Plantation Settled at Plymouth in New England, By Certain English Adventurers Both Merchants and Others.* Edited from the original printing of 1622.

God that the next day, being Saturday the 16th day, the wind came fair and we put to sea again, and came safely into a safe harbor. . . .

This harbor is a bay greater than Cape Cod, compassed with a goodly land, and in the bay, two fine islands uninhabited, wherein are nothing but wood, oaks, pines, walnuts, beech, sassafras, vines, and other trees which we know not. This bay is a most hopeful place, innumerable store of fowl, and excellent good, and cannot but be of fish in their seasons; skote [*skate*], cod, turbot, and herring, we have tasted of, abundance of mussels the greatest and best that ever we saw; crabs and lobsters, in their time infinite. . . .

Monday the 18th day,   we went a-land, manned with the master of the ship and three or four of the sailors. We marched along the coast in the woods some seven or eight miles, but saw not an Indian nor an Indian house; only we found where formerly had been some inhabitants and where they had planted their corn. We found not any navigable river, but four or five small running brooks of very sweet fresh water, that all run into the sea. . . . That night, many being weary with marching, we went aboard again.

The next morning, being **Tuesday the 19th of December,** we went again to discover further; some went on land, and some in the shallop. The land we found as the former day we did, and we found a creek, and went up three English miles. . . . This place we had a great liking to plant in, but that it was so far from our fishing, our principal profit, and so encompassed with woods that we should be in much danger of the savages, and our number being so little, and so much ground to clear, so as we thought good to quit and clear that place till we were of more strength. . . .

That night we returned again a-shipboard, with resolution the next morning to settle on some of those places; so in the morning, after we had called on God for direction, we came to this resolution: to go presently ashore again, and to take a better view of two places which we thought most fitting for us, for we could not now take time for further search or consideration, our victuals being much spent, especially our beer, and it being now the 19th of December. After our landing and viewing of the places, so well as we could we came to a conclusion, by most voices, to set on the mainland, on the first place, on a high ground, where there is a great deal of land cleared, and hath been planted with corn three or four years ago, and there is a very sweet brook runs under the hill side, and many delicate springs of as good water as can be drunk, and where we may harbor our shallops and boats exceeding well, and in this brook much good fish in their seasons. . . . What people inhabit here we yet know not, for as yet we have seen none. So there we made our rendezvous, and a place for some of our people, about twenty, resolving in the morning to come all ashore and to build houses.

But the next morning, being **Thursday the 21st of December,** it was stormy and wet, that we could not go ashore. . . .

An idealized view of the Pilgrims' landing at Plymouth. *(Library of Congress)*

Friday, the 22nd,   the storm still continued, that we could not get a-land. . . .

Saturday, the 23rd,   so many of us as could, went on shore, felled and carried timber, to provide themselves stuff for building.

Sunday, the 24th,   our people on shore heard a cry of some savages (as they thought) which caused an alarm, and to stand on their guard, expecting an assault, but all was quiet.

Monday, the 25th day,   we went on shore, some to fell timber, some to saw, some to rive, and some to carry, so no man rested all that day. But towards night some, as they were at work, heard a noise of some Indians, which caused us all to go to our muskets, but we heard no further. . . .

Thursday, the 28th of December,   so many as could went to work on the hill where we purposed to build our platform for our ordnance, and which doth command all the plain and the bay, and from whence we may see far into the sea, and might be easier impaled, having two rows of houses and a fair street. So in the afternoon we went to measure out the grounds, and first we took notice how many families there were, willing all single men that had no wives to join with some family, as they thought fit, that so we might build fewer houses, which was done, and we reduced them to nineteen families. To greater families we allotted larger plots, to every person half a pole in breadth, and three in length [*8¼ by 49½ feet*], and so lots were cast where every man should lie, which was done, and staked out. We thought this proportion was large enough at the first for houses and gardens . . . considering the weakness of our people, many of them growing ill with cold . . . the cause of many of their deaths.

/////

Thursday, the 4th of January,   Captain Miles Standish with four or five more, went to see if they could meet with any of the savages in that place where the fires were made. They went to some of their houses, but not lately inhabited, yet could they not meet with any. . . .

Tuesday, the 9th of January,   was a reasonable fair day, and we went to labor that day in the building of our town, in two rows of houses for more safety. We divided by lot the plot of ground whereon to build our town. After the proportion formerly alloted, we agreed that every man should build his own house, thinking by that course men would make more haste than working in common. . . .

Saturday, 20th,   we made up our shed for our common goods. . . .

Monday, the 22nd,   was a fair day. We wrought on our houses, and in the afternoon carried up our hogsheads of meal to our common storehouse. The rest of the week we followed our business likewise. . . .

Tuesday and Wednesday, 30th and 31st of January,   cold frosty weather and sleet, that we could not work. In the morning the master and others saw two savages that had been on the island near our ship. What they came for we could not tell; they were going so far back again before they were descried, that we could not speak with them.

Sunday, the 4th of February,   was very wet and rainy, with the greatest gusts of wind that ever we had since we came forth, that though we rid in a very good harbor, yet we were in danger, because our ship was light, the goods taken out, and she unballasted. . . .

Friday, the 9th,   still the cold weather continued, that we could do little work. That afternoon our little house for our sick people was set on fire by a spark that kindled in the roof, but no great harm was done. That evening the master going ashore, killed five geese, which he friendly distributed among the sick people. He found also a good deer killed; the savages had cut off the horns, and a wolf was eating of him. . . .

Friday, the 16th,   was a fair day, but the northerly wind continued, which continued the frost. . . . Captain Miles Standish and Francis Cook, being at work in the woods, coming home, left their tools behind them, but before they returned their tools were taken away by the savages. This coming of the savages gave us occasion to keep more strict watch. . . .

Saturday, the 17th day,   in the morning we called a meeting for the establishing of military orders among ourselves, and we chose Miles Standish our captain, and gave him authority of command in affairs. And as we were in consultation hereabouts, two savages presented themselves upon the top of a hill, over against our plantation, about a quarter of a mile and less, and made signs unto us to come unto them; we likewise made signs unto them to come to us, whereupon we armed ourselves, and stood ready, and sent two over the brook towards them, to wit, Captain Standish and Stephen Hopkins, who went towards them. Only one of them had a musket, which they laid down on the ground in their sight, in sign of peace, and to parley with them, but the savages would not tarry their coming. A noise of a great many more was heard behind the hill, but no more came in sight. This caused us to plant our ordnances in places most convenient. . . .

Friday, the 16th [*March*], a fair warm day towards; this morning we determined to conclude of the military orders, which we had begun to consider of before but were interrupted by the savages, as we mentioned formerly. And whilst we were busied hereabout, we were interrupted again, for there presented himself a savage [*Samoset*], which caused an alarm. He very boldly came all alone and along the houses straight to the rendezvous, where we intercepted him, not suffering him to go in, as undoubtedly he would, out of his boldness. He saluted us in English, and bade us welcome, for he had learned some broken English among the Englishmen that came to fish at Monchiggon, and knew by name the most of the captains, commanders, and masters that usually come. He was a man free in speech, so far as he could express his mind, and of a seemly carriage. We questioned him of many things; he was the first savage we could meet withal. He said he was not of these parts, but of Morattiggon, and one of the sagamores or lords thereof, and had been eight months in these parts, it lying hence of a day's sail with a great wind, and five days by land. He discoursed of the whole country, and of every province and of their sagamores, and their number of men, and strength. The wind beginning to rise a little, we cast a horseman's coat about him, for he was stark naked, only a leather about his waist, with a fringe about a span [*9 inches*] long, or little more; he had a bow and two arrows, the one headed, and the other unheaded. He was a tall straight man, the hair of his head black, long behind, only short before, none on his face at all; he asked some beer, but we gave him strong water [*liquor*] and biscuit, and butter, and cheese, and pudding, and a piece of mallard, all which he liked well, and had been acquainted with such amongst the English. He told us the place where we now live is called Patuxet and that about four years ago all the inhabitants died of an extraordinary plague, and there is neither man, woman, nor child remaining, as indeed we have found none, so as there is none to hinder our possession, or to lay claim unto it. All the afternoon we spent in communication with him; we would gladly have been rid of him at night, but he was not willing to go this night. . . . We lodged him that night at Stephen Hopkins' house, and watched him.

The next day he went away back to the Massasoits, from whence he said he came, who are our next bordering neighbors. They are sixty strong, as he saith. The Nausets are as near southeast of them, and are a hundred strong, and those were they of whom our people were encountered, as we before related. They are much incensed and provoked against the English, and about eight months ago slew three Englishmen, and two more hardly escaped by flight to Monchiggon. . . . These people are ill affected towards the English, by reason of one [*Thomas*] Hunt [*captain in Captain John Smith's company*], a master of a ship, who deceived the people, and got them under color of trucking [*trading*] with them, twenty out of this very place where we inhabit, and seven men from the Nausets, and carried them away, and sold them for slaves [*in Spain*] like a wretched man (for twenty pound a man) that cares not what mischief he doth for his profit.

Saturday,   in the morning we dismissed the savage, and gave him a knife, a bracelet, and a ring; he promised within a night or two to come again, and to bring with him some of the Massasoits, our neighbors, with such beavers' skins as they had to truck with us.

Saturday and Sunday,   reasonable fair days. On this day came again the savage, and brought with him five other tall proper men; they had every man a deer's skin on him, and the principal of them had a wild cat's skin, or such like on the one arm. They had most of them long hosen [*leggings*] up to their groins, close made; and above their groins to their waist another leather, they were altogether like the Irish-trousers. They are of complexion like our English gypsies, no hair or very little on their faces, on their heads long hair to their shoulders, only cut before, some trussed up before with a feather, broad-wise, like a fan, another a fox tail hanging out. These left (according to our charge given him before) their bows and arrows a quarter of a mile from our town. We gave them entertainment as we thought was fitting them; they did eat liberally of our English vituals. They made semblance unto us of friendship and amity; they sang and danced after their manner, like antics [*clowns*]. They brought with them in a thing like a bow-case (which the principal of them had about his waist) a little of their corn pounded to powder, which, put to a little water, they eat. He had a little tobacco in a bag, but none of them drank [*smoked*] but when he listed. Some of them had their faces painted black, from the forehead to the chin, four or five fingers broad; others after other fashions, as they liked. They brought three or four skins, but we would not truck with them at all that day, but wished them to bring more, and we would truck for all, which they promised within a night or two, and would leave these behind them, though we were not willing they should, and they brought us all our tools again which were taken in the woods, in our men's absence. . . .

Thursday, the 22nd of March,   was a very fair warm day. About noon we met again about our public business, but we had scarce been an hour together, but Samoset came again, and Squanto, the only native of Patuxet, where we now inhabit, who was one of the twenty captives that by Hunt were carried away [*kidnapped*] and had been in England, and dwelt in Cornhill with Master John Slanie, a merchant, and could speak a little English, with three others, and they brought with them some few skins to truck, and some red herrings newly taken and dried, but not salted, and signified unto us, that their great sagamore Massasoit was hard by, with Quadequina his brother, and all their men. They could not well express in English what they would, but after an hour the king came to the top of a hill over against us, and had in his train sixty men, that we could well be hold them and they us. . . . We sent to the king a pair of knives, and a copper chain with a jewel at it. To Quadequina we sent likewise a knife and a jewel to hang in his ear, and withal a pot of strong water, a good quantity of biscuit, and some butter, which were all willingly accepted.

Our messenger made a speech unto him, that King James saluted him with words of love and peace, and did accept of him as his friend and ally, and that our governor desired to see him and to truck with him, and to confirm a peace with him, as his next neighbor. He liked well of the speech and heard it attentively, though the interpreters did not well express it. . . . After salutations, our governor kissing [*the king's*] hand, the king kissed him, and so they sat down. The governor called for some strong water, and drunk to him, and he drunk a great draught that made him sweat all the while after; he called for a little fresh meat, which the king did eat willingly, and did give his followers. Then they treated of peace, which was:

1. That neither he nor any of his should injure or do hurt to any of our people.
2. And if any of his did hurt to any of our, he should send the offender, that we might punish him.
3. That if any of our tools were taken away when our people were at work, he should cause them to be restored, and if our did any harm to any of his, we would do the like to them.
4. If any did unjustly war against him, we would aid him; if any did war against us, he should aid us.
5. He should send to his neighbor confederates, to certify them of this, that they might not wrong us, but might be likewise comprised in the conditions of peace.
6. That when their men came to us, they should leave their bows and arrows behind them, as we should do our pieces when we came to them.

Lastly, that doing thus, King James would esteem of him as his friend and ally.

All which the king seemed to like well. . . .

So after all was done, the governor conducted him to the brook, and there they embraced each other and he departed. . . .

Questions for Discussion

1. What was the initial response of the Pilgrims and Native Americans to each other? Were those responses warranted? Does the Pilgrim treaty with the Native Americans seem fair to both sides?
2. What problems did the Pilgrims face in the New World? How do those problems differ from later migrations to "new worlds"?

2.
John Winthrop

A New England Governor's Diary, 1633–1648

John Winthrop was born in England and educated in the law at Cambridge. He sailed for New England in 1630, landed at Salem, Massachusetts, and made his home in what became the city of Boston. Winthrop was selected by London's Massachusetts Bay Company to govern its colony, and was subsequently elected to that office twelve times from 1630 to 1649. While Massachusetts prospered under his leadership, his Puritan ethic and strict religious governance left little room for the kind of democracy America was later to enjoy.

Winthrop's diaries are rich in graphic examples of life in colonial America: the smallpox epidemic that ravaged Native Americans and colonists; native enslavement; and rulings of the colony's Court of Assistants on a wide range of individual and social behavior, including the banishment of Anne Hutchinson for her religious dissent, and the death penalty for witchcraft and adultery. The following excerpts reflect those events.

Thousands Die from Smallpox

December 5 [*1633*]. John Sagamore died of the small pox, and almost all his people (above thirty buried by Mr. Maverick of Winesemett in one day). The towns in the bay took away many of the children; but most of them died soon after.

John Winthrop. *Winthrop's Journal, "History of New England," 1630–1649.* James Kendall Hosmer, ed. Volumes I and II. New York: Charles Scribner's Sons, 1908.

11

James Sagamore of Sagus died also, and most of his folks. . . . This infectious disease spread to Pascataquack, where all the Indians (except one or two) died. . . .

/////

20 [*January, 1634*].   Hall and the two others, who went to Connecticut November 3, came now home, having lost themselves and endured much misery. They informed us, that the small pox was gone as far as any Indian plantation was known to the west, and much people dead of it, by reason whereof they could have no trade.

At Naragansett, by the Indians' report, there died seven hundred; but, beyond Pascataquack, none to the eastward.

/////

30 [*January, 1634*].   John Seales, who ran from his master to the Indians, came home again. He was at a place twelve miles off, where were seven Indians, whereof four died of the pox while he was there.

February 1 [*1634*].   . . . Such of the Indians' children as were left were taken by the English, most whereof did die of the pox soon after, three only remaining. . . .

/////

War and Slavery: The Pequot Tribe

[*June 3, 1637*].   . . . Upon our governor's letter to Plymouth, our friends there agreed to send a pinnace, with forty men, to assist in the war against the Pequots. . . .

15 [*June, 1637*].   There was a day of thanksgiving kept in all the churches for the victory obtained against the Pequots, and for other mercies.

/////

Mo. 5 [*July, 1637*].   . . . Capt. Stoughton and his company, having pursued the Pequots beyond Connecticut, and missing of them, returned to Pequot River, where they were advertised, that one hundred of them were newly come back to a place some twelve miles off. So they marched thither by night, and surprised them all. They put to death twenty-two men, and reserved two sachems, hoping by them to get Sasacus (which they promised). All the rest were women and children, of whom they gave the Naragansetts thirty, and our Massachusetts Indians three, and the rest they sent hither.

A pinnace, returning, took a canoe with four Indians near Block Island. We sent to Miantunnomoh to know what they were, and after we discharged all save one, who was a Pequot, whom we gave Mr. Cutting to carry into England. . . .

6 [*July, 1637*].   There were sent to Boston forty-eight women and children. There were eighty taken, as before is expressed. These were disposed of to particular persons in the country. Some of them ran away and were brought again by the Indians our neighbors, and those we branded on the shoulder.

/////

The Case Against Mrs. Hutchinson[1]

9 (November) [*1637*].   . . . The court . . . sent for Mrs. Hutchinson and charged her with divers matters, as her keeping two public lectures every week in her house, whereto sixty or eighty persons did usually resort, and for reproaching most of the ministers (viz., all except Mr. Cotton) for not preaching a covenant of free grace, and that they had not the seal of the spirit, nor were able ministers of the New Testament; which were clearly proved against her, though she sought to shift it off. And, after many speeches to and fro, at last she was so full as she could not contain, but vented her revelations; amongst which this was one, that she had it revealed to her, that she should come into New England, and should here be persecuted, and that God would ruin us and our posterity, and the whole state, for the same. So the court proceeded and banished her; but because it was winter, they committed her to a private house, where she was well provided, and her own friends and the elders permitted to go to her, but none else. . . .

/////

[*January*] 16 [*1638*].   . . . Upon occasion of the censures of the court upon Mrs. Hutchinson and others, divers other foul errors were discovered, which had been secretly carried by way of inquiry, but after were maintained by Mrs. Hutchinson and others; and so many of Boston were tainted with them, as Mr. Cotton, finding how he had been abused. . . .

---

[1]Anne Hutchinson had done a number of things to offend the authorities. It was not considered proper for women to take a leading role in religious discussion. She charged that most ministers did not preach a sufficiently strict "covenant of free grace," i.e., the belief that God has decided who would be saved, and that individuals could not affect their salvation. Finally, she was suspected of antinomianism, the belief that an individual who was saved was freed from man-made laws and was directed instead by revelations from God.

Some of the secret opinions were these:—

That there is no inherent righteousness in a child of God.

That neither absolute nor conditional promises belong to a Christian.

That we are not bound to the law, not as a rule, etc.

That the Sabbath is but as other days.

That the soul is mortal, till it be united to Christ, and then it is annihilated, and the body also, and a new given by Christ.

That there is no resurrection of the body.

/////

[*March*] 22 [*1638*].   Mrs. Hutchinson appeared again. . . . She impudently persisted in her affirmation, to the astonishment of all the assembly. So that, after much time and many arguments had been spent to bring her to see her sin, but all in vain, the church, with one consent, cast her out. Some moved to have her admonished once more; but it being for manifest evil in matter of conversation, it was agreed otherwise. . . .

After she was excommunicated, her spirits, which seemed before to be somewhat dejected, revived again, and she gloried in her sufferings, saying, that it was the greatest happiness, next to Christ, that ever befel her. Indeed, it was a happy day to the churches of Christ here, and to many poor souls, who had been seduced by her, who, by what they heard and saw that day, were (through the grace of God) brought off quite from her errors, and settled again in the truth. . . .

/////

A Question of Fashion

25 [*September, 1638*].   . . . The court, taking into consideration the great disorder through the country in costliness of apparel, and following new fashions, sent for the elders of the churches, and conferred with them about it, and laid it upon them, as belonging to them, to redress it, by urging it upon the consciences of their people, which they promised to do. But little was done about it; for divers of the elders' wives, etc., were in some measure partners in this general disorder.

/////

A Law Abolishing Toasting One's Health

[*December 10, 1639*].   At the general court, an order was made to abolish that vain custom of drinking one to another, and that upon these and other grounds:

1. It was a thing of no good use.
2. It was an inducement to drunkenness, and occasion of quarrelling and bloodshed.
3. It occasioned much waste of wine and beer.
4. It was very troublesome to many, especially the masters and mistresses of the feast, who were forced thereby to drink more oft than they would, etc. Yet divers (even godly persons) were very loath to part with this idle ceremony, though (when disputation was tendered) they had no list, nor, indeed, could find any arguments, to maintain it. . . .

/////

Capital Punishment for Adultery

[*March 7, 1644*].   . . . At this court of assistants one James Britton, a man ill affected both to our church discipline and civil government, and one Mary Latham, a proper young woman about 18 years of age, whose father was a godly man and had brought her up well, were condemned to die for adultery, upon a law formerly made and published in print. It was thus occasioned and discovered. This woman, being rejected by a young man whom she had an affection unto, vowed she would marry the next that came to her, and accordingly, against her friends' minds, she matched with an ancient man who had neither honesty nor ability, and one whom she had no affection unto. Whereupon soon after she was married, divers young men solicited her chastity, and drawing her into bad company, and giving her wine and other gifts, easily prevailed with her, and among others this Britton. But God smiting him with a deadly palsy and fearful horror of conscience withal, he could not keep secret, but discovered this, and other the like with other women, and was forced to acknowledge the justice of God in that having often called others fools, etc., for confessing against themselves, he was now forced to do the like. The woman dwelt now in Plymouth patent, and one of the magistrates there, hearing she was detected, etc., sent her to us. Upon her examination, she confessed he did attempt the fact but did not commit it, and witness was produced that testified (which they both confessed) that in the evening of a day of humiliation through the country for England, etc., a company met at Britton's and there continued drinking sack, etc., till late in the night, and then Britton and the woman were seen upon the ground together, a little from the house. It was reported also that she did frequently abuse her husband, setting a knife to his breast and threatening to kill him, calling him old rogue and cuckold, and said she would make him wear horns as big as a bull. And yet some of the magistrates thought the evidence not sufficient against her, because there were not two direct witnesses; but the jury cast her, and then she confessed the fact, and accused twelve others, whereof two were married men. Five of these were apprehended and committed, (the rest were gone,) but denying it, and there being no other witness against them than the testimony of a condemned person, there could be no proceeding against them. The woman proved very penitent, and had deep apprehension of the foulness of her sin, and at length attained to hope of pardon by the blood of Christ, and was willing to die in satisfaction to justice. The man also was very much cast down for his sins, but was loth to die, and petitioned the general court for his life, but they would not grant it, though some of the magistrates spake much for it, and questioned the letter, whether adultery was death by God's law now. This Britton had been a professor in England, but coming hither he opposed our church government, etc., and grew dissolute, losing both power and profession of godliness.

[*March 21, 1644*].   They were both executed, they both died very penitently, especially the woman, who had some comfortable hope of pardon of her sin, and gave good exhortation to all young maids to be obedient to their parents, and to take heed of evil company. . . .

/////

The Death Penalty for Witchcraft

4 [*June 1648*].   At this court one Margaret Jones of Charlestown was indicted and found guilty of witchcraft, and hanged for it. The evidence against her was, 1. that she was found to have such a malignant touch, as many persons (men, women, and children) whom she stroked or touched with any affection or displeasure, or, etc., were taken with deafness, or vomiting, or other violent pains and sickness, 2. she practising physic, and her medicines being such things as (by her own confession) were harmless, as aniseed, liquors, etc., yet had extraordinary violent effects, 3. she would use to tell such as would not make use of her physic, that they would never be healed, and accordingly their diseases and hurts continued, with relapse against the ordinary course, and beyond the apprehension of all physicians and surgeons, 4. some things which she foretold came to pass accordingly; other things she could tell of (as secret speeches, etc.) which she had no ordinary means to come to the knowledge of, 5. she had (upon search) an apparent teat in her secret parts as fresh as if it had been newly sucked, and after it had been scanned, upon a forced search, that was withered, and another began on the opposite side, 6. in the prison, in the clear day-light, there was seen in her arms, she sitting on the floor, and her clothes up, etc., a little child, which ran from her into another room, and the officer follow-

John Winthrop. *(New York Public Library)*

ing it, it was vanished. The like child was seen in two other places, to which she had relation; and one maid that saw it, fell sick upon it, and was cured by the said Margaret, who used means to be employed to that end. Her behavior at her trial was very intemperate, lying notoriously, and railing upon the jury and witnesses, etc., and in the like distemper she died. The same day and hour she was executed, there was a very great tempest at Connecticut, which blew down many trees, etc. . . .

Questions for Discussion

1. What do the laws of the Massachusetts Bay Colony suggest about Winthrop, along with the conduct and values of these early settlers?
2. What does Winthrop's diary suggest about the relationship between the Puritans and the Native Americans?
3. What is your view of the evidence used in the witch trials?

3.
Sarah Kemble Knight
A Colonial Woman's Journey, 1704–1705

Sarah Kemble Knight was born in Boston in 1666, married Richard Knight, and had one daughter before she was widowed. Her home in Boston appears to have contained a shop and also served as a boarding house which earned a modest income from several rentors.

The diary excerpts that follow describe her five-month journey from Boston, Massachusetts to New Haven, Connecticut (traveling briefly to New York) to conduct family business. They include a depiction of the people she encountered and reveal a woman of wit and humor who ventured into what was a man's world.

MONDAY, OCTB'r Ye SECOND, 1704. About three o'clock afternoon, I begun my Journey from Boston to New-Haven; being about two Hundred Mile. My Kinsman, Capt. Robert Luist, waited on me as farr as Dedham, where I was to meet ye Western post.

I vissitted the Reverd. Mr. Belcher, ye Minister of ye town, and tarried there till evening, in hopes ye post would come along. But he not coming, I resolved to go to Billingses where he used to lodg, being 12 miles further. But being ignorant of the way, Madm Billings, seing no persuasions of her good spouses or hers could prevail with me to Lodg there that night, Very kindly went wyth me to ye Tavern, where I hoped to get my guide, And desired the Hostess to inquire of her guests whether any of them would go

Sarah Kemble Knight. *The Journal of Madam Knight.* Boston: David R. Godine, 1972.

with mee. But they being tyed by the Lipps to a pewter engine, scarcely allowed themselves time to say what clownish . . . [*the next half page of the manuscript is missing*].

. . . to my no small surprise, son John arrose, and gravely demanded what I would give him to go with me? Give you, sais I, are you John? Yes, says he, for want of a Better; And behold! this John look's as old as my Host, and perhaps had bin a man in the last Century. Well, Mr. John, sais I, make your demands. Why, half a pss. of eight and a dram, sais John. I agreed and gave him a Dram (now) in hand to bind the bargain. . . .

. . . My Guide dismounted [*in Billinges*] and very Compasantly help't me down and shewd the door, signing to me wth his hand to Go in; wch I Gladly did—But had not gone many steps into the Room, ere I was Interogated by a young Lady I understood afterwards was the Eldest daughter of the family, with these, or words to this purpose, (viz.) Law for mee—what in the world brings You here at this time a night?—I never see a woman on the Rode so Dreadfull late, in all the days versall life. Who are You? Where are You going? I'm scar'd out of my witts—with much now of the same Kind. I stood aghast, Prepareing to reply, when in comes my Guide—to him Madam turn'd, Roreing out: Lawfull heart, John, is it You?—how de do! Where in the world are you going with this woman? Who is she? John made no Ansr. but sat down in the corner . . . she then turned agen to mee and fell anew into her silly questions, without asking me to sit down.

I told her shee treated me very Rudely, and I did not think it my duty to answer her unmannerly Questions. But to get ridd of them, I told her I come there to have the post's company with me to-morrow on my Journey &c. Miss star'd awhile, drew a chair, bid me sitt. . . . I paid honest John wth money and dram according to contract, and Dismist him, and pray'd Miss to shew me where I must Lodg. Shee conducted me to a parlour in a little back Lento, wch was almost fill'd wth the bedsted, wch was so high that I was forced to climb on a chair to gitt up to ye wretched bed that lay on it; on wch having Stretcht my tired Limbs, and lay'd my head on a Sadcolourd pillow, I began to think on the transactions of ye past day.

TUESDAY, OCTOBER Ye THIRD   . . . About Three afternoon went on with my Third Guide, who Rode very hard; and having crossed Providence Ferry, we come to a River wch they Generally Ride thro'. But I dare not venture; so the Post got a Ladd and Cannoo to carry me to tother side, and hee rid thro' and Led my hors. The Cannoo was very small and shallow, so that when we were in she seem'd redy to take in water, which greatly terrified mee, and caused me to be very circumspect, sitting with my hands fast on each side, my eyes stedy, not daring so much as to lodg my tongue a hair's breadth more on one side of my mouth then tother, nor so much as think on Lott's wife, for a wry thought would have oversett our wherey: But was soon put out of this pain, by feeling the Cannoo on shore. . . . Rewarding my sculler, [*we*] again mounted and made the best of our way forwards.

. . . wee rode on Very deliberatly . . . when we entered a Thickett of Trees and Shrubbs, and I perceived by the Hors's going, we were on the descent of a Hill, wch, as wee come neerer the bottom, 'twas totaly dark wth the Trees that surrounded it. But I knew by the Going of the Hors wee had entered the water, wch my Guide told mee was the Hazzardos River he had told me off; and hee, Riding up close to my Side, Bid me not fear—we should be over Imediatly. I now ralyed all the Courage I was mistriss of, Knowing that I must either Venture my fate of drowning, or be left like ye Children in the wood. So, as the Post bid me, I gave Reins to my Nagg; and sitting as Stedy as Just before in the Cannoo, in a few minutes got safe to the other side, which hee told mee was the Narragansett country.

. . . I was very civilly Received, and courteously entertained, in a clean comfortable House. . . .

WEDNESDAY, OCTOBr 4TH.   About four in the morning, we set out for Kingston (for so was the Town called) with a french Docter in our company. Hee and ye Post put on very furiously, so that I could not keep up with them, only as now and then they'd stop till they see mee. This Rode was poorly furnished wth accommodations for Travellers, so that we were forced to ride 22 miles by the post's account, but neerer thirty by mine, before we could bait so much as our Horses. . . .

FRIDAY, OCTOBr 6th.   I got up very early, in Order to hire somebody to go with mee to New Haven, being in Great parplexity at the thoughts of proceeding alone; which my most hospitable entertainer observing, himselfe went, and soon return'd wth a young Gentleman of the town, who he could confide in to Go with mee; and about eight this morning wth Mr. Joshua Wheeler my new Guide, takeing leave of this worthy Gentleman, Wee advanced on towards Seabrook. The Rodes all along this way are very bad, Incumbred wth Rocks and mountainos passages, wch were very disagreeable to my tired carcass; but we went on with a moderate pace wch made ye Journy more pleasent. . . .

SATURDAY, OCT. 7th.   . . . about two a clock afternoon we arrived at New Haven, where I was received with all Possible Respects and vivility. Here I discharged Mr. Wheeler with a reward to his satisfaction, and took some time to rest after so long and toilsome a Journey. . . .

They [*the people of New Haven*] are Govern'd by the same Laws as wee in Boston, (or little differing,) thr'out this whole Colony of Connecticot, And much the same way of Church Government, and many of them good, Sociable people, and I hope Religious too: but a little too much Independant in their principalls, and, as I have been told, were formerly in their Zeal very Riggid in their Administrations towards such as their Lawes made Offenders, even to a harmless Kiss or Innocent merriment among Young people. Whipping being a frequent and counted an easy Punishment, about wch as other Crimes, the Judges were absolute in their Sentances. . . .

Their Diversions in this part of the Country are on Lecture days and Training days mostly: on the former there is Riding from town to town.

And on training dayes The Youth divert themselves by Shooting at the Target, as they call it, (but it very much resembles a pillory,) where hee that hitts neerest the white has some yards of Red Ribbin presented him, wch being tied to his hattband, the two ends streeming down his back, he is Led away in Triumph, wth great applause, as the winners of the Olympiack Games. They generally marry very young: the males oftener as I am told under twentie than above; they generally make public wedings. . . . Just before Joyning hands, the Bridegroom quitts the place, who is soon followed by the Bridesmen, and as it were, dragg'd back to duty—being the reverse to ye former practice among us, to steal ms Pride. . . .

There are every where in the Towns as I passed, a Number of Indians the Natives of the Country, and are the most salvage of all the salvages of that kind that I had ever Seen: little or no care taken (as I heard upon enquire) to make them otherwise. They have in some places Landes of their owne, and Govern'd by Law's of their own making; they marry many wives and at pleasure put them away, and on the ye least dislike or fickle humour, on either side, saying *stand away* to one another is a sufficient Divorce. And indeed those uncomely *Stand aways* are too much in Vougue among the English in this (Indulgent Colony) as their Records plentifully prove, and that on very trivial matters, of which some have been told me, but are not proper to be Related by a Female pen, tho some of that foolish sex have had too large a share in the story. . . .

Their Cheif Red Letter day is St. Election, wch is annualy Observed according to Charter, to choose their Govenr: a blessing they can never be thankfull enough for, as they will find, if ever it be their hard fortune to loos it. The present Govenor in Conecticott is the Honble John Winthrop Esq. A Gentleman of an Ancient and Honourable Family, whose Father was Govenor here sometimes before, and his Grand father had bin Govr of the Massachusetts. This gentleman is a very curteous and afable person, much Given to Hospitality, and has by his Good services Gain'd the affections of the people as much as any who had bin before him in that post.

DECr 6TH.   . . . . Dec. 6th we set out from New Haven. . . .

The Cittie of New York is a pleasant, well compacted place, situated on a Commodius River wch is a fine harbour for shipping. The Buildings Brick Generaly, very stately and high, though not altogether like ours in Boston.

The Bricks in some of the Houses are of divers Coullers and laid in Checkers, being glazed look very agreeable. The inside of them are neat to admiration. . . .

They are Generaly of the Church of England and have a New England Gentleman for their minister, and a very fine church set out with all Customary requisites. There are also a Dutch and Divers Conventicles as they call them, viz. Baptist, Quakers, &c. They are not strict in keeping the Sabbath as in Boston and other places where I had bin, But seem to deal with great exactness as farr as I see or Deall with. They are sociable to one another and Curteos and Civill to strangers and fare well in their houses. The English go very fashionable in their dress. But the Dutch, especially the middling sort, differ from our women, in their habitt go loose, wear French muches wch are like a Capp and a head band in one, leaving their ears bare, which are sett out wth Jewells of a large size and many in number. And their fingers hoop't with Rings, some with large stones in them of many Coullers as were their pendants in their ears, which You should see very old women wear as well as Young. . . .

Having here transacted the affair I went upon and some other that fell in the way, after about a fortnight's stay there I left New-York with no Little regrett, and Thursday, Dec. 21, set out for New Haven wth my Kinsman Trowbridge. . . .

/////

JANUARY 6th [*1705*]. Being now well Recruited and fitt for business I discoursed the persons I was concerned with, that we might finnish in order to my return to Boston. . . . I stayed a day here Longer than I intended by the Commands of the Honble Govenor Winthrop to stay and take a supper with him whose wonderful civility I may not omitt. . . . the next day being March 3d we got safe home to Boston, where I found my aged and tender mother and my Dear and only Child in good health with open arms redy to receive me, and my Kind relations and friends flocking in to welcome mee and hear the story of my transactions and travails I having this day bin five months from home and now I cannot fully express my Joy and Satisfaction. But desire sincearly to adore my Great Benefactor for thus graciously carying forth and returning in safety his unworthy handmaid.

Questions for Discussion

1. What do we learn about colonial society from this diary?
2. How might you characterize Sarah Kemble Knight within this society?

4.
William Byrd
Diary of a Virginia Planter and Politician, 1709–1712

William Byrd was born in Virginia in 1674 of a wealthy and influential family and educated from the age of seven in England, where he would later occasionally serve the colony's interests. He inherited his father's fortune and in 1726 settled in Virginia and made his Westover plantation a permanent home. Ultimately, he expanded his properties to include numerous plantations and thousands of acres of land, principally in Richmond, a city he had founded. Byrd was an honored member of the Council of State in Virginia, and in the last year of his life its president.

These diary excerpts, covering the years 1709 to 1712, provide a picture of a witty, intellectual, philandering plantation owner, as well as a public servant and member of colonial Virginia society.

April 19, 1709   I rose at 5 o'clock and read in Homer and a chapter in Hebrew. I said my prayers and ate rice milk for breakfast. . . . In the afternoon I played at piquet with Mr. W-l-s. We dined very late and I ate nothing but fowl and bacon. When that was over we went to Mr. David Bray's where we danced till midnight. I had Mrs. Mary Thomson for my partner. I recommended myself to the divine protection. I had good thoughts, good health, and good humor, thanks to God Almighty. . . .

Louis B. Wright and Marion Tinling, eds. *The Great American Gentleman; William Byrd of Westover in Virginia: His Secret Diary for the Years 1709–1712*. New York: G.P. Putnam's Sons, 1963. Reprinted by permission.

/////

June 14, 1709 . . . We heard guns this morning, by which we understood that the fleet was come in and I learned the same from Mr. Anderson. I ate bacon and chicken for dinner. I began to have the piles. I read some Greek in Homer. I heard guns from Swinyard's and sent my boat for my letters. In the meanwhile I walked about the plantation. In the evening the boat returned and brought some letters for me from England, with an invoice of things sent for by my wife which are enough to make a man mad. It put me out of humor very much. . . .

/////

June 16, 1709 . . . Mr. Bland's boy brought me abundance of letters from Williamsburg, out of the men-of-war. I spent all the morning in reading them. My orders for being of the Council arrived among the rest. By these letters I learned that tobacco was good for nothing, that protested bills would ruin the country, that our trade with the Carolina Indians was adjusted in England, that my sister Braynes was in prison by the cruelty of C-r-l-y, that my salary was in a fair way of being increased, that the College was like to be rebuilt by the Queen's bounty, that there was a probability of peace next winter. . . .

/////

June 27, 1709 . . . I made an invoice of the things that my wife could spare to be sold. I settled the accounts of protested bills. I ate mutton for dinner. My wife was in tears about her cargo but I gave her some comfort after dinner. . . . Tom was whipped for not telling me that he was sick.

/////

September 3, 1709 . . . I said my prayers and ate chocolate with Mr. Taylor for breakfast. Then he went away. I read some geometry. We had no court this day. My wife was indisposed again but not to much purpose. I ate roast chicken for dinner. In the afternoon I beat Jenny [*a slave*] for throwing water on the couch. I took a walk to Mr. Harrison's who told me he heard the peace was concluded in the last month. After I had been courteously entertained with wine and cake I returned home, where I found all well, thank God. . . .

/////

September 12, 1709 . . . I went to Mr. President's where I found several of the Council. The President persuaded me to be sworn, which I agreed to, and accordingly went to Council where I was sworn a member of the Council. God grant I may distinguish myself with honor and good

William Byrd. *(Library of Congress)*

conscience. We dined together and I ate beef for dinner. In the evening we went to the President's where I drank too much French wine and played at cards and I lost 20 shillings. I went home about 12 o'clock at night. . . .

/////

October 15, 1709   I rose at 3 o'clock and recommended my family to the divine protection. Then I was set over the creek and proceeded towards Williamsburg by moonshine. I got as far as C-ler before the rising of the sun and to Williamsburg by 10 o'clock. I waited on the President and found five of the Council there. A letter came from Colonel Parke that informed us that he had like to have been assassinated by a negro hired for that purpose who shot at him and broke his arm. I was sworn a judge of the General Court and took my place on the bench. . . .

October 16, 1709   . . . I went to the President's and waited on him to church where we heard Mr. Gray preach, who did not attack his sermon well. It rained much in the night and good part of the day. I dined with the President and ate roast chicken for dinner and then ran through the rain home. . . .

/////

October 23, 1709   . . . I went in the evening to Colonel Bray's where we found abundance of company and agreed to meet there the next day and have a dance. About 10 o'clock I came home and neglected to say my prayers and for that reason was guilty of uncleanness. I had bad thoughts, good health and good humor, thanks be to God Almighty.

/////

November 2, 1709   . . . In the evening I went to Dr. [*Barret's*] where my wife came this afternoon. Here I found Mrs. Chiswell, my sister Custis, and other ladies. We sat and talked till about 11 o'clock and then retired to our chambers. I played at [*r-m*] with Mrs. Chiswell and kissed her on the bed till she was angry and my wife also was uneasy about it, and cried as soon as the company was gone. I neglected to say my prayers, which I should not have done, because I ought to beg pardon for the lust I had for another man's wife. However I had good health, good thoughts, and good humor, thanks be to God Almighty.

/////

November 6, 1709   . . . About 11 o'clock we rode to the church of Abingdon Parish which is the best church I have seen in the country. We heard a sermon of Parson Smith. After church we returned to Mr. Burwell's and Mr. Berkeley and his wife with us. We dined late and I ate boiled beef and pudding. In the evening we sat and talked till 10 o'clock and I told abundance of lies by way of diversion. . . .

/////

December 24, 1709   . . . I rose about 8 o'clock and read in my commonplace and said my prayers. I cast water over a negro maid that was passing under the window. I ate custard for breakfast. Then we took a walk about the pasture and about 11 o'clock went to dinner. . . .

/////

January 1, 1710   . . . In the afternoon we took a walk about the plantation. The weather was very warm. In the evening we drank a bottle of wine and were merry. I said my prayers and had good health, good thoughts, and good humor, thanks be to God Almighty. I gave my wife a flourish this morning.

/////

January 3, 1710   I gave my wife a flourish and then rose at 7 o'clock. . . . News was brought that the distemper was at Captain Stith's where he had ten negroes sick of it. God of his excessive goodness deliver from it! Mr. Mumford and I played at billiards till dinner after we had settled our accounts. My wife was very sick. I ate hashed turkey. My son began to breed teeth which disordered him. In the afternoon Mr. Mumford went away and I took a walk about the plantation and when I came home

I gave vomit to six of my people by way of prevention. God send it may succeed. . . .

/////

April 18, 1710   . . . I went to the capitol about 8 o'clock and settled my accounts till 9. Then I went to the President's where I found several of the Council and about 10 we went to Council where among other things we directed the negroes to be arraigned for high treason. . . .

/////

April 21, 1710   . . . About 8 o'clock I went to see the President and then went to court. I settled some accounts first. Two of the negroes were tried and convicted for treason. . . . About 3 o'clock I returned to my chambers again and found above a girl who I persuaded to go with me into my chambers but she would not. . . . I went to the President's where we were merry till 11 o'clock. Then I stole away. I said a short prayer but notwithstanding committed uncleanness in bed. I had good health, bad thoughts, and good humor, thanks be to God Almighty.

/////

June 1, 1710   . . . In the evening I took a walk and met the new negroes which Mr. Bland had bought for me to the number of 26 for £23 apiece. . . .

June 2, 1710   . . . Robin Hix asked me to pay £70 for two negroes which he intended to buy of John [*Evans*] which I agreed to in hope of gaining the trade. I neglected to say my prayers but was griped in my belly and had indifferent bad humor.

June 3, 1710   I rose at 6 o'clock and as soon as I came out news was brought that the child was very ill. We went out and found him just ready to die and he died about 8 o'clock in the morning. God gives and God takes away; blessed be the name of God. Mrs. Harrison and Mr. Anderson and his wife and some other company came to see us in our affliction. My wife was much afflicted but I submitted to His judgment better, notwithstanding I was very sensible of my loss, but God's will be done. . . . My poor wife and I walked in the garden. . . .

/////

June 6, 1710   I rose at 6 o'clock and read two chapters in Hebrew and no Greek because we prepared to receive company for the funeral. I said my prayers and ate cake and water gruel for breakfast. . . . About 2 o'clock we went with the corpse to the churchyard and as soon as the service was begun it rained very hard so that we were forced to leave the parson and go into the church porch but Mr. Anderson stayed till the service was finished. . . . Mr. Custis and I took a walk about the plantation. Two of the new negroes were taken sick and I gave each of them a vomit which worked well. . . .

/////

July 8, 1710 . . . Two negroes of mine brought five of the cows that strayed away from hence and told me all was well above, but that Joe Wilkinson was very often absent from his business. It rained all the afternoon, that I could not walk. The negro woman was found and tied but ran away again in the night. . . .

/////

August 5, 1710 . . . Dr. Bowman came to tell me that my negro boy which he had was too big for him to manage, and therefore desired me to send for him, which I did. . . .

/////

November 13, 1710 . . . Colonel Digges sent for a white negro for us to see who except the color was featured like other negroes. She told us that in her country, which is called Aboh near Calabr, there were many whites as well as blacks. We played at dice till about 12 o'clock and then we [*went*] to Williamsburg. . . . I had a letter from home which told me all was well except a negro woman who ran away and was found dead. . . .

/////

February 6, 1711 . . . I went to the President's where I drank tea and went with him to the Governor's and found him at home. . . . About 7 o'clock the company went in coaches from the Governor's house to the capitol where the Governor opened the ball with a French dance with my wife. . . . The President had the worst clothes of anybody there.

/////

February 25, 1711 . . . In the afternoon I took a walk about the plantation and met negro P-t-s-n who had been off the plantation and brought some bacon with him, for which I threatened to whip him. Then I found also that John was riding out with the stallion without leave, for which I threatened him likewise. Then I returned home and read some English and then walked out with my wife. . . .

/////

March 4, 1711 . . . Little Peter came from above and brought news another negro died, which makes 17 this winter; God's will be done. Several others are sick. The Lord have mercy on them, and spare them if it be His will. . . .

A Southern plantation. *(Metropolitan Museum of Art)*

/////

April 15, 1711 . . . I had a letter from the Falls which told me another negro was like to die. God preserve her and all the rest. I ate some bacon and eggs for dinner. . . .

/////

August 15, 1711 . . . In the afternoon I received a letter from the Governor with orders to exercise all the milita under my command because we were threatened with an invasion, there being 14 French men-of-war designed for these parts. I immediately [*sent*] to Colonel Eppes to get the militia of this county together and sent orders to Colonel Frank Eppes to do the same in Henrico County. In the evening I wrote a letter to the Governor, to make my excuses for not going to council tomorrow. . . .

/////

October 11, 1711 About 10 o'clock came Captain H-n-t to buy planks and soon after him came Captain Drury Stith and after him Captain John Eppes, Captain Sam Harwood and Captain Hamlin. I persuaded them to stay and dine before we went to the martial court and fined as many people as came to 4500 pounds of tobacco. We made an order that the fines returned by each captain should go towards his trophies. Mr. Bland called on his way to Williamsburg. In the evening I took a walk and beat Jenny for being unmannerly. At night I read some latin in Terence. . . .

/////

February 5, 1712   I rose about 8 o'clock, my wife kept me so long in bed where I rogered her. I read nothing because I put my matters in order. I neglected to say my prayers but ate boiled milk for breakfast. My wife caused several of the people to be whipped for their laziness. . . . In the afternoon I ordered my sloop to go to Colonel Eppes' for some poplar trees for the Governor. . . .

February 7, 1712   . . . Tom returned about 11 o'clock and brought me several letters by which I learned that the Indians continued still their hostilities in Carolina. . . .

/////

February 14, 1712   . . . I gave directions about everything and promised Tom Addison I would take him for my overseer next year for two of my plantations there. About 10 o'clock I got a man to show me the way across the country to the falls of James River. . . . I got to my plantation called Shockoe about 12 o'clock, where I found all well, thank God. I went to my two other plantations on that side and found all things well, only little tobacco made. About 6 o'clock I returned to Shockoe and ate some boiled beef for supper. . . . I had not seen this place since the house was built and hardly knew it again. It was very pretty. . . .

/////

May 22, 1712   . . . My wife caused Prue to be whipped violently notwithstanding I desired not, which provoked me to have Anaka whipped likewise who had deserved it much more, on which my wife flew into such a passion that she hoped she would be revenged of me. I was moved very much at this but only thanked her for the present lest I should say things foolish in my passion. I wrote more accounts to go to England. My wife was sorry for what she had said and came to ask my pardon and I forgave her in my heart but seemed to resent, that she might be the more sorry for her folly. She ate no dinner nor appeared the whole day. . . . I said my prayers and was reconciled to my wife and gave her a flourish in token of it. I had good health, good thoughts, but was a little out of humor, for which God forgive me.

May 23, 1712   My wife and I were very good friends again. . . .

/////

June 23, 1712   . . . I wrote several notes wherein I promised to give £5 for each of my negroes run away. . . .

/////

September 18, 1712 . . . My man John was incommoded still with the piles. Mr. Catesby and I took a walk and I found Eugene asleep instead of being at work for which I beat him severely. . . . In the afternoon came Sam Good and bought two negroes of me for £60 towards paying for the land which I had of him. . . .

/////

September 29, 1712 . . . I said my prayers and ate boiled milk for breakfast. I danced my dance. . . . The weather was cold, the wind northeast. My wife was pretty well. About 11 o'clock I was a little fevered and my head ached a little; however I would not give way to it. I had not much stomach to dinner; however I ate some broiled beef. In the afternoon I put several things in order in the library. . . . I said my prayers and had good health, good thoughts, and good humor, thank God Almighty.

Questions for Discussion

1. What does Byrd's diary tell us about the kind of man he was and the life of this Southern politician and plantation owner?
2. How might you compare Byrd's life and attitudes with those of John Winthrop?

5.
John Harrower
Diary and Letters of an Indentured Servant, 1774–1776

Indentured servitude was a common way of getting to America in the colonial period. In exchange for passage to the colonies, the indentured servant agreed to work for a purchaser for a set period, usually from four to seven years. The word "indentured," like the common word "indent," is related to dent for "tooth," and refers to the toothlike effect of an indented surface. The contract between employer and indentured servant would be torn in two, one piece going to each party. Matching the torn edges at the appropriate time would demonstrate that the two holders of the paper were parties to the same contract.

John Harrower was from the Shetland Islands off Scotland. Forced to leave home to seek work, he made his way first to London and in desperation finally boarded ship for Virginia, arriving just in time to witness the beginnings of the American Revolution. As a literate man he had a more privileged position in the colonies than most of his fellow indentured servants, but in other ways his experience reflects that of many immigrants to America.

[*Tuesday, January*] 18th [*1774*].   This day I got to London and was like a blind man without a guide, not knowing where to go and being friendless and having no more money but fifteen shillings and eight pence farthing a small sum to enter London with; But I trust in the mercys of God who is

---

For more information on Harrower, see Thomas Dublin, ed. *Immigrant Voices: New Lives in America, 1773–1986*. Urbana: University of Illinois Press, 1993.

a rich provider and am hopefull before it is done some way will cast up for me. I took up my lodging at the old ship Tavern in little Hermitage street, Mr. George Newton being the landlord, but in Prison for debt at present.

/////

Thursday, 20th.   This morning breakfast at home and paid 6d. for it. At noon called at the Jamaica Coffee House and soon after seed Capt. Perry [*an acquaintance Harrower hoped could find him work*] and waited here and Change [*exchange time, when merchants gathered*] until 3 pm but no appearance of any Business for me. the time I was in the Coffee house I drank 3 ds. worth of punch, and I was obliged to make it serve me for Dinner. at night I hade 1/2d. worth of bread and 1 d. of Cheese and a poynt of Porter for supper it being all I cou'd afford.

/////

Munday, 24th.   This morning I wrote six tickets to give to shipmasters at Change seeking a steward's birth onbd. some ship, but could not get a birth. I also wrote a petition to any Mercht. or Tradesman setting forth my present situation, and the way in which I hade been brought up and where I hade served and in what station, at same time offering to serve any for the bare support of life fore some time. But all to no effect, for all places here at present are intierly carried by freinds and intrest, And many Hundreds are sterving for want of employment, and many good people are begging.

/////

Wednesday, 26th.   This day I being reduced to the last shilling I hade was obliged to engage to go to Virginia for four years as a schoolmaster for Bedd, Board, washing and five pounds during the whole time. I have also wrote my wife this day a particular Accot. of every thing that has happened to me since I left her untill this date; At 3 pm this day I went on board the *Snow Planter* Capt. Bowers Comr. for Virginia now lying at Ratcliff Cross, and imediatly as I came Onbd. I recd. my Hammock and Bedding. at 4 pm came Alexr. Steuart onbd. the same ship. he was Simbisters Servt. and had only left Zetland [*the Shetland Islands*] about three weeks before me. we were a good deall surprised to meet with one another in this place.

/////

Sunday, [*February*] 6th.   At 7 AM got underway with a fair wind and clear wr. and at 11 AM came to an anchor off Gravesend and immediately the Mercht. came onboard and a Doctor and a clerk with him and while the Clerk was filling up the Indentures the doctor search'd every serv't. to see that they were sound when . . . seventy five were Intend to Capt. Bowres for four years.[1]

/////

Sunday, 13th.   . . . At noon the Indented servants was like to mutiny against the Capt. for putting them to Allowance of bread and Mate [*meat*], but it was soon quelled, our Mace [*mess*] not joining with the rest. in the afternoon he went ashore, But before he left the Ship he called me and begged I wou'd stand by the Mate if there arose any disturbance among the rest of the servants.

/////

Saturday, 26th.   . . . at 10 AM the Capt. went ashore to get more fresh provisions, at 4 pm he came onbd. from Portsmouth with Bread, Beiff Pork and Water and then immediately got under sale and stood out to sea [*the ship had been delayed by unfavorable winds*]. At this time we hade three men sick onbd. one with the flux, one with the fever and Ego [*Ague*], and one frost bitt on his feet . . .

/////

Freiday, March 11th.   . . . The wind blowing excessive hard and a verry high sea running still from the westward. at 8 pm was obliged to batten down both fore and main hatches, and a little after I really think there was the odest shene [*scene*] betwixt decks that I ever heard or seed. There was some sleeping, some spewing . . . some daming, some Blasting their leggs and thighs, some their liver, lungs, lights and eyes, And for to make the shene the odder, some curs'd Father, Mother, Sister, and Brother.

/////

Tuesday, [*May*] 10th.   At 2 AM weigh'd and stood up with the tide, came to anchor at 6 AM and lay untill Do. 8 when we weigh'd with a fair wind and got to our Moorings at 6 pm at the Toun of Frederisckburgh.

Wednesday, 11th.   At 10 AM Both Coopers and the Barber from our Mace went ashore upon tryall. At night one Daniel Turner a servt. returned onbd. from Liberty so drunk that he abused the Capt. and chief Mate and Boatswan to a verry high degree, which made to be horsewhipt. put in Irons and thumb screwed on houre afterward he was unthumbscrewed, taken out of the Irons, but then he was hand cuffed, and gagged all night.

---

[1]This was the procedure by which servants became officially indentured. The sick were taken ashore.

/////

Monday, 16th. This day severall came onbd. to purchase servts. Indentures and among them there was two Soul drivers. they are men who make it their business to go onbd. all ships who have in either Servants or Convicts and buy sometimes the whole and sometimes a parcell of them as they can agree, and then they drive them through the Country like a parcell of Sheep untill they can sell them to advantage, but all went away without buying any.

/////

Monday, 23rd. This morning a great number of Gentlemen and Ladies driving into Town it being an annuall Fair day and tomorrow the day of the horse races . . . at the same time all the rest of the servants were ordered ashore to a tent at Fredericksbg. and severall of their Indentures were then sold. at about 4 pm I was brought to Colonel Dangerfield, when we imediatly agreed and my Indenture for four years was then delivered him and he was to send for me the next day. at the same time ordred to get all my dirty Cloaths of every kind washed at his expense in Toun; at night he sent me five shillings onbd. by Capt. Bowers to keep my pocket.

Thursday, 24th. This morning I left the Ship at 6 AM having been sixteen weeks and six days on board her. I hade for Breackfast after I came ashore one Chappin [*about one quart*] sweet milk for which I paid 3 1/2 Cury. . . .

/////

Tuesday 14th. . . . This day I wrote my wife a particular Accot. of all my transactions since I wrote her from London 26th Jany. last, the Coppy of which I have by me [*the letter was inserted later in the diary*].

Belvidera 14th June 1774

My Dearest Life,

I wrote you from London on Wednesday 26th Jany. last which Im hopefull came safe to hand, and found you and my dear Infants in perfect health. . . . I have a Journal of every days transactions and remarcable Occurrances since the morning I left you which will be amusing to you when please God we are spared to meet, for I design to see and prepare a way for you all in this Country how soon I am able.— I shall now aquant you with my situation in this Country. I am now settled with on Colonel Wm. Dangerfield Esqr. of Belvidera, on the banks of the Rappahanock about 160 miles from the Capes or sea mouth, and seven Miles below the town of Fredericksburgh. My business is to teach his Children to read write and figure. . . . I am also obliged to talk english the best I can, for Lady Dangerfield speacks nothing but high english, and the Colonel hade his Education in England, and is a verry smart Man. As to my agreement it is as follows Vizt. I am obliged to continue with Coll. Dangerfield for four years if he insists on it, and for teaching his own children I have Bed, Board, washing and all kinds of Cloaths during the above time, and for what Schoolars I can get more than his Children I have five shillings currency per Quarter for each of them, which is equal to four shillings sterling, and I expect ten or twelve to school next week. . . .

As to my living I eat at their own table, and our witualls are all Dressed in the English taste. wee have for Breackfast either Coffie or Jaculare [*chocolate*], and warm Loaf bread of the best floor, we have also at table warm loaf bread of Indian corn, which is extreamly good but we use the floor bread always at breackfast. for Dinner smoack'd bacon or what we cal pork ham is a standing dish either warm or cold. when warm we have greens with it, and when cold we have sparrow grass. we have also either warm roast pigg, Lamb, Ducks, or chickens, green pease or anything else they fancy. As for Tea there is none drunk by any in this Govenment since 1st June last, nor will they buy a 2ds worth of any kind of east India goods, which is owing to the difference at present betwixt the Parliment of great Britton and the North Americans about laying a tax on the tea; and I'm afraid if the Parliment do not give it over it will cause a total revolt. . . .

. . . I thank God I want for nothing that is necessary, But it brings tears from my eyes to think of you and my infants when at the same it is not in my power at present to help you. But how soon I am able you may depend upon it. . . .

/////

Belvidera 6 Dec. 1774.

My Dearest Life,

Since my aravil here I wrote you 14. June and 7. Aug. last to both which I shall partly refer you. I now rite you with a shaking hand and a feeling heart to enqair of your and my D. Infants welfare, this being the return of the day of the year on which I was obliged to leave you and my D. Infants early in the morning which day will be ever remembred by me with tears untill it shall please God to grant us all a happy meeting again. I trust in the mercies of a good God this will find you and my D. Infants in perfect health as I am and have been ever since I came here, for neither the heat in summer nor what I have as yet felt of the cold in winter gives me the least uneasiness I thank God for it. . . . I wrote you in my first letter, that I was designed Please God to prepare a way for you and my Infants in this Country. . . . But this you are not to attemp untill I have your thoughts upon it and I send you a recomendation to a Merch. in Glasgow and cash

A British satire of American women protesting the tax on tea. *(Library of Congress)*

to bear your expences. I have as yet only ten scollars One of which is both Deaff and Dumb and his Father pays me ten shilling per Quarter for him he has been now five M. with [*me*] and I have brought him tolerably well and understands it so far, that he can write mostly for anything he wants and understands the value of every figure and can work single addition a little. he is about fourteen years of age. . . .

The Col. Children comes on pretty well. the Eldest is now reading verry distinctly in the Psalter according to the Church of England and the other two boys ready to enter into it; the Col. and his Lady being extreamly well satisfied w. my Conduct in every respect. . . .

You no doubt have heard of the present disturb. Betwixt Great Britain and the Collonys in N. America, Owing to severall Acts of Parliment latly made greatly infringing the rights and Liberties of the Americans, and in order to enforce these Acts, The Harbour and Toun of Boston are at present blockt up by a fleet and armie under the Command of Gen. Gage. The

Americans are determined to Act with Caution and prudence in this affair, and at same time are resolved not to lose an inch of their rights or liberties, nor to submit to these Acts. And in order to enforce a repeal of them, A Generall Congress was held at Philadelphia . . . And it is resolved that they will allow no goods to be imported into America from Great Britain, Ireland, or any of the Islands thereto belong. . . . Nor will they export from America to Great Britain or Ireland or any of the Islands thereto belonging any goods after the 1. Dec. 1775 during which time any that are indebted to Great Britain may pay up their ballances. Ma[n]y and pretty are the resolves of August Assembly, but room wou'd fail me here to insert them. By the Congress the Bostonians are desired not to leave the Toun nor to give any offence to Gen. Gage or the troops under his Command, But if he or they offers to commit the least Hostielyties in order to enforce any to the Obedience of these Acts, they are to repel force by force and the Bostonians can raise in their Collony in 24 Hours warning ods of 60 M [*60,000*] men well disiplined and all readdy provided w. arms and amunition. And the resolves of the Congress every one of the above Collonys and each man in every Collony are determined to abide by. And it is my oppinion that the laboring part and poor of Boston are as well supplied at present by controbutions sent free to them from the other Collonys as when their trade was oppen. M. Daingerfield this year for his own hand gives them fifty Bushels of wheat and One Hundred Bushels of Indian Corn, By which ye may Judge of the rest. . . .

. . . Pray my Dearest let me know what my D. Boys and Girle are doing. I hope Jock and George are still at school and I begg of you to strain every nerve to keep them at it untill I am able to assist you, for he who has got education will always gain Bread and to spare, and that in a genteel way in some place or other of the World. I supose Betts is at home with yourself, but pray keep her tight to her seam and stockin and any other Housold affairs that her years are capable of and do not bring her up to Idleness or play or going about from house to house which is the first inlet in any of the sex to laziness and vice. Send me an Acco. of their Ages from the Bible which ye may do verry short by saying Jo: Born _____ day Nov. 1762 Geo: Born &.

I yet hope please God, if I am spared, some time to make you a Virginian Lady among the woods of America which is by far more pleasent than the roaring of the raging seas round abo't Zetland, And yet to make you eat more wheat Bread in your old age than what you have done in your Youth. But this I must do by carefullness, industry and a Close Application to Business, which ye may take notice of in this letter I am doing Sunday as well as Saturday nor will I slip an honest method nor an hour whereby I can gain a penny for yours and my own advantage. . . .

/////

Munday, 28th. Coppy of my 4th Letter wrote this day to my wife.

My Dearest Life

Your most agreeable favours I rec. 27. May last, which was dated 1. March, And you may belive me it gave me the greatest satisfaction I have hade for twelve months past to hear from your own hand that you my Dearest Jewell and my sweet Infants are and has been in a good state of health since I left you, As I still am and has been for the above time. . . .

. . . As to M. Forbes pray make my Compt. to him and spouse and tell him from me that I make no doubt from the information I have of his making good bread in this Country for that a Journaman Bricklayer here has no less than five shillings a day Currancy which is equall to four Shillings St. . . . And I am aquanted with an Undertaker in that branch of business who is now set down on good Estate and rides in his Chair every day. But if he was to come over he must resolve to give closs application to business and keep from drinking. About 7 months ago a Gentleman in Fredericksb. hade his two sons taken from the high school there and put under my care for which he pays me £5 a year. He is an English man himself and his Lady from Edinburgh, and I have the pleasure to have given the parents such satisfaction that I hade sent me in a present two silk vestcoats and two pair of britches ready to put on for changes in summer. . . . I wou'd have you at all events Make your Brother apply for your Passage with the Children and a servant and imediatly dispose of every article in the house your Feather Bedds Bedding and Cloaths excepted, and if any money to spare lay it out in Linen; and write me imediatly on your Aravell here by post and I shou'd soon be with you. May God grant that such a cast may happen to you . . . my blesing to you my sweet life and my Dear Infants is all at present from, My Dearest Jewell, your ever affectionate Husband while—Signed J.H.

/////

My Dearest Life, Yours of the 12. May last I received 2 Ins. immediatly after sending off one for you and one for your Aff. brother dated 28. last M. Both which will come to your hand I imagine at the same time that this will as I am obliged to send this to New York by post in order to come to London by the Pacquet, There being no more Opportunities from this Collony to Glasgow this season, by reason that the Nonimportation and Non-exportation Acts of the Continental Congress now takes place and will continue untill the disputes betwixt Great Britain and the Colonys be settled. . . . As my principal Design of writing you this so soon after my last is to make you as easy as possible I can, both with respect to my not sending for you and making you a remittance. As to the first of these I cou'd not be certain if you wou'd come to this Country or not untill I rec. your last letter. But as I find by it you are satisfied to come here, you may believe me nothing in this world can give me equall satisfaction to my having you and my D. Infants with me. As a proof of which I have ever signified the same in my letters to your brother. An I now declare unto you as I sinceerly write from my heart before God, that I will how soon I am able point out the way to you how you may get here, and at same time make you what remittance I can in order to Assist you on your way. But you must consider this as I hade not a shilling in my pocket when I left you It must take me some time befor I can be able to make you a remittance. Therefore I even pray you for Gods sake to have patience and keep up your heart and no means let that fail you: For be asured the time is not Longer to you than me, And the National disputes and the stopage of trade betwixt this and the Mother Country if not soon settled will of course make the time longer as your bro. will inform you. As to your Jocks [*jokes*] upon me with respect to my getting a Virginian Lady it is the least in all my thoughts and am determined to leave that Jobb for you by aiding your sons with your advice to them in their choise of wifes among the Virginian Ladys: For I am resolved (as at first) to do as much for you as God is pleased to put in my power. . . .

[John Harrower died in 1777 before he could bring his family to Virginia.]

Questions for Discussion

1. Why did Harrower come to America? What did he think of his new country?
2. What is Harrower's opinion of the beginnings of the American Revolution?

6.

Diary of the Slave Ship *St. John*, 1659

These diary excerpts about the slave ship St. John *provide a graphic description of the marketing of slaves by Dutch traders through Curacao in the Virgin Islands and then to auction in Virginia. Covering the period from March to November 1659, the diarist describes the voyage to purchase slaves, the unsuccessful attempts to obtain food, and the many lives lost. Crowded into the hold of a ship unworthy of an ocean voyage, and without adequate food or water, the slaves were extremely vulnerable to illness. Indeed, the loss of life took fifty-six percent of the slaves during this voyage, as an accounting of deaths indicates. (The material presented here was written by the ship's captain or a crew member.)*

1659 Mar. 17 Arrived at *Rio Reael*, in front of a village called *Bany* where we found the Company's Yacht, named the *Peace*, which was sent out to assist us to trade for Slaves.

April Nothing was done except to trade for Slaves.

/////

May 22 Again weighed Anchor and ran out of *Rio Reael* accompanied by the Yacht *Peace*; purchased there *two hundred and nineteen* head of Slaves, men, women, boys and girls, and proceeded on our course for the

Edmond Bailey O'Callaghan, ed. *Voyages of the Slavers St. John and Arms of Amsterdam, 1659, 1663: With Additional Papers Illustrative of the Slave Trade Under the Dutch*. Albany: J. Munsell, 1867.

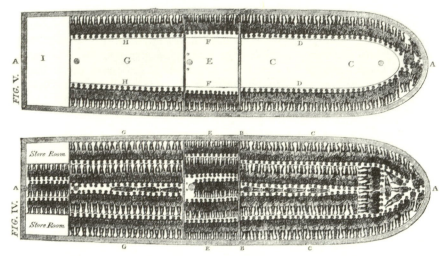

Architect's drawing of a slave ship. *(Peabody Museum of Salem)*

High land of *Ambosius*, for the purpose of procuring food there for the Slaves, as nothing was to be had at *Rio Reael*.

May 26   Arrived under the High land of *Ambosius* to look there for Victuals for the Slaves, and spent *seven* days there, but with difficulty obtained enough for the daily consumption of the Slaves, so that we resolved to run to *Rio Commerones* to see if any food could be had there for the Slaves.

June 5   Thursday, Arrived at the *Rio Commerones* and the Yacht *Peace* went up to look for provisions for the Slaves. . . .

June 29   Sunday. Again resolved to proceed on our Voyage, as but little food was to be had for the Slaves in consequence of the great Rains which fell every day, and because many of the Slaves were suffering from the Bloody Flux in consequence of the bad provisions we were supplied with at *El Mina,* amongst which were several barrels of Groats, wholly unfit for use.

We then turned over to *Adriaen Blaes*, the Skipper, *One hundred* and *five* Women, *six* boys and *three* girls for which Bills of lading were signed and sent, one by the Yacht *Peace* to *El Mina* with an account of, and receipts for, remaining Merchandize.

/////

Nov. 2   Lost our ship on the Rifts of *Rocus*, and all hands immediately took to the Boat, as there was no prospect of saving the Slaves, for we must abandon the Ship in consequence of the heavy Surf.

Nov. 4   Arrived with the Boat at the Island of *Curacao*; the Honble Governor *Beck* ordered two sloops to take the Slaves off the wreck, one of which sloops with *eighty four* slaves on board, was captured by a Privateer.

LIST OF THE SLAVES
Who died on board the Ship *St. John* from
30th June to 29th October in the Year 1659.

1659	Men	Women	Children
June 30	3	2	
July 1	2	1	
3		1	
5		2	1
6		1	
7	1		
8	2	1	
9	2		
10		2	
12		1	
13	2		1
14	1		
16	3	2	
17	2		
18	3	1	
19	1	3	
20	1		
21	1	1	
23		2	
24	1	1	
25	2	1	
26	1		
28	3		
29		2	
Aug. 2	2		
3	1		
6	1		
8	2		1
9		1	
11		1	
16	1 man leaped overboard		
18	1		
20		1	
22		1	
23		1	
24	1		
29	1		
31	1	1	
Sept. 3		1	
6	2		
7	1		
8	1	1	
13	1	1	
14	2	2	1
16	1		
19	1		

(continued)

1659		Men	Women	Children
	23		2	
	24	1	3	
	26		1	
Oct.	1	2		
	3	1	1	
	4		1	
	10	1	2	
	12	1		
	13	1		
	19		1	
	23	1		
	29	1		
		59	47	4

Emaciated slaves on the deck of a slave ship. (Harpers Weekly. *May 20, 1860)*

On the *first* of November, two hours before day, have we lost the Ship *St. John,* upon the Reef of *Rocus* and fled with the Boat to the Island of *Curacao*, and left in the Ship *eighty five* Slaves, including Men, Women, Boys and Girls, and arrived on the *fourth* of this instance at *Curacao*.

Questions for Discussion

1. What is the diarist's attitude toward the slaves? How does the diary reflect that attitude?
2. Are there details about the slave trade that were new to you?

7.
Peter Stuyvesant and Dutch Slave Traders

Letters Concerning the Slave Trade, 1653–1664

While not alone in the marketing of slaves, the Dutch were leaders in slave trading from Africa to America. These letters written by traders and Peter Stuyvesant, Director General of New Nether-land (now New York), capture the business of slavery and the traders' indifference to its inhumanity.

[This letter notes the contract with Holland in slave trading.]

Directors at Amsterdam to Director Stuyvesant

We have by contract given and granted to some private Merchants permission empowering them to repair to the Coast of Africa to trade for Slaves there, and to carry and convey them to the West Indies and the Islands situate thereabout, and as we expect that the aforesaid Ships or some of them will go to New Netherland to sell their Slaves also to the Inhabitants there, in such case we desire and request that Your Honor will not demand any duties from them, but lend them all reasonable Assistance, in order to the removal of every obstacle which might prove a hinderance to Agriculture. This for your information and notification.

Amsterdam, this 6th June, 1653.

Edmond Bailey O'Callaghan, ed. *Voyages of the Slavers St. John and Arms of Amsterdam, 1659, 1663: With Additional Papers Illustrative of the Slave Trade Under the Dutch.* Albany: J. Munsell, 1867.

Peter Stuyvesant.
*(New-York Historical
Society, New York City)*

*[This letter to the Directors of the West India Company reports
the loss of the* St. John *and progress made in the slave trade.]*

Vice Director Beck to the Directors of the West India Company
Curacao, 4th Feb., 1660.

Noble, Honorable, Respected, Wise, Prudent and most Discreet Gentlemen.

My last to your honors, dated 5. January, as per copy enclosed, was
by the Ship *Gideon,* Skipper Simon Cornelissen by way of the Caribbean
Islands. . . .

You will learn from my last letters, and from the annexed papers sent
again herewith, the fate of the Ship *St. John* which was due here from
Guinea with Negroes, and which according to your Honors' orders was to
replace the Ship *Diemen* here. What causes us most grief here is, that your
Honors have thereby lost such a fine lot of Negroes and such a fast sailing
Bark which has been our right arm here.

Although I have strained every nerve to overtake the Robbers of the
Negroes and Bark, as stated in my last, yet have I not been as successful as
I wished. I shall communicate the particulars to your Honors, God willing,
by the Ship *St. George,* which is about to sail direct from hence this month.
If no remedy can be found to prevent such Robberies, and villainous crimes
as the carrying away of the Company's Slaves and Bark, and no prosecution

and redress follow, they will not only persist therein, but even strike terror into the Spanish merchants who come here to trade. . . .

I have witnessed with pleasure your Honors' diligence in providing us here from time to time with Negroes. . . . The more . . . quietly the trade to and on this Island can be carried on, the better will it be for this place and yours. . . . [*An apparent reference to limiting competition from Spain.*]

. . . What with the Cape Verde Negroes, and those of the Company, I have collected together with great trouble Sixty two head. As there were among them some old and some young, *two* were deducted for them, as appears by the original Receipt transmitted herewith. They have accordingly paid me here for *Forty-six* head, as per contract, @ *One hundred* and *twenty* pieces of Eight, amounting to *Five thousand, five hundred and twenty* pieces of Eight, leaving *Fourteen* head of Negroes, for which the aforesaid Messrs. Hctor Pietersen and Guillaume Momma are to pay your Honors in Holland, as is more full set forth in the receipt. . . .

[In the following letter, Peter Stuyvesant receives slaves and discusses the cost.]

Director Stuyvesant to Vice Director Beck
17 February 1660

Four Negro Boys and *one* Negro Girl have, as you advised, been sent to, and received by me [*from*] the ship *Sphera Mundi*; 3 on mine and 2 on Commissary Van Brugge's account, their price being left to our discretion. Upon this subject I must say, that the assignment sent to me by Frans Bruyn is unsigned. However, in order to avoid any difficulty, I left this time the choice to the Commissary who took the Negro Girl and one of the stoutest Boys. But greater difficulties have arisen in this wise: One of the *Five* died on the passage hither; some were sick or have become so after arriving. To prevent any misunderstanding in future, the sold Negroes ought to be consigned to the purchaser by their names or marks. . . .

. . . I am willing to take my share of the expense and risk of their passage hither, because I desired the Negroes for my own service and the promotion of Agriculture, not in the expectation of any gain, and therefore sent for young ones, in which regard the worthy Inhabitants, Christians, and those of the Honble. Company, ought, I think, to be preferred before Spaniards and unbelieving Jews.

You will see by the enclosed extracts from my letter covering yours to the Honble Directors, what I have proposed to them. It is therefore desirable and somewhat necessary that a fixed price should be set on Horses conveyed hither, or ordered from Curacao, by private persons, as well as on Negroes as far as practicable, according to their ability and age, because the one as well as the other are most urgently required here for purposes of Agriculture and its advancement, and finally would tend to the greater advantage trade and prosperity of the Honble. Company and its subjects.

In regard to the Negroes which the Honble Directors ordered to be sent hither, they ought to be stout and strong fellows, fit for immediate employment on this Fortress and other works; also, if required, in war against the Wild Barbarians, either to pursue them when retreating, or else to carry some of the Soldiers' baggage; it being very apparent that we shall be constrained to wage a righteous and offensive War against them, for the peaceable possession once of the Land, and the avenging of numerous suffered affronts and murders. An important service would be conferred on the Company, on us and the Country if there were among the sold Negroes, some of experience who had resided a certain time in Curacao.

[In this letter to Vice Director Beck, Stuyvesant responds to the receipt and sale of the slaves and recommends identifying marks to distinguish their slaves from those of other companies.]

Director Stuyvesant to Vice Director Beck

Honorable, Wise, Prudent, right
   Discreet Sir.

Your welcome Letter of the 31st of August of last Year, was handed to us in due course by the Bearer, in which is first mentioned the unfortunate loss for the Company on the Horses sent hither in the Ship *Eyckenboom* and Galiot *New Amstel*. You[r] Honor will learn from the annexed return of the public sale, what they brought here in consequence of their emaciated appearance after having been refreshed during two or three months.

We have had better luck with the few Slaves sent hither at the same time. They were sold to the highest bidder, chiefly at Beaver's value, which differs little from Silver pay. I have retained some of the best for the Company. One with another they brought about fl.440 [*$176*] a head, less the freight.

On this point, we must not neglect to recommend ... that ... the Negroes sent for account of the Company, or Individuals, may be distinguished the one from the other by some particular marks or tokens, either by a stripe on the clothing or otherwise, in order to prevent disputes and differences here, which we might easily have had here with the Owners of the Ship *Indian* if any had fallen sick or died on the passage, since they claimed to be entitled to the first choice, leaving the rest for the Company. This choice I also have allowed them, as there were no certain marks to guide us. . . .

Amsterdam in New Netherland,
16th April, 1661.

[The following letter from Beck to Stuyvesant notes an error in the selling of slave children who, having received baptism, should not have been sold.]

Vice Director Beck to Peter Stuyvesant
Curacao, in Fort Amsterdam the
15 Novembr., Ano 1664.

Sir,

I have remarked among other things in your Honor's acceptable Letter, the serious mistake that has been committed here in the sale of your Slaves; expecially of the little Children, since with great forethought on the part of Madam Stuyvesant, your Honor's spouse, they were presented at the baptismal Font. If we had had the least knowledge of the Fact, the mistake would not have occurred. To my grief, a great error has been committed which I fear is irreparable: for so long an interval has elapsed, it will be very difficult to ascertain where they have been finally landed. But I shall have inquiries made by the first Ship that leaves here for Carthagena and Porto Bello, and if it be possible, endeavor to get them back, even if I should have to give two full grown Slaves and more for them.

Questions for Discussion

1. In what ways is language in these letters reflective of a mentality guided by the details of business and law? What inferences can be drawn from this usage?
2. What do these letters reveal about the slave trade that is new to you?

Part 2

Era of the American Revolution

Beginning in the 1760s Great Britain attempted to exert more control over her American colonies, including the imposition of taxes. Many Americans, perceiving a threat to the liberties they had long enjoyed, organized in strenuous opposition. Fighting began in 1775 and skirmishes continued until 1783, when the Treaty of Paris recognized American independence.

Among the events preparing the way for the Revolution was the Great Awakening, a religious revival that swept the colonies in the 1730s and 1740s. At the time of the Revolution, its effects were still strong. The Awakening emphasized in highly emotional terms the terrors of hell but also the possibility of salvation, and appealed to many for whom established religion had grown stale and formal. Others, however, regarded the Awakening as a dangerous outbreak of mass hysteria. The result was a split in many religious denominations and a decline in the position of the clergy, some of whom were abruptly dismissed by their congregations when they failed to provide the intensity of religious feeling their parishioners craved. In the 1760s and 1770s, those who had challenged religious authority would not find it difficult to challenge political authority as well. Excerpts from Jonathan Edward's letters and John Cleaveland's diary illustrate the religious intensity and divisiveness of the time.

Soldiers who fought in the Revolution experienced great hardships. Many would serve for a while, return home, and perhaps come back to fight again. Jeremiah Greenman, however, was a common soldier who stayed throughout the war. The selections from his diary describe the hardships of some of his campaigns.

Civilians, too, suffered during the war. The diary of the patriot Grace Barclay tells of depredations at the hands of the British, while that of Catherine Van Cortlandt describes the harassment experienced by loyalists. The loyalists are often neglected in accounts of the Revolution, but it is likely that half a million Americans, or nearly twenty percent of the population, remained faithful to Great Britain. By the end of the war as many as eighty thousands had left or been driven out of the colonies.

Despite the assertion in the Declaration of Independence that "all men are created equal," the Revolution in the short run led to few substantive changes in American society. But the ideas that inspired the Revolution strongly influenced the nation's history. The exchange of letters between Abigail and John Adams illustrates the potential for social change inherent in the ideas of the era.

8.
Jonathan Edwards
Letter on the Great Awakening, 1735

The Great Awakening began in 1734 with a series of sermons by Jonathan Edwards in Northhampton, Massachusetts, and spread among the New England Congregationalists and the middle-colony and southern Presbyterians. Edwards' revival sermons were intended, in part, as a doctrinal correction to Arminianism, the belief that good works and a free spirit were sufficient for salvation.

Edwards was important in these revivals not only as a revival preacher, but as a historian and theologian, documenting, defending, promoting, but also criticizing the revivals. His first reports of the revival in the Connecticut River Valley during 1734 and 1735 were in this letter to the Rev. Dr. Benjamin Colman, pastor of the Brattle Street Church in Boston.

Northhampton, May 30, 1735

Dear Sir:

In answer to your desire, I here send you a particular account of the present extraordinary circumstances of this town, and the neighboring towns with respect to religion. I have observed that the town for this several years have [*sic*] gradually been reforming; there has appeared less and less of a party spirit, and contentious disposition, which before had prevailed for many years between two parties in the town. . . . The winter before last

---

Jonathan Edwards. "Unpublished Letter of May 30, 1735." *The Works of Jonathan Edwards*. Vol. 4, *The Great Awakening*. C. C. Goen, ed. (New Haven: Yale University Press, 1972), 99–109.

their appeared a strange flexibleness in the young people of the town, and an unusual disposition to hearken to counsel, on this occasion. It had been their manner of a long time, and for aught I know, always, to make Sabbath-day nights and lecture days to be especially times of diversion and company-keeping. I then preached a sermon on the Sabbath before the lecture, to show them the unsuitableness and inconvenience of the practice, and to persuade them to reform it; and urged it on the heads of families that it should be a thing agreed among them to govern their families, and keep them in at those times. . . .

But the parents found little or no occasion for the exercise of government in the case; for the young people declared themselves convinced by what they had heard, and willing of themselves to comply with the counsel given them. . . .

After this there began to be a remarkable religious concern among some farm houses at a place called Pascommuck, and five or six that I hoped were savingly wrought upon there. And in April [1734] there was a very sudden and awful death of a young man in town, in the very bloom of his youth, who was violently seized with the pleurisy and taken immediately out of his head, and died in two days; which affected many young people in the town. This was followed with another death of a young married woman, who was in great distress in the beginning of her illness, but was hopefully converted before her death; so that she died full of comfort . . . which I believe much contributed to the solemnizing of the spirits of the young people in the town; and there began evidently to appear more of a religious concern upon people's minds. In the fall of the year I moved to the young people that they should set up religious meetings, on evenings after lectures, which they complied with. . . . About that time began the great noise that there was in this part of the country about Arminianism, which seemed strangely to be overruled for the promoting of religion. People seemed to be put by it upon inquiring, with concern and engagedness of mind, what was the way of salvation, and what were the terms of our acceptance with God. . . .

And then a concern about the great things of religion began, about the latter end of December and the beginning of January [1735], to prevail abundantly in the town, till in a very little time it became universal throughout the town, among old and young, and from the highest to the lowest. All seemed to be seized with a deep concern about their eternal salvation; all the talk in all companies, and upon occasions was upon the things of religion, and no other talk was anywhere relished; and scarcely a single person in the whole town was left unconcerned about the great things of the eternal world . . . no one family that I know of, and scarcely a person, has been exempt. And the spirit of God went on in his saving influences, to the appearance of all human reason and charity, in a truly wonderful and

Jonathan Edwards. *(Special Collections, Columbia University)*

astonishing manner. The news of it filled the neighboring towns with talk, and there were many in them that scoffed and made a ridicule of the religion that appeared in Northampton. But it was . . . very frequent and common that those of other towns that came into this town, and observed how it was here, were greatly affected, and went home with wounded spirits, and were never more able to shake off the impression that it made upon them, till at length there began to appear a general concern in several of the towns in the county.

In the month of March the people in New Hadley seemed to be seized with a deep concern about their salvation, all as it were at once, which has continued in a very great degree ever since. About the same time there began to appear the like concern in the west part of Suffield, which has since spread into all parts of the town. It next began to appear at Sunderland, and soon became universal, and to a very great degree. . . . About three weeks ago the town of Enfield were struck down as it were at once, the worst persons in the town seemed to be suddenly seized with a great degree of concern about their souls, as I have been informed. . . . Mr. Noyes writes me word that there is a considerable revival of religion at New haven. . . . I yesterday saw Mr. White of Bolton, and also last night saw a young man that belongs to [*the church at*] Coventry, who gave a very remarkable account of that town, of the manner in which the rude debauched young people there were suddenly seized with a concern about their souls.

As to the nature of persons' experiences, and the influences of that spirit that there is amongst us, persons when seized with concern are brought to forsake their vices, and ill practices; the looser sort are brought to forsake and to dread their former extravagances. Persons are soon brought to have done with their old quarrels; contention and intermeddling with other men's matters seems to be dead amongst us. . . .

People are brought off from inordinate engagedness after the world, and have been ready to run into the other extreme of too much neglecting their worldly business and to mind nothing but religion. . . . They generally seem to be united in dear love and affection one to another, and to have a love to all mankind. I never saw the Christian spirit in love to enemies so exemplified in all my life as I have seen it within this half year. . . .

There is an alteration made in the town in a few months that strangers can scarcely conceive of; our church I believe was the largest in New England before, but persons lately have thronged in, so that there are very few adult persons left out. . . . The town seems to be full of the presence of God; our young people when they get together instead of frolicking as they used to do are altogether on pious subjects; 'tis so at weddings and on all occasions. The children in this and the neighboring towns have been greatly affected and influenced by the spirit of God, and many of them hopefully changed; the youngest in this town is between nine and ten years of age. . . . And there have been many old people, many above fifty and several near seventy, that seem to be wonderfully changed and hopefully newborn. . . .

This work seems to be upon every account an extraordinary dispensation of providence. 'Tis extraordinary upon the account of [the] universality of it in affecting all sorts, high and low, rich and poor, wise and unwise, old and young, vicious and moral; 'tis very extraordinary as to the numbers that are hopefully savingly wrought upon, and particularly the number of aged persons and children and loose livers; and also on the account of the quickness of the work of the spirit on them. . . . The extraordinariness of the thing has been, I believe, one principal cause that people abroad have suspected it. . . . Thus, Sir, I have given you a particular account of this affair which Satan has so much misrepresented in the country. This is a true account of the matter as far as I have opportunity to know, and I suppose I am under greater advantages to know than any person living. . . .

Jonathan Edwards

Questions for Discussion

1. What ages or groups of people were affected by the revival?
2. How does Edwards account for the spread of the revival? What seems to be his purpose in writing this letter?
3. Identify some effects of the revival.

9.
John Cleaveland
Diary of a Student During the Great Awakening, 1742

John Cleaveland's diary for 1742 illustrates the effect of the Great Awakening on a young man at Yale University, where religious divisions caused by the Awakening were so severe that for a while in 1742 the school was forced to close. Cleaveland, like his family, was sympathetic to the Awakening. He was tormented by what he saw as his inability to receive the salvation God was offering him. His emotional struggle and the divisions at Yale typify what was happening in many other places. The diary ends with Cleaveland still in spiritual despair. He was suspended from Yale for his religious activities in 1745, though he eventually received his degree in 1763. Until his death in 1799 at the age of seventy-six, he served as pastor of churches sympathetic to Awakening ideas. (Spelling in the diary is unchanged, but corrections have been made in capitalization and punctuation).

[January] 1741–2.

15)   This day is Fryday and I Declamd the first time that Ever I Declamed & all the time and was Something affrited, and Bett was very much affrited, but before I was up out of my bed in the morning I had many thoughts about my [*illegible*]ing from god my first husband, and all this I have bin very headless about Spiral things. This night after prayers in the hall Jones prayed in Halls rome very affectionatly. After I Came home I

Ross W. Beales, ed. "The Diary of John Cleaveland, January 15–May 11, 1742." *Essex Institute Historical Collections.* Vol. 107 (1971) 143–172.

and Whilliams Sang a Hymn and that there Came up five more and we Sang a hymn and So the[y] Departed and went away and Whilliams and I had A Considerable Discourse Cons[ern]ing religion, & after he went away we prayed, and I was the mouth to Speek but was Exsceding blind in Spiritual things. Johnson [Sam?] this day I have heard a horruble Story Conscerning Branard[1] how that people Suppert that he Sat up a Letter or paper upon a mans Door and Said we are Stoute men and the first time that we meet with whether by night or by Day we will pull out your tonge out of you[r] throte and brake Every boon that you have in your boday and Cleer the town of Mr. Wrascull.

18)   This day being Monday I have bin very Cold in religion, and as it ware a runing down hill and from the Lord Jesus Christ. O that the Lord would Smite my Dead Soul with his Spirit and Cause me to hear his voice that the bones which he hath broken may rejoyce. The day has bin wett Lousy day Some Snow and Some rain. This day I have heard the Seniors disputte upon the words *istud homini Indubitabile esset quod non Cognoscitur*. This day Lord primus was Called before the Seniors for Carr[y]ing himself unbecomingly and this night I Spent with the Lymans and Ely, and we had Some Discourse Conserning removeing out of the College if we Could See our way Clear and if we Could have some ministers on our Side. I dranke tea this night with Ely, and after I came home I discoursed with Mr. Mix Conserning giting out of Commons, and this night Dickinson went and talked with Mr. Clapp[2] about going into the College in the place of Britt.

/////

23)   This day being Saterday Mr. Clapp Expounded in·the hall upon the free Will of man. This night Wee had a meeting in Hawleys room and we Sange first and then prayed twice. This day I have heard Some presious news Conserning the Lord Jesus Christs Wriding upon the word of truth att Wathersfield, and a fame of the wrks Spreding att Norwalk. O that I might hear Such news Every day and not only hear of it but [see it?].

/////

26)   This day [has] bin attended with much Disturbance in this town. This night Sir Woodbrige preached in the hall upon Hebrues the 3rd. 12 the third time that Ever he preached. This night we had a battle Conserning

---

[1]David Brainerd, an advocate of the Great Awakening, was expelled from Yale in 1742 for his suggestion that one of his tutors had no more grace (in religious terms) than a chair.
[2]Mr. Clapp was a University rector who believed the Awakening was a subversive conspiracy.

George Whitefield, a lead-
ing preacher during the
Great Awakening.
*(National Portrait Gallery,
London)*

riligion, about Branard and many others of the Same Class or of the Same
Sorte. Landlord Mix Simed to talke as if the work which is in the Land was
of the Divil. And I thought that my Landlord was Disturbed, and I was
very plain with him planer then ever I was with him.

/////

28)   This day being the Thirdsday in the morn after prayers in the Hall
I received a Letter from my brother Elisha Cleaveland and it was full of
gall and hunny full of bitter and Sweet. I heard that the Lord by Death had
taken away my brother Moses. O that the Lord would Sanctifie the Death
of my brother to the Salvation of my Soul. After that read this bitter news
I heard that Lord had Smiled upon my fathers family with the mercys of
David: I heard that the blessed worke of the Lord had gone through my
fathers family: O that it may be a Saving worke upon Each of their hearts.
This night Mr. Whitelsey preached in the Hall and I thought he was a very
good orator but for a preacher I did take no Liking to him. After the
meeting was over I went into Foullers Room and Set with him and Tracey
and Spent the night until twelve a Clock in Discourseing on religion and
we prayed once.

/////

[*Illegible*] February 1741/2.

1)   This day being Monday and the first day of the month I have Spent it very odly and in a Dead and Slugesh manner in the things of a religious natur. O that my Soul might be drawn out in Love to the god of heaven and Earth. O that I might See and tast that the Lord is plesent. O that I might have raptours of Joy Let into my Soul that my Soul might be Drawn out in a reflection of Love to the god of heaven.

This day Mr. Clapp gave us a Lectour Conserning these new Lights [*New Lights were advocates of the Great Awakening*] as people Call them in a Reflecting way. He Seemed to talk as if these people ware quakers who go under the name of new Lights. I think he Saide that [*they*] had taken oath against the religion of the Country, and also he Saide it would not do for the Colony to bring up or the Colony would not bringe up Scholars to Sware against the Religion of the Colony and also he Said he believed that our religion was the true religion [*of*] Jesus Christ and we Should find it So if we would Compare it with the word of god.

/////

18)   In the fore parte of the day I Remember nothing Remarkable. But this afternoon I had Some Discourse with Lockwood; and after I Came home I Received a Letter from Sir Lewis from Canterbury and there I heard of the Conversions of my bretheren and Sisters and also of the wonderfull [*Ex?*]ploites of the Lord.

/////

20)   This morning having the Care of the buttery I was to Ring the bell; but over Slept my self, So the Rector Called me a Slepy head for it. This day Mr. Clapp Expound[*ed*] on adoption Justification and Sanctification, and this afternoon I Spent with Branard primus and heard Some heavenly news from Canterbury [*Canterbury, Connecticut was Cleaveland's home town*] Conserning my brother and Sister how Remarkable full they are; this night after meeting I Spent with Lockwood in discourseing on Religion and our Dead Souls how that we are Conforming to the world.

/////

March Anno Domini 1741/2

1)   This day hath passed over with much Commotion. I went in the morning to the Seperate [*meeting*] to hear Mr. Bellamy, and he preached from, [*blank*] the words of Paul that I glory in nothing Save in the Cross of christ. He preacht Excellent well and I was under Some Convictions, but it Soon wore off. In the afternoon I went again to hear him and he preacht from the words of Christ (viz) Strive to enter in at the Strate grate, for many Shall Seek but few Shall enter. Many of the Children of god ware inlivened and Stured up by the Spirite of god; after prayers in the Hall the Seniors had a meeting and Throop was filled very full by the Spirite of god. We ware Called Down by Some of the Siniors, and it was the Sweetest meeting we have had Sence we Came to College. Mr. Bellamy and Mr. Perpoint Came to visit us in College. We Sined a Letter to Send to Mr. Tennant.

/////

[In April, John Cleaveland returned home to Canterbury, Connecticut.]

April
13)   This morning I had a Considerable discourse with unkle Solomon Paine about Religion. He Related to me his Experiences. This afternoon Mr. Mills preacht from I Cor. 1.30 of him are you in Christ Jesus who of god are made wisdom Riteousness, Sanctification and Redeemtion. After him Mr. Baker preacht from the words Conserning the five [*illegible*] His words Seemed to have a very great affect upon the audience. I was in Considerable Distress for my Self, but many more were more Distrest for me then I was: there were a very great Stir indeed.

/////

24)   This morning I have been in a Dreadfull Senceless Condition full of all manner of wickedness, and full of all Dronenishness, and Sloth. [*It*] Seems to me Sometimes [*as*] if my Case was irrecoverable, and Disperate indeed for a glance as it were. This afternoon Samuel Adams Dyed.

/////

30)   This day in the forenoon I have been a wandring about almost Like Caine. This afternoon Mr. Wadsworth preach'd from Romans 8 Chap, 9 verse (viz) but ye are not in the flesh, but in the Spirit, if So be that the Spirit of god Dwell in you. There was Something of a Revival amonge the Christians: after meeting a Company of us went to uncle Henry Cleaveland's and Seem'd to have a Considerable meeting; I Seem'd to be a Cast away: I Could not Joyn with them in praising the Lord. This night I was wonderfully Called upon by god to Repent and except of Christ: but I would not. Pompey Exhorted me Ebenezer Bacons wife and Sir Lewis: but I Seem'd to Refuse all. There were a great Revival among them there: we pray'd three times there: but [*I*] felt as Stuped as Stone. O when Shill I Returne from my wickedness unto the Liveing and true god. This night Sir Lewis Stay'd at father's and he was prity full of the Spirit of god, as I trusted. This month is Ended etcatera finis.

May

3)   This day I went to Trooping, and Stay'd there a few minutes and then went with Sir Sprout and Sir Lewis to uncle Johnson's: and there Sir Sprout Exhorted me Exceeding well: but how did I Receive it o but poorly: I did Seem at first Something prest at my heart and as I Came home I felt very much Consern'd: o what Shall I do that I may be Saved, what Shall I do, that I may obtain Eternal Salvation.

/////

6)   This day Mr. Mosley preach'd from Luke 22.48 but Jesus said unto him, Judas, betrayest thou the Son of man with a kiss? He preach'd Exceeding well: and he was very Earnest that Souls Should flee to the Lord Jesus Christ for Salvation: but I Still Refused his glorious Calls and envitations. There ware a Considerable Revival amonge the Christians; and Something of a Stir among Sinners: but I was Like a Stuped Stone having a heart as heard as an Adimant.

Questions for Discussion

1. What is the nature of the religious dispute Cleaveland describes?
2. John Cleaveland seems to modern eyes an intensely religious person. Why is he in despair over his salvation?

10.
Jeremiah Greenman
Diary of a Common Soldier, 1775-1782

Born in Newport, Rhode Island, on May 7, 1758, Jeremiah Greenman had some education in a public school, but had not yet prepared for a trade or career when the Revolution began. Thus for Greenman, the war may have been a means of earning a living as well as an opportunity for patriotic service. Greenman joined the army just after his seventeenth birthday and served during the entire war, traveling north to Quebec and south as far as Philadelphia and experiencing two lengthy stays in British prisons. After his imprisonment in Quebec, Greenman reenlisted in the Rhode Island Continentals and remained in active service until after the definitive treaty of peace was signed, having risen in rank from sergeant to first lieutenant, and finally to regimental adjutant.

Like most Revolutionary War diaries, Greenman's was kept in a pocket notebook with scribbled entries related to travel, the weather, and the length of the marches. His observations also take in the hard life of a soldier, the suffering of civilians displaced from their homes and livelihood, the indiscipline of many of the troops, and the harsh treatment of offenders by the officers who judged them.

In these excerpts, spelling and capitalization have been regularized and punctuation added.

Robert C. Bray and Paul E. Bushnell, eds. *The Diary of a Common Soldier in the American Revolution, 1775–1783: An Annotated Edition of the Military Journal of Jeremiah Greenman.* Dekalb, Illinois: Northern Illinois University Press, 1978. Reprinted by permission.

The Quebec Campaign, 1775–1776

During this campaign, a thousand men marched nearly four hundred miles under Benedict Arnold to attack the British stronghold. Many died of starvation, and three companies turned back. Afterwards, most either quit the army or stopped keeping their diaries.

September 1775, Cannabeck [*Kennebec*]

M 18   Had orders for to be in readiness for to embark. In the evening went all on board our fleet consisting of about eleven in number. Our troops consist of 13 hundred, 11 [*companies*] of musket men, 3 of rifle. We lay in the river on board of our Shipping [*ships*].

T 19   Early this morn. weighed anchor with the wind at SE, a fresh gale, our colors flying, drums a-beating, fifes a-playing, the hills and wharfs a-cover with people bidding their friends farewell. At night foggy. Hove to till next morning then set sail, went into the mouth of Cannabeck river and came to an anchor.

///////

S 23   This day pushed to Hollow Wils [*Hallowell*] where we landed a Lieut and 20 men; ordered to stay here to see that the flour was baked into bread to proceed up the river with.

S 24   This morn marched up to Fort Weston [*Western*] which was about four miles where encamped 48 miles up the river. So far this river is navigable with good pilots.

///////

T 26   . . . Continuing at Fort Weston. In the afternoon a man belonging to Capt Goodrich's Company, James McArn being in liquor shot Serj't Bishop belonging to Capt Williams Company. He was set upon [*the gallows ?*] 10 minutes; then was taken down, sent to Cambridge to have another trial.

W 27   . . . Embarked in my bateau 4 barrels & a tent for Fort Halifax. Had to get out and draw our bateau over rips and rocks in the room of rowing. Up to our armpits in water and very cold.

T 28   This morn proceeded on with the bateaus. Very swift water indeed and rocky. Came over two pair falls. Got forward 12 miles and encamped in the woods where we made up fires to dry our selves by.

///////

October 1775, Cannebeck

T 3   Carried our bateaus & provision a 100 hundred [*rods ?*] & put them into the river again. . . . One of Capt. Hendricks Company killed a young moose weighing 200 weight.

Greenman's drawing of the *Liberty*, possibly a ship he saw on either the Kennebec River or the St. Lawrence. *(From his diary)*

/////

S 7   . . . This day left all inhabitants & entered an uncultivated country and a barren wilderness. . . . There are some places on the river where maple trees grew where the inhabitants made sugar. . . .

/////

T 10   This morn found a place where there was troughs made of birch bark and two old wigwams and a number of small bowls which we supposed they cooked their maple juice in to make sugar of. . . .

W 11   . . . This day a man was passing when a tree that some of the men was cutting fell on him & wounded him so that he died. We buried him there. . . .

/////

T 31   Set out this morn very early. Left 5 sick men in the woods that was not able to march. Left two well men with them but what little provision they had did not last them very long. We gave out of our little. Every man gave some but the men that was left was obliged to leave them to the mercy of wild beast. . . . We had very bad travelling through the woods and swamps. Our provision being very short here we killed a dog. I got a small piece of it and some broth that it was boiled with a great deal of trouble. Then, lay down took our blankets and slept very hearty for the times.

November 1775 by Shedore
W 1   . . . In a very miserable situation. Nothing to eat but dogs. Here we killed another and cooked. I got some of that by good luck with the head of a squirrel with a parcel of candle wicks boiled up together which made very fine soup without salt. Here on this we made a noble feast without bread or salt thinking it was the best that ever I eat & so went to sleep contented. . . .

T 2   This morn when we arose many of us so weak that we could hardly stand. We staggered about like drunken men. How somever we made shift to get our pack on, them that did not throw them away. We marched off hoping to see some inhabitants by night. I hap to get a pint of water that a partridge was boiled in. . . . In the afternoon when we came in sight of the cattle which the advance party had sent out, it was the joyfullest sight that I ever saw and some could not refrain from crying for joy. . . . Here we killed a creature and some of the men were so hungry before this critter was dressed they had the skin and all entrails guts and everything that could be eat on the fires a boiling. . . .

F 3   This morn thick raining weather. We set out for to reach inhabitants, it being 20 miles where we was obliged to wade several small river.

Some of them up to our middles & very cold. We met some Indians on the march that had some flour cakes & some potatoes which we bought of them giving a very great price. Then we came in sight of a house, the first I had seen in 27 days where there was beef and bread for us which we cooked very plenty of. Some of the men made theirselves sick eating so much. At night snow but we slept very hearty in the woods.

S 4   Continuing at Setigan [*Sertigan*] in the province of Canada. Very cold & snowing. Only one house here; & some Indians' wigwam.

/////

M 6   . . . Came up with Colonel [*Benedict*] Arnold the advance party marched off together. The roads very bad half leg deep with mud and water. Marched till 2 o'clock at night. March 17 miles.

/////

[Crossed the St. Lawrence by canoes]

M 13   . . . We got all over. Landed our men at Wolf's Cove where landed his army. Marched up the bank which was very steep. Came on Abraham's Plains where Wolfe had his battle, where we formed. Marched back and forth to keep from freezing while the officer held a counsel whether to storm the city or not & the most part said not storm. Then we march about a mile to some very good houses which was forsaken by the owners, Major Colwils house for one. He had just gone as we got to the house. Here was a number of teams loaded with potatoes for to carry into the city. We took the teams and dealt out the potatoes to the soldiers &c.

T 14   . . . About ten o'clock we was paraded. Marched up close by the walls of the city gave three cheers. The enemy not being fixed, we stayed there a small spell till they fixed a cannon but was obliged to go to a barn to get word before they could fire at us. Then they fired a few shot among us but did no damage. Then we returned to our quarters again.

W 15   This day very pleasant but cool. . . . We made an attempt to sent a flag into the city but they fired at the flag & would not receive it.

T 16   We took this day a quantity of flour belonging to the enemy & some sheep. . . . A sergeant of the rifle men had leg shot off and died with the wound.

/////

S 18   This day there was a counsel held whether we should storm the city or retreat back till Gen'l Montgomery's forces could join us. They consulted to march 209 miles back in the country. . . .

/////

F 24   This day there was a counsel held concerning our allowance. We were ordered to have one pound & a quarter of beef & the same of flour. Here we got moccasins made of half tanned leather which made us comfortable for we was very bad off for clothes &c forth.

/////

S 26   . . . News came that Gen'l Montgomery's cannon was landed. Orders was given for a hundred men to be attached as quick as possible for to meet Gen'l Montgomery. Very cold and poor off for clothing.

M 27   This day the French inhabitants sent to Colonel Arnold for assistance to prevent the kings' troops from burning and plundering their houses.

/////

December 1775, Point Aux
S10   This day we began the siege on Quebec. . . . At night our people sent in to the city very plenty of shells. The enemy keep a continual fire all day. Set a number of houses on fire. Killed a French woman.

M 11 to the 21   During our time we stayed we took several prisoners and cannoned & bombarded each other both night & day. . . . We hear that the two men that was left back with Lieut McCleland and other sick returned. Inform'd that Capt McCleland was [*buried*?] at the first French inhabit and the others died in the woods. . . . Made another attempt to send a flag into the city but they would not receive it. The smallpox very plenty among us. . . .

/////

S 23   . . . Gen'l Montgomery asked us if we were willing to storm the city & the bigger part of them seem willing for to storm the city . . .

/////

T 28 and 29   Very pleasant. Some of our company dieth with the smallpox. A very brisk cannonading both sides.

S 30 and S 31   . . . At 2 o'clock at night we turn'd out, it snowing and blowing very hard. Got all in readiness with our ladders, spears and so forth. With hearts undaunted to scale the walls . . . we sent off an advance guard of 50 men which soon alarmed the town at which all the bells rang. They . . . keep a continual fire on us but we got up to their two gun battery after losing a great number of men. We soon got into their battery which was two nine pounders. . . . Then our men's arms being wet we could not do much. Howsoever we tried to force the gate to get into the upper town but all in vain. Gen'l Montgomery being killed, all the men retreated and left us to fight for ourselves. Then they sent a flag to us to give up. Our Col. Arnold wounded, Col. Green took command. Then the officers held a counsel. Agree to give up. They marched us into a French Jesuit College after taking away our arms. Here we were very much crowded. No room for us to stir and very cold.

January 1776 in Quebec

M 1   We were put all into a French Convent. . . . We were allowed by the Gen'l: 1 pound of bread and a half a pound of meat, 6 ounces of butter a week, a half a pint of boiled rice in a day.

T 2   This day the Gen'l sent for all our names, places of abodes and our occupations and list of the old country men [*prisoners born in England or Ireland*] by themselves. . . . We live very uncomfortable for we have no room. Not enough to lay down to sleep.

T 9 to S 21   . . . Two of our men put in irons for talking of deserting. Got overheard. Hubard died with his wound that was in his heel.

M 22 to W 31   . . . 8 of the old country men that listed out[1] ran away. 2 of our men taken that was a-going to set fire to their shipping. We live very happy & contented though we are in such a dismal hole, hoping the first dark night that our people will be in & redeem us. Here we continue very lousy making wooden spoons & one notion and another to employ our very disagreeable time.

February 1776 in Quebec Prison

T 1 to T 15   . . . The smallpox very brief [*prevalent*] among us. 40 men sick in prison with it now, very cold & a very heavy storm of ice. There was 3 men perished on sentry. Some more of the old country men that listed out ran away. . . .

F 16 to T 29   Very cold indeed. We get some wheat that is in bags below where we go after wood and burn it which maketh very good coffee and selling some of our thing we get some money & so we have once in awhile some coffee.

March 1776, Quebec Prisoner

F 1 to T 14   1 of the prisoners was put in irons for talking with one of the sentries. We are pleased with a notion we hear that the enemy is left Boston & 2 thousand men on the march for here. The carpenter order'd to

---

[1]Prisoners born in England or Ireland were told that while they deserved death for fighting against their countrymen, if they enlisted in the British service until the following June, they would be reprieved.

nail slabs of boards across our windows to keep us from looking out of them & they are very strict among us.

/////

June 1776 in Quebec Prison
S 1 to T 4   . . . Gen'l Carleton with a number more of officers . . . came into prison to see us. . . . Then he asked us if he let us go whether or no we thought we could lay at home & not come there to trouble him. He likewise said he did not take us as enemy & hoped we [*would not take up arms* ?] any more and if he could rely on our honors he would send us home.

W 5 to W 12   . . . After the provost master came in we gave this as follows to him: May it please you Excellency we the prisoner in his Majesty's jail . . . return your Excellency's thanks for your offer made to us yesterday & having a desire to return to our friends & families again will promise not to take up arms against his majesty but remain peaceful & quiet in our respective places of abode & we further assure your Excellency that you may depend on our fidelity. . . . Signed in behalf of the prisoner.

/////

M 17 to S 30   . . . We begin to think that we are not to be sent home. We are put off from one day to another and next week but we keep our hearts up all we can for our situation for we are very unhealthy by keeping us in such a hole not fit for dogs much more for men. . . .

July 1776 in Quebec Prison
M 22 to W 31   This day we are told by the provost master that we are to be put on board the transports in a week or ten day at which we are all very glad. . . . Then again to comfort us we heard that the militia officers of the town . . . held a council concerning our going away & they think is best not to send us home. . . . One of our prisoner taken crazy . . .

/////

September 1776 on Passage for New York
F 13 to F 20 September   . . . We see English Colours flying at the town which we did not like very well. We hear that a flag is gone to Gen'l Washington to see where we shall be landed. We hear that the enemy is killed & taken great numbers of our people. An officer came on board to get all our names & told us we should go home in a few days. 2 of our prisoners in the night stole a boat & ran away. Our time seen to be very long staying here on board of this ship, almost out of patience.

S 21 to S 22   There came on board an officer told us we should all be landed a Monday at night. A very great fire broke out in the town and by looks of it burnt the bigger part of the town. The river & harbor full of shipping going up to the town. We hear that the 200 houses burnt down in the city. We hear that the man was catched that set the houses on fire by the sentry and run through by a bayonet & then the next day he was hung.

M 23 to T 24 . . . About 12 o'clock we heft up our anchor came to Elizabethtown where we land one boat. Lord we lay here drinking grog &c that we got out of the steward's room. All hands on deck dancing & carousing all night.

W 25 This morn very early remainder of us was landed to the greatest of our joy after being prisoner almost 9 month. Here we was carried to the barracks where we drawed 1 pound of bread & the same of beef. We were order'd by our officers to be in readiness to march in the morn up to headquarters.

T 26 This morn very cold. Two or three of us went about 2 miles into the country where we bought a fine breakfast of bread & milk &c. Then return'd to the barracks took our packs what small ones we had, & came to Newark . . . then to Seconnector [*probably Secaucus, New Jersey*] where we put up. Came all the way barefooted.

F 27 to M 30 This morn set off from Seconnector . . . very hard without shoes. . . . In the morn came to New Rochelle where the paymaster gen'l was but could not get our money till then. We was paid off 9 month pay. Then I proceeded on. . . . Stopped in Greenwich in Connecticut where I got me a pair of shoes.

October 1776 on a March for Newingland [*New England*]
T 1 to T 3 and W 16 . . . Came to Bethlehem in Woodbury where I continued til the 16 at one of my Relations where I began to live well & have on clean cloth which was a rarity after going lousy & dirty almost 9 months.

/////

June 1778 Valley Forge
T 4 This day there was a man executed for a spy.

/////

T 11 to S 14 . . . We hear . . . that four men is gone to the Congress to try to settle a peace.

M 15 . . . a number of prisoners came from Philadelphia who informs us that the enemy is getting everything in readiness to go to New York & we hear that the French is proclaimed war against Great Britain.

/////

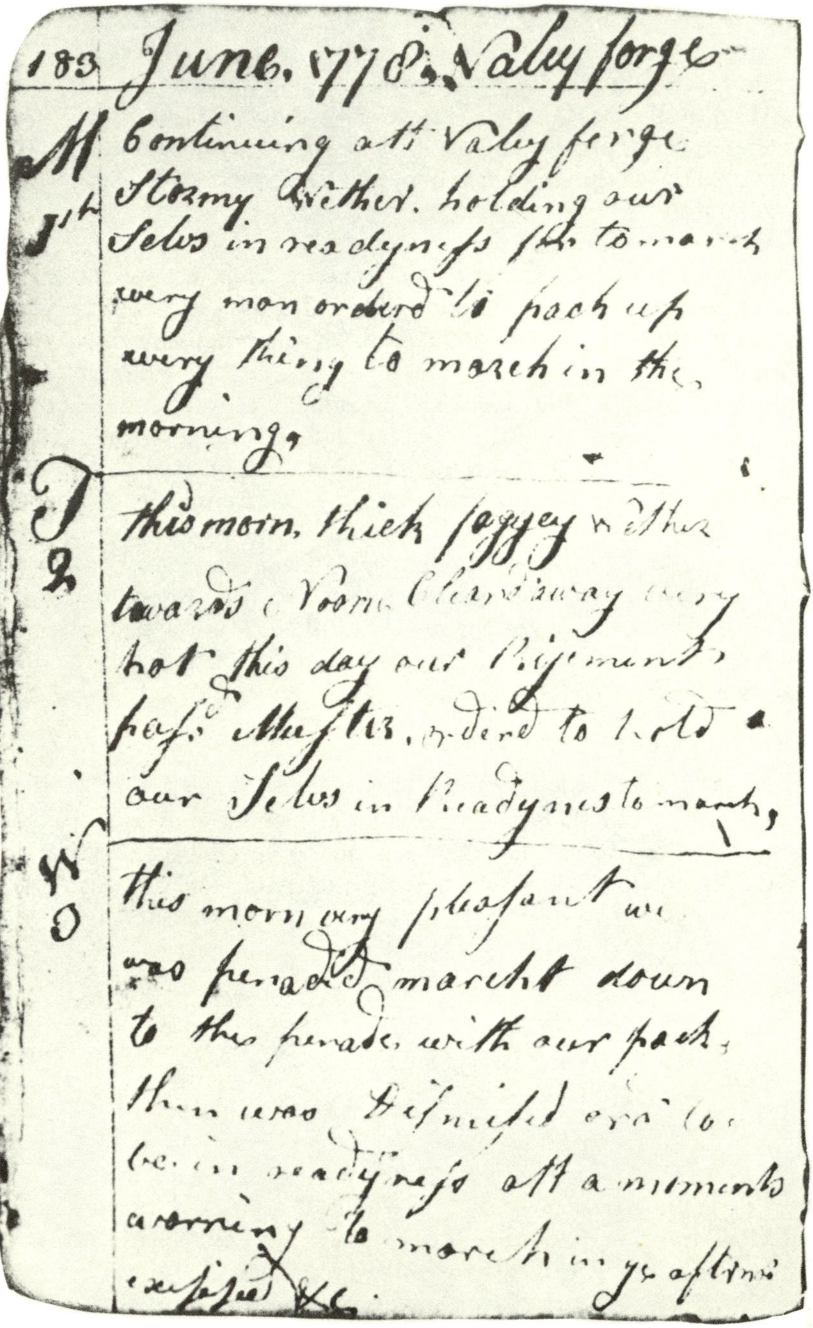

183 June. 1778. Valey forge

M 1st Continuing att Valey forge Stormy wether. holding our Selves in readynefs for to march every man ordered to pack up every thing to march in the morning.

T 2 this morn thick foggey wether towards noon cleard away very hot this day our Rigement pass'd Muster. ordered to hold our Selves in Readynes to march,

W 3 this morn very pleasant we was peraded marcht down to the perade with our packs then was Dismissed ord to be in readynefs att a moments warning to march in ye afternoon excepted &c.

A page from Greenman's diary.

M 22   . . . Gen'l Washington crossed the river [*Delaware*] with a large number of troops. There is 4 hundred of the enemy deserted with two commissioned officers.

/////

S 28 Englishtown . . . Our division under the command of General Lee advanced towards the enemy. After firing a number of rounds we was obliged to retreat. A number of our men died with heat a-retreating. . . . Left the ground with about a thousand killed & wounded. On our side about two hundred killed & wounded & died with heat. . . . We went back to . . . English town. . . . Here received a ball in my left thigh.

M 29 . . . Very hot indeed so that the men that went on a march retreating yesterday throwed away their packs & so forth and a number died before the enemy retreated back.

T 30 . . . Such a number of soldiers that water is almost as scare as liquor . . .

/////

July 1778 on a March
S 4 . . . In the afternoon the whole of the army paraded and formed two lines ware they fired thirteen pieces of cannon & the whole of the army fired the three rounds and gave 3 cheers in memory of Independence.

/////

December 1778, Warrine
S 12 to S 26 Laying in our barracks which is very bad indeed, & cold snowy weather. Two or three men froze to death. We hear no stir of the enemy. We hear that they have no stores of provision, only what they bring from New York as they want to use it which gives us reason to think they are a-going off in the Spring—

/////

January 1779, Warrin
F 1 to S 31 . . . We hear once in a great while from the western army. We hear they are in great confusion there concerning the pay, being so depreciated, times very dull indeed. . . . Hear that Gen'l Washington is gone to the congress to try to get the soldiers' pay made up to them. . . .

February 1779, Warren
M 1 to T 11 . . . Was alarmed by some of the enemy that landed on Poppaqua [*Poppasquash Neck*] which we supposed was come to plunder. . . . Informed . . . that the bigger part of the regiment had turned out in mutiny. I received orders to march with my men to camp. . . . Then

marched in pursuit of the mutineers which had marched off for Greenwich to take a man from the guard that was under sentence of death for mutiny. . . .

/////

December 1779 on a March
[*At this point, Greenman has been promoted in rank.*]
S 18 to F 31   Continuing near Morris. . . . Very cold & almost starved for want of provision & as the mens' huts was near completed, moved up into one of the sergeant's huts, putting them amongst the men till our hut could be fit to move into. At the same time to work on my hut when the weather would admit of it. . . .

/////

Morristown to the Hudson Highlands, 1780

January 1780
S 15   . . . Here we dug the snow off the ground & built up fires and tarried all night and very cold with a number of our mens' feet frozed.
S 16   . . . About break of day we paraded expecting we was to storm the works immediately. Receiving orders that if any man quit his platoon he was to be put immediately to death. Marched about a quarter of a mile & wheeled off by platoons & marched across the river & came to Elizabethtown where we made a small halt & drew provision. At our halt we found that one third of our mens' feet was frozed. . . .

/////

May 1780, Morris Town
F 26   This day the eleven men that was under sentence of death for desertion & other crimes was ordered to be executed near the grand parade. 50 men was ordered to attend to the execution. After arriving on the grand parade, they was all pardoned except one. . . .

/////

June 1780
T 8   . . . Proceeded toward the enemy near Elizabeth where made a small halt where found the enemy had burned a number of houses & ravished one or two women cutting open feather beds & strewing the feathers about the road . . .

/////

March–April 1781, Rhode Island Village
F 13   This day set on gen'l court martial of which Major E. Flag was president. Tried Jack Champlin for stealing, Benjn. Buffington for Deser-

tion & Mathew Henly, Corlinius Driskill, Charles Stevens, & James Single-ton, all of which plead guilty and was sentenced to receive 100 lashes—tried Cuff Roberts for stealing and was sentenced to receive 100 lashes—Nathan Gale was tried by the same court for repeat'd desertion, plead guilty & threw himself on the mercy of the court, the court . . . do sentence him to suffer death—

/////

February 1782, Philadelphia

W 6 . . . Tried 5 soldiers of the light company on suspicion of stealing wood from the public. All acquitted—

T 7 . . . Tried 6 Soldiers for being drunk on duty—and one of the light company for damning Congress—all sentenced to receive 60 stripes. . . .

/////

T 12 Set on Court Martial. Tried 2 soldiers, one for being [*blank*] when on guard, the other for begging money of the inhabitants of the city.

Questions for Discussion

1. In what ways do these entries enlarge your perspective on the Revolutionary War? What kinds of hardships did the soldiers suffer?
2. Do you notice any changes in Greenman during the course of his diary? How would you account for the increasing emphasis on court martials toward the end of the war?
3. What do you learn from this diary about the methods of warfare employed in this conflict? What has changed since that time?

11.
Grace Barclay
A Civilian's Diary, 1776–1783

During the years of the Revolutionary War, Grace Barclay lived on Long Island, New York, with her son, Charles, and her father, a retired Anglican clergyman and native of England who, like their Quaker neighbors, maintained neutrality during the war. Each day Grace, herself an American patriot, wrote a page in her journal as a letter to her husband, an officer in the Revolutionary army. The diary describes the suffering of Long Island residents during the British occupation, as well as incidents of robbery and looting when outlaws or "runners" from the mainland periodically attacked and harassed Long Island households.

Sept., 1776 In this quiet nook where we had hoped to find peace and safety, we shall have disturbance, fear, and danger; since the enemy have possession of the island, there can be no doubt of it, but to some extent my father's neutral stand, and sacred profession, will protect us. . . . My father tells me the news, which he gathers in his walks in the neighborhood; and I read to him portions of your letters, which indeed is but seldom, because they are so few. His breast is, I think, agitated by contending emotions. He is attached to the land of his adoption, and can sympathize in her distress, but naturally his first, his dearest affections, were given to the land of his birth. . . . They seem (the English) the foes of our own household to him; brother lifting up sword against brother, in unnatural warfare, which he prays may speedily come to an end!

Grace Barclay's Diary, or Personal Recollections of the American Revolution, 2nd ed. Sidney Barclay, ed. (pseudonym). New York: D.F.Randolph, 1866.

British troops occupy New York City, 1776. *(Library of Congress)*

///////

Oct. 3, 1776   Dear, dear husband! was there ever anything so sorrowful, so dreadful, as young Nathan Hale's fate? Tears are running down
while I write.

Would that the enemy's designs could have been discovered without so
costly a sacrifice! Gen. Washington desired, for he knew it to be of vital
importance to the Continental Forces, that some one should penetrate the
British Camp, to discover their plans. . . .

Young Captain Hale left the camp at Harlem Heights under General
Washington's orders, late in last month, I believe.

Before reaching the British lines he assumed the dress of a school master; he wore a suit of brown broad-cloth, and a round broad-brimmed hat.

He took off his silver shoe buckles too. His college diploma was in his
portmanteau, signed by the Reverend Doctor Napthali Daggett of Yale
University.

He passed, so Rhoda tells me, safely through the British lines, every
where, along the posts, and among the tents and barracks, to Huntingdon,
about nine miles from this place. It was the place from which he started a
short time before. A boat was to meet him, to sail over to Connecticut
Main.

The young man went down to the shore at day-break in perfect security;
no doubt buoyed with joy at the success of his enterprise.

He saw a boat moving shoreward. *It was the enemy!* He did retreat, but they cried out "Surrender, or Die."

An armed vessel, the "Halifax," stood around the neck, out of sight. Thither the young man was taken, and put in irons.

His papers, written in some dead language (Latin I believe), were under the soles of his pump. They betrayed him.

The next morning at daybreak, after he received sentence, he was executed.

"I only regret," he said, just before he ascended to the gibbet, "that I have but one life to lose for my country." . . .

It was on the 21st of September '76. They tore up the letter he wrote to his family, saying, "the rebels should never know they had a man in their army who could die with such firmness."

Tuesday, 1776   The Hessians have been ordered to cut down all the saplings they can find. They pile them along the road about twelve feet high, then by pressing teams and wagons, they cart it away to forts and barracks at a distance.

It is a serious loss; in a few years our farms will be without wood for use. They (the Hessians) burn an immense quantity—even the rail-fences, unless we take care to cut and cart wood for their constant use. . . .

/////

Wednesday, 1776   Charles accompanied John Harris home from school, with my permission, last night. He returned this morning, with a story of the night, which he related to me in breathless excitement.

A family living a mile from us were quietly sitting together in the evening, when a noise was heard at the door like that of a sharp instrument thrust into it. On opening the door, there stood a redcoat with his sabre in his hand, which he had stuck into the wood an inch or two. He was backed by a dozen men. They pushed their way in, and were very unruly, rummaging and ransacking every drawer and closet; but the family had long before taken the precaution to place all their valuables and money in a small room, which opened out of the common sitting-room, putting a large cupboard before the door, which covered it entirely, so that the Hessians quartered there last winter never discovered the existence of the room. A cunning device.

The red-coats, highly enraged at finding nothing, began to threaten terrible things if they did not divulge the hiding place. Mr. W. told them, that if they dared do any violence he would report them to the commanding officer; whereupon they actually went into the kitchen, kindled some light wood, came out, and set a burning brand at each corner of the house. The family were exceedingly alarmed. . . .

A new source of trouble has appeared on the south side—kidnapping negroes.

The ruffians come in sloops from the Delaware and Maryland country, and landing on the island in the night, they steal the poor creatures while asleep, after the labor of cutting the salt meadow grass for their masters. When they get them away, they sell them at the South.

A week since, while the men were at work, four persons, in broad day, their faces blackened, and dressed like negroes, appeared suddenly, each armed with a gun, and before the others could come to the rescue, a man and a boy were forcibly taken, put in a boat, and rowed off to a cutter out at sea. On the deck the villains could be seen putting chains on the poor creatures. I tremble at the thought of the future.

Saturday, Nov. 27, 1776 Received a few hasty lines from White Plains. They mention an engagement on the 28th October; "retreated with loss." The aspect of affairs is gloomy indeed. . . . The army is greatly reduced by killed, wounded, and taken and those whose enlistments have expired daily leaving; the poor creatures remaining, many without shoes or comfortable clothing, are sadly disheartened. The enemy have possession of the city of New York, of Staten Island, and of Long Island. Who can look without trembling at the failure of this struggle to throw off our yoke? . . .

December, 1776 The depredations, robberies, and not seldom murders, committed by the Cow-Boys and Runners, are alarming, and exasperating the people in the extreme. The farmers suffer dreadfully from the levying, taxing, and quartering upon them of the Hessians and British soldiers. They are very insolent, making most unreasonable demands, and the meek-spirited, unresisting Quakers are martyrs to their lawlessness and rapacity. . . .

Monday, 1776 Henry Pattison, the nearest neighbor, has eight sturdy sons, and one little timid daughter. He belongs to the Society of Friends, is a fine specimen of humanity, owns a valuable farm, yet has a pretty hard struggle to bring up his large family. He was beginning to prosper a little, when the war began. . . . He is called hereabouts The Peace-Maker.

Friend Pattison appears to have neither "part nor lot" in the struggle in which the country is engaged. How strange! *To be a man, and remain neutral!* His soul abhors War. This principle of their sect is enrooted in his breast. Yet he is a severe sufferer from it. Six Hessians are quartered upon him. They took possession of the kitchen; swung up their hammocks; cook his (the farmer's) food, and hang about, smoking and drinking the live-long day. Dear, how annoying! When shall we be rid of them?

/////

Thursday, 1776 . . . It is said that many wealthy and influential persons have deserted the American cause. It is indeed a gloomy hour! But we *must* triumph. The descendants of those who sought here a peaceful asylum from oppression, —Huguenots, Puritans, Covenanters, —will not submit to oppression here. They will defend it with their lives. . . .

Monday, 1776   The impressments of men, horses, and wagons, to carry provender, hat, and soldiers, about the country, are unceasingly going on. When the dreadful work begins, the light-horseman is seen flying like lightning from house to house; the men take the alarm, and make every effort to get out of the way, and to hide their horses and wagons. It is very difficult. Many a noble animal is ruined, worked to death. . . .

/////

Tuesday, 1776   Oh, dear husband, war is a weariness! its effects sickens the soul. Every hour some fresh account of murder, robbery, wounding, destroying, depredating!

When will this unnatural warfare be at an end?

/////

Dec. 30th, 1776   The year has closed disastrous, gloomy; panic and despair reign in many a breast. All the future is uncertain; none can foretell what another year may bring forth. . . . If Congress would appropriate more money, and men could be enlisted on longer terms, say, during the war, and properly equipped, greater things could be done. Now, no sooner are they organized, and become a little drilled, than the term of enlistment expires, and raw recruits take their place.

Jan. 15th, 1777   News of the Battle of Princeton. My husband safe, thank Heaven! General Washington victorious; General Mercer mortally wounded! . . . The Commander-in-Chief, by his judgment, skill, and cool intrepidity, has struck the enemy with surprise. They have looked with contempt on our raw men, many of whom never saw a battle. They expected to crush us; to quell with ease, by their giant power, the rebels, as the lord of the forest crushes the insects beneath his feet. . . .

/////

Tuesday, 1777   Congress has passed important resolutions, and increased General Washington's power, investing him with unlimited command. They are endeavoring to rouse the people by an impressive Address. Benjamin Franklin, Silas Deane, and Arthur Lee, are sent to solicit aid of foreign powers.

/////

Monday, 1777   On every Monday exercising is practiced opposite our house. Today, when the manoeuvering was over, a man who had been found intoxicated the night before, was stripped and whipped severely, with a rattan, till the blood streamed down his back. Oh, it is dreadful to witness such horrors!

Friday, 1777   Days of agony and nights of tears are my experience; the agony of suspense, the tears of widowhood! In imagination I have no longer a husband! He is slain on the field of battle, of which no tidings have come; or the victim of neglected wounds and disease, he is in the hands of the enemy. If alive and at liberty, we surely should long ago have heard from him. How *can* I endure it? Oh, God, endue me with patience, or I sink! . . .

/////

Sunday Evening, 1778   A tale of horror has just come to our ears: we have not heard the details nor do I wish to they are so horrible. It seems the Runners entered the house of John Wilson, and threatened, until the wife, to save the life of her husband, revealed the hiding-place. But it was too late; he died the next morning from a sabre-cut which he then received, cleaving the skull and occasioning so great loss of blood. The villains took a large sum of money, which was in silver coin, in bags under the hearth-stone. Mr Wilson was much beloved in the neighborhood; his death produced the greatest excitement and indignation.

/////

Wednesday, 1778   Last night the Runners appeared round a house near West-Town, and were about forcing a door in front when they were discovered. John Rawlins, the owner, sent a negro up stairs to fire when the word was given. It was a bright moonlight night, and he saw the creatures step up to the door from a window near it with a pane of glass out. In alarm, he looked out for something wherewith to defend himself; seeing the broom, he took it for want of something better, and ran it through the broken window. It touched the shoulder, and grazed the cheek of one of the villains, who, supposing it to be a loaded gun, cried out piteously, "Oh, heavens, don't kill me!" as though he had never an evil intention towards any one.

The signal was now given, and the man above fired; they soon scattered, leaving John Rawlins aiming his broomstick through the broken window-pane!

/////

Friday, 1778   . . . Received a condoling and scolding letter from Aunt Barbara. She dwells feelingly on you, in that you have joined the rebels, whose cause, she appears to think, is that of anarchy, confusion, and insubordination. . . .

Dear, simple soul! The possibility of the struggle being successful, and the yoke shaken off, never seems to have entered her imagination. . . .

/////

Tuesday, 1778   Papa and Charles safely returned [*from a journey to New York*]; the latter much excited by all he saw. . . .

He saw a sight . . . in New York, which, with your republican notions, dearest Edward, would excite little emotion; but the very mention of which made the blood tingle in my veins. They saw a Prince of the blood royal! Prince William Henry [*afterwards King William IV of England*].

He is about seventeen years old, very stout (my father thinks) for that age. The royal family are said to be inclined that way. King George is portly. The young Prince . . . has a pleasant countenance, but very crooked, knock-kneed legs, of which you must know papa is a keen observer, a handsome limb being in *his* eyes of no small importance in view of personal appearance.

/////

Monday, 1780   This neighborhood is still infested with the odious Hessians. They are so filthy and lazy, lounging about all day long, smoking and sleeping. The patience of the good Friends is inexhaustible. After filling up their parlors, kitchens, and bed-rooms, the whole winter with chests, liquor-casks, hammocks, bird-cages, guns, boots, and powder-flasks, they were last week ordered to Jamaica. Oh the rejoicing! It *would* flash out of the eye, though their discreet tongues spake it not.

The moment the Hessians took their leave Friend Pattison caused the broken places in the wall to be repaired, for the Colonel's lady had the room ornamented all around with stuffed parrots, perched on sticks driven in the wall. . . .

Well, all were putting their houses in order, when the appalling news spread like wildfire — *The Hessians are coming back!* . . . They had indeed been ordered back. How many tears of vexation I shed!

/////

August 10th, 1782   News of Lord North's resignation of the office of Prime Minister, and the forming of a new cabinet, who advise His Majesty to discontinue the war. Glorious news! Heaven grant it may be true. It is certain the war has proved but great loss of life and treasure, without any real gain to English valor, or concession on the part of the Colonies. . . .

/////

April 23, 1783   The cry of peace resounds! The news came to-day. The children ran from school, dismissed by the teacher, that all might share in the general joy. They are told that some great good has happened, they know not what. The time will come when they will experience and treasure it as the highest favor vouchsafed by a kind Providence. God be praised!

The soldiers and Hessians are moving off in bands, and the sick are left behind to follow after. Many of the poor creatures have formed attachments, and the ties of kindness and gratitude are hard to break. The human heart, of whatever clime or station, *will* respond to good treatment; and it is cheering and delightful to observe that, in spite of the greatest personal inconvenience, by patience and good offices, we may awaken interest and gratitude in those beneath us.

Many of them begged to be permitted to remain in some menial capacity; but the ties of kindred prevailed with the greater part.

Questions for Discussion

1. Describe some of the hardships experienced by civilians, especially Quakers, during the Revolutionary War.
2. Describe some of the contradictory attitudes toward the war, even within the same household. What feelings or attitudes toward war seem to be universal, transcending this particular time?
3. In what ways did the British occupation enhance the spirit of resistance among the colonists?

12.
Catherine Van Cortlandt
Letters of a Loyalist Wife, 1776–1777

In 1776, Catherine Van Cortlandt, her husband Philip, and their nine children were living in relative affluence on a large estate in Hanover, New Jersey. Philip Van Cortlandt, employed in the West India trade, had recently come under suspicion for his Tory views and had refused to take up arms against the British. On December 8, 1776, having been warned by a neighbor boy of his imminent arrest, Van Cortlandt fled to Governor William Franklin's headquarters in New York, where he received a commission in the New Jersey Brigade.

These letters, written by Catherine, were sent secretly by messenger to her husband in New York. They describe the effects of this period on a loyalist woman and her children. The final letter describes the family's journey, traveling by special permission of George Washington, to join Van Cortlandt in New York. (The family never returned to New Jersey, but moved to Nova Scotia and then to England.)

December 15, 1776, Hanover N.J.

My dearest love,

    You had not left us ten minutes last Sunday when a party of Light Horsemen, headed by Joseph Morris, came to our once peaceful mansion all armed, who said they had positive orders to take you, my dear Philly,

---

H. O. H. Vernon-Jackson, ed. "A Loyalist's Wife: Letters of Mrs. Philip Van Cortlandt, December 1776–February 1777." *History Today* 14 (1964): 574–580.

Punishment of a loyalist
during the Revolution.
(Library of Congress)

prisoner to Easton, and your favourite horse Sampson to be carried to Morristown for the use of General Lee from whom these cruel mandates were issued. What were my emotions on seeing these wretches alight and without ceremony enter the doors you can only conceive, you who know their base characters and how their present errand must be received by your beloved family. When these bloody minded men came into the dining room our little flock gathered around me and with anxious eyes watched my looks, whilst I was answering questions. . . . One of them (flourishing his sword) swore bitterly that, if you was to be found alive on earth, he would take you or have your heart's blood. This was too much. They fled into their nursery, bursting into tears; screams out, 'Oh my dear Pappa, they will kill him, they will kill him.' One of the inhuman men seemed touched and endeavoured an excuse by saying they were sent by their General and therefore were obliged to do their duty, even though against a person they formerly much esteemed, but had been represented to General Lee as one too dangerous to be permitted to stay in the country. Finding you was certainly gone . . . they went off and left me in a situation . . . scarce to be described. My first care was the nursery to comfort those innocent pledges of our mutual love. . . . Their sobbing and crying had almost overcome them; and they would not be persuaded from a belief that the wretches were gone to murder their dear Pappa. . . .

. . . The house is surrounded by eighteen or twenty armed men every night in expectation of intercepting you, as they observed that you was too much attached to your family to be long absent. Our dear children are again taken from school in consequence of the cruel insults they daily receive for the principles of their parents.

I now write in fear and trembling and venture this by an honest Dutch farmer who says he will deliver it into your hands.

January 20, 1777, Hanover, New Jersey

My beloved Philly,

. . . The arrival of the Rebel Troops in this neighbourhood has been severely felt by us. Parties continually passing this way were always directed by officious people to stop at our house to breakfast, dine, or stay the night; the horses from the teams were put into our barns to feed, without even the ceremony of asking liberty. During the stay of the officers of the hospital we had some protection. But immediately on their removal, several field officers from the New England line and a company of privates took posses-sion. . . . They were the most disorderly of their species and their officers were from the dregs of the people. Indeed, two lieutenants messed and slept in the kitchen altogether, and would not be prevailed upon to leave their quarters . . . a French general has also come on the hill at Dashwood, and daily draws his supply for his numerous cavalry from our granary and barrack.

Many of our female neighbours have been here, but I find their visits are only to gratify curiosity and to add insult to our unremitted distress. One of them who lives across the river, whose family we took so much pleasure in relieving when friendless . . . said that formerly she always respected you and loved the ground over which you walked, but now could with pleasure see your blood run down the road. . . . The pious, devout and Reverend Mr. Green is very industrious in promoting your ruin by declaring you an enemy to their cause. The farmers are forbid to sell me provisions, and the millers to grind our grain. Our woods are cut down for the use of their army, and that which you bought and left corded near the river my servants are forbid to touch, though we are in the greatest distress for the want of it . . . our dear children have been six weeks without any other covering to their tender feet but woollen rags sewed round them to keep them from freezing.

A few days ago, the colonel and other officers quartered here told me they expected some of their brother officers to dine and spend the evening with them. This I understood as a hint to provide accordingly, which I was determined to do to the utmost of my powers, *though from necessity.* . . . After removal of the cloth, I took the earliest opportunity . . . to absent myself; and then they set in for a drinking match, every few minutes calling aloud upon the *landlady* to replenish the decanters which were kept continually going. . . . At length, one of them [*the children*] observed that the Gentlemen who used to dine with Papa never did so; and if these were not his friends, why did Mamma treat them so well. . . .

A Servant came down and said the Gentlemen desired my company, as they were going to dance. This confounded me. . . . Though I was much distressed, my resolution supported me whilst I told him that the present situation of myself and children would sufficiently apologize for my refusing to partake of any scenes of mirth where my husband could not attend me. . . . near ten o'clock . . . he returned and entreated me to honour the Company for a few minutes as a Spectator. . . . The Officers were dancing Reels with some tawdry dressed females I had never seen. . . .

February 12, 1777
Hanover, New Jersey

. . . The narrow escape of your last was something remarkable. I was sitting about the dusk of evening in my room, very disconsolate with our dear children around me, reflecting on our deplorable situation and the gloomy prospects before me, when I heard a sudden rap at the street door. . . . I went myself to see who it was, and lucky I did. A tall, thin man presented himself, and on my stooping to unbolt the door whispered, he had a letter for me. My heart fluttered. The sentry was walking before the door, and two of the Officers were coming towards me. I recollected myself and *'desired the good man to walk into my room until I could give him a little wine for the sick woman.'* He took the hint, and as soon as he came to my fireside gave me a letter, the outside of which I just looked at and threw it under the head of my bed and immediately set about getting him some wine for his wife to prevent suspicion. . . . The honest man after taking a dram went away, being followed out of doors and questioned by the Officers, who had been venting, cursing, and swearing against the sentry for permitting anyone to approach the house or speak to me without their first being acquainted with it. . . . The frequent frolics of the Officers in the house, the Soldiers in the Nursery, and Cattle constantly fed here has reduced our late Stock of plenty to a miserable pittance. The other day was almost too much for me. We had been several days without bread and were subsisting upon a half bushel of Indian meal which had been given me by a Dutch farmer I did not know, who said he had heard of our situation and would take no pay. . . . Our stock of meal had been expended five days and the Soldiers not being about, our little Sally immediately went into the Nursery, and picking up a piece of dirty bread which had been trod under their feet came running up to me, wiping it with her frock, and with joy sparkling in her eyes presented it to me crying out, 'Do eat it, Mamma. 'Tis good. 'Tis charming good bread. Indeed it is. I have tasted it.' This was too much.

The next day Doctor Bond . . . came to the house, and passing me suddenly went into the back room and taking from under his coat a loaf of bread he gave it to the children and before I could thank him he ran past me with his handkerchief and hat before his face. . . .

A few days after, Doctor Bond came here and with a faltering voice told me he was sent by General Washington to inform me that it was his positive orders that our house should be taken as an Hospital to innoculate his Army with the smallpox, and if I chose he would innoculate my family at the same time. . . . He . . . promised to use his influence with the General to obtain the only favour I had now to ask of him; which was, to go to my husband with my children, servants, and such effects as I could take with me. . . .

February 19, 1777
Hoboken Ferry

My beloved husband,

Doctor Bond succeeded and with orders for my removal brought me General Washington's pass which I now enclose.

To describe the scene at parting with our few though sincere friends, the destruction of our property, the insulting looks and behaviour of those who had been accessory to our ruin . . . is more than I dare attempt. At four in the afternoon, a cold, disagreeable day, we bid adieu to our home to make room for the sick of General Washington's Army and, after an unpleasant and fatiguing journey, arrived at twelve o'clock at night at the Fork of the Rivers Rockaway, Pompton and Haakinsack. A Young Woman, whose father and brother were both in the Rebel service, was much affected with my situation and endeavoured to remove me into another room. The next evening, after a most distressing ride through snow and rain . . . we arrived at Campbell's Tavern at Haakinsack, the mistress of which refused me admittance when she was informed whose family it was, alleging as an excuse that she expected a number of Officers. . . .

The town was filled with Soldiers and the night advancing . . . a person came up to me, looked me in the face, and asked me to accompany him to his Uncle's house with my whole family. On entering a room with a large fire, it had an effect on the children, whose stomachs had been empty the greatest part of the day, that caused instant puking, and was near proving fatal to them.

The next morning early, we again set off in a most uncomfortable sleet and snow. . . . Our youngest children could not pass a farm yard where they were milking cows without wishing for some. My little Willing was almost in agonies, springing in my Arms and calling for milk. I therefore rode up and requested the good man to let me have some from one of his pails. . . . The man stopped, asked who we were, and . . . swore bitterly he would not give a drop to any Tory Bitch. I offered him money, my children screamed; and, as I could not prevail, I drove on.

. . . the servants . . . had been obliged to leave me soon after setting off from Haakinsack, on account of the baggage and the badness of the roads. About two hours ago, they came in and inform me that, crossing the river on the ice at the ferry, they were stopped and fired upon by a party of armed Rebels, nearly killing several of them. . . . Upon being shewn a copy of General Washington's pass, . . . they damned the General 'for giving the mistress a pass' and said they were sorry they had not come a little sooner as they would have stopped the whole . . . and immediately fell to plundering chests, trunks, boxes, etc., throwing the heavy Articles into a hole in the ice, and breaking a barrel of old fashioned China into a thousand pieces. . . .

. . . be not surprised, my dear Pappa, if you see your Kitty altered. Indeed, I am much altered. But I know your heart, you will not love me less, but heal with redoubled affection and tenderness the wounds received in your behalf for those principles of loyalty which alone induced you to leave to the mercy of Rebels nine innocent children and your fond and ever affectionate Wife,

C.V.C.

Questions for Discussion

1. What kinds of pressures—economic, social, emotional—did the community and former friends exert on this loyalist family?
2. What qualities of character did the writer employ during this stressful period? What part, if any, do you think her letter writing played in her ability to cope with her changed situation?
3. How would you describe the degree of tolerance shown to those who disagreed with the Revolution?

13.
Abigail and John Adams
Letters on Women's Rights, 1776

Frequently separated by his attendance at the First and Second Continental Congresses, Abigail and John Adams wrote letters that provide a vivid picture of the future president (1797–1801) and first lady.

The following excerpts reflect their views of women's rights, a subject that Abigail raised in response to her husband's support of America's rights and independence from England. While Abigail justifies equal rights for women, John's response is one of amusement at what he apparently sees as rather audacious, a proposal not to be taken seriously. Included here also are letters on this issue from Abigail to Mercy Otis Warren and John to James Sullivan.

Abigail to John Adams

Braintree March 31, 1776

—I long to hear that you have declared an independency—and, by the way, in the new Code of Laws, which I suppose it will be necessary for you to make I desire you would remember the ladies, and be more generous and favourable to them than your ancestors. Do not put such unlimited power into the hands of the Husbands. Remember all Men would be tyrants if they could. If particular care and attention is not paid to the ladies we are determined to foment a rebellion, and will not hold ourselves bound by any Laws in which we have no voice, or Representation.

Alice S. Rossi, ed. *The Feminist Papers from Adams to de Beauvoir.* New York: Bantam, 1973.

Abigail and John Adams. *(Massachusetts Historical Society)*

That your Sex are Naturally Tyrannical is a Truth so thoroughly established as to admit of no dispute, but such of you as wish to be happy willingly
give up the harsh title of Master for the more tender and endearing one of
Friend. Why then, not put it out of the power of the vicious and the Lawless
to use us with cruelty and indignity with impunity. Men of Sense in all Ages
abhor those customs which treat us only as the vassals of your Sex. Regard
us then as Beings placed by providence under your protection and in imita-
tion of the Supreem Being make use of that power only for our happiness.

John to Abigail Adams

Ap. 14, 1776

As to Declarations of Independency, be patient. Read our Privateering
Laws, and our Commercial Laws. What signifies a Word.

As to your extraordinary Code of Laws, I cannot but laugh. We have
been told that our Struggle has loosened the bands of Government every
where. That Children and Apprentices were disobedient—that schools and
colledges were grown turbulent—that Indians slighted their Guardians and
Negroes grew insolent to their Masters. But your Letter was the first Intimation that another Tribe more numerous and powerfull than all the rest were
grown discontented.—This is rather too coarse a Compliment but you are
so saucy, I wont blot it out.

Depend upon it, We know better than to repeal our Masculine systems. Altho they are in full Force, you know they are little more than theory. We dare not exert our Power in its full Latitude. We are obliged to go fair, and softly, and in Practice you know We are the subjects. We have only the Name of Masters, and rather than give up this, which would completely subject Us to the Despotism of the Petticoat, I hope General Washington, and all our brave Heroes would fight. I am sure every good Politician would plot, as long as he would against Despotism, Empire, Monarchy, Aristocracy, Oligarchy, or Ochlocracy.

Abigail to Mercy Otis Warren

Braintree April 27 1776

He is very saucy to me in return for a List of Female Grievances which I transmitted to him. I think I will get you to join me in a petition to Congress. I thought it was very probable our wise Statesmen would erect a New Government and form a new code of Laws. I ventured to speak a word in behalf of our Sex, who are rather hardly dealt with by the Laws of England which gives such unlimitted power to the Husband to use his wife Ill.

I requested that our Legislators would consider our case and as all Men of Delicacy and Sentiment are averse to Exercising the power they possess, yet as there is a natural propensity in Humane Nature to domination, I thought the most generous plan was to put it out of the power of the Arbitrary and tyranick to injure us with impunity by Establishing some Laws in our favour upon just and Liberal principals.

I believe I even threatened fomenting a Rebellion in case we were not considered, and assured him we would not hold ourselves bound by any Laws in which we had neither a voice, nor representation.

In return he tells me he cannot but Laugh at My Extrodonary Code of Laws. That he had heard their Struggle had loosned the bands of Government, that children and apprentices were dissabedient, that Schools and Colledges were grown turbulant, that Indians slighted their Guardians, and Negroes grew insolent to their Masters. But my Letter was the first intimation that another Tribe more numerous and powerfull than all the rest were grown discontented. This is rather too coarse a complement, he adds, but that I am so sausy he wont blot it out.

So I have help'd the Sex abundantly, but I will tell him I have only been making trial of the Disintresstedness of his Virtue, and when weigh'd in the balance have found it wanting.

It would be bad policy to grant us greater power say they since under all the disadvantages we Labour we have the assendancy over their Hearts.

And charm by accepting, by submitting sway.

Abigail to John Adams

B[*raintre*]e May 7, 1776

I can not say that I think you very generous to the Ladies. For, whilst you are proclaiming peace and good will to Men, Emancipating all Nations, you insist upon retaining an absolute power over Wives. But you must remember that Arbitrary power is like most other things which are very hard, very liable to be broken—and notwithstanding all your wise Laws and Maxims we have it in our power not only to free ourselves but to subdue our Masters, and without violence throw both your natural and legal authority at our feet—

"Charm by accepting, by submitting sway
Yet have our Humour most when we obey."

John Adams to James Sullivan

Philadelphia, 26 May, 1776

It is certain, in theory, that the only moral foundation of government is, the consent of the people. But to what an extent shall we carry this principle? Shall we say that every individual of the community, old and young, male and female, as well as rich and poor, must consent, expressly, to every act of legislation? No, you will say, this is impossible. How, then, does the right arise in the majority to govern the minority, against their will? Whence arises the right of the men to govern the women, without their consent? Whence the right of the old to bind the young, without theirs?

But let us first suppose that the whole community, of every age, rank, sex, and condition, has a right to vote. This community is assembled. A motion is made, and carried by a majority of one voice. The minority will not agree to this. Whence arises the right of the majority to govern, and the obligation of the minority to obey?

From necessity, you will say, because there can be no other rule.

But why exclude women?

You will say, because their delicacy renders them unfit for practice and experience in the great businesses of life, and the hardy enterprises of war, as well as the arduous cares of state. Besides, their attention is so much engaged with the necessary nurture of their children, that nature has made them fittest for domestic cares. And children have not judgment or will of their own. True. But will not these reasons apply to others? Is it not equally true, that men in general, in every society, who are wholly destitute of property, are also too little acquainted with public affairs to form a right judgment, and too dependent upon other men to have a will of their own? If this is a fact, if you give to every man who has no property, a vote, will you not make a fine encouraging provision for corruption, by your fundamental law? Such is the frailty of the human heart, that very few men who have no property, have any judgment of their own. They talk and vote as they are directed by some man of property, who has attached their minds to his interest.

Upon my word, Sir, I have long thought an army a piece of clock-work, and to be governed only by principles and maxims, as fixed as any in mechanics; and, by all that I have read in the history of mankind, and in authors who have speculated upon society and government, I am much inclined to think a government must manage a society in the same manner; and that this is machinery too. . . .

Depend upon it, Sir, it is dangerous to open so fruitful a source of controversy as would be opened by attempting to alter the qualifications of voters; there will be no end of it. New claims will arise; women will demand a vote; lads from twelve to twenty-one will think their rights not enough attended to; and every man who has not a farthing, will demand an equal voice with any other, in all acts of state. It tends to confound and destroy all distinctions, and prostrate all ranks to one common level.

Questions for Discussion

1. How does Abigail justify her proposal for equal rights for women? What do her letters reveal about the future first lady?
2. How does John's letter to James Sullivan differ from those he writes to Abigail? What can we infer about early American society from John's comments?

Part 3

The New Nation

The decades between the Revolution and the Civil War were a time of enormous growth, as the nation expanded its geographic boundaries, its economy, and its population. Restless Americans moved from place to place and from occupation to occupation, believing that the next stop, or the next job, would provide them with the happiness and security they sought. At the same time, the promise of economic opportunity attracted millions of immigrants to the new nation. Americans were optimistic about the future of their democratic system, whose benefits some sought to extend to women and even to slaves.

There was a darker side to the era as well. Geographic expansion sometimes meant appropriation of land claimed by others, including Native Americans. The dreams of immigrants were not always fulfilled, while the expansion of industry could mean a hard life for those who worked in the factories. And over everything lurked the shadow of slavery.

The selections that follow illustrate the complexity of life in the new country. As the American population grew, the original inhabitants living east of the Mississippi found it more and more difficult to keep their land. Two letters from Native-American leaders explain their views on the loss of their ancestral homes.

Meanwhile, expansion beyond the Mississippi was already beginning. The Lewis and Clark expedition awakened the nation to the opportunities in the land to the west, and soon other Americans began to follow. First just a trickle, the movement to the West became a flood by the 1840s.

Between 1840 and 1870 a quarter of a million Americans crossed the continent, traveling about 2,400 miles from Independence, Missouri, to Oregon or California. The diary of Mary Louisa Black describes the hardships of the journey.

Increasing numbers of immigrants, almost all from northern and western Europe, helped swell the nation's population. Particularly after 1840, economic hard times and political instability in Europe led to a vast increase in the numbers of people seeking opportunity and security in the United States. In 1820, for instance, only about 8,400 had emigrated. During the 1840s an average of over 170,000 a year arrived, and by the early 1850s over 300,000 were leaving Europe annually for America. Some found success; others disillusionment and hardship. The diary of Abraham Kohn and letters of Jens Gronbek and Syver Christopherson reflect some of the varieties of immigrant experiences.

The economy, too, was changing and expanding. While the South grew ever more committed to cotton, in the North a significant manufacturing sector was developing. The beginnings of a modern urban and industrial economy led to changes in family relationships. Women in families that could afford it remained at home, while men went out into the world to work. The diary and letters of Henry and Mary Lee reflect the lives of one such couple. Not all women could afford or wished to remain at home. The early factories, including the famous Lowell mills, often relied on the labor of women and children. Mary Paul was one of the women who moved to Lowell to work in the mills, and her letters describe both the pleasures and hardships of her new life.

Many Americans, while proud of their country's achievements, realized that there was still much to be done if America was to fulfill its democratic promise. A wave of reform movements swept American society, especially in the North, from the 1820s to the 1860s. Abolitionism and women's rights were prominent among reform goals. The letters of Sarah and Angelina Grimké describe their involvement in these movements, while the pastoral letter from the Massachusetts Congregationalist clergy illustrates the opposition to them. Other Americans believed that piecemeal reforms could not achieve the perfection they desired, and chose to live in communes ordered to reflect an ideal arrangement of society. Mary Paul, tiring of the mills, found refuge in one of these, and described life there in letters to her family. Mary Paul's restless search for a better life reflected the hopes and aspirations of many Americans in the early decades of the nineteenth century.

14.
Big Tree, Cornplanter, Half-Town, and George W. Harkins
Letters from Indian Leaders, 1790 and 1832

Throughout early American history, the struggle over land was one of the major issues between Native Americans and the United States government. The letters printed here illustrate Indian views of this conflict.

The Seneca, the most powerful members of the Iroquois confederacy, had taken the side of the British during the American Revolution, and paid a heavy price for it. The United States was deeply in debt following the Revolution, and the acquisition of Indian lands to be sold to settlers was a way of bolstering the country's finances. Arguing that the treaty of 1783 with Great Britain had given it ownership of the land of Britain's Native-American allies, the United States in 1784 imposed the Treaty of Fort Stanwix on the Seneca. The treaty, negotiated at gunpoint, required the Seneca to give up much of their land. In 1790, three Seneca leaders wrote to President Washington protesting the treaty.

The story of the Choctaw is similar. In 1830 The United States Congress enacted the Indian Removal Bill. As President Andrew Jackson interpreted it, this bill required removal of Indians in the eastern United States to lands west of the Mississippi. In December 1830, Choctaw leaders bribed by the federal agents were the first to sign away their land. As the midwinter move was about

Wayne Moquin with Charles Van Doren, eds. *Great Documents in American Indian History.* New York: Praeger Publishers, 1973. Reprinted by permission.

to take place, a dissenting Choctaw leader, George W. Harkins,
expressed his views in a letter to the American people.

Letter to President Washington, 1790
Big Tree, Cornplanter, and Half-Town (Seneca)

Father: The voice of the Seneca nations speaks to you; the great coun-
sellor, in whose heart the wise men of all the *thirteen fires* [*the thirteen
states*] have placed their wisdom. It may be very small in your ears, and we,
therefore, entreat you to hearken with attention; for we are able to speak
of things which are to us very great.

When your army entered the country of the Six Nations [*the Iroquois
confederacy*], we called you the *town destroyer*; to this day, when your name
is heard, our women look behind them and turn pale, and our children cling
close to the necks of their mothers.

When our chiefs returned from Fort Stanwix, and laid before our council what had been done there, our nation was surprised to hear how great
a country you had compelled them to give up to you, without your paying
to us any thing for it. Every one said, that your hearts were yet swelled with
resentment against us for what had happened during the war, but that one
day you would consider it with more kindness. We asked each other, *What
have we done to deserve such severe chastisement?*

Father: when you kindled your 13 fires separately, the wise men assembled at them told us that you were all brothers; the children of one great
father, who regarded the red people as his children. They called us brothers,
and invited us to his protection. They told us that he resided beyond the
great water where the sun first rises; and that he was a king whose power
no people could resist, and that his goodness was as bright as the sun. What
they said went to our hearts. We accepted the invitation, and promised to
obey him. What the Seneca nation promises, they faithfully perform. When
you refused obedience to that king, he commanded us to assist his beloved
men in making you sober. In obeying him, we did no more than yourselves
had led us to promise. We were deceived; but your people teaching us to
confide in that king, had helped to deceive us; and we now appeal to your
breast. *Is all the blame ours?*

Father: when we saw that we had been deceived, and heard the invitation which you gave us to draw near to the fire you had kindled, and talk
with you concerning peace, we made haste towards it. You told us you
could crush us to nothing; and you demanded from us a great country, as
the price of that peace which you had offered to us: *as if our want of strength
had destroyed our rights.* Our chiefs had felt your power, and were unable
to contend against you, and they therefore gave up that country. What they
agreed to has bound our nation, but your anger against us must by this time

Cornplanter. *(New-York Historical Society)*

be cooled, and although our strength is not increased, nor your power become less, we ask you to consider calmly—*Were the terms dictated to us by your commissioners reasonable and just? . . .*

Father: you have said that we were in your hand, and that by closing it you could crush us to nothing. Are you determined to crush us? If you are, tell us so; that those of our nation who have become your children, and have determined to die so, may know what to do. In this case, one chief has said, he would ask you to put him out of his pain. Another, who will not think of dying by the hand of his father, or his brother, has said he will retire to the Chataughque, eat of the fatal root, and sleep with his fathers in peace.

All the land we have been speaking of belonged to the Six Nations. No part of it ever belonged to the king of England, and he could not give it to you.

Hear us once more. At Fort Stanwix we agreed to deliver up those of our people who should do you any wrong, and that you might try them and punish them according to your law. We delivered up two men accordingly. But instead of trying them according to your law, the lowest of your people took them from your magistrate, and put them immediately to death. It is just to punish the murder with death; but the Senecas will not deliver up their people to men who disregard the treaties of their own nation.

Farewell Letter to the American People, 1832
George W. Harkins (Choctaw)

To the American People.

It is with considerable diffidence that I attempt to address the American people, knowing and feeling sensibly my incompetency; and believing that your highly and well improved minds could not be well entertained by the address of a Choctaw. But having determined to emigrate west of the Mississippi river this fall, I have thought proper in bidding you farewell, to make a few remarks of my views and the feelings that actuate me on the subject of our removal.

Believing that our all is at stake and knowing that you readily sympathize with the distressed of every country, I confidently throw myself on your indulgence and ask you to listen patiently. I do not arrogate to myself the prerogative of deciding upon the expediency of the late treaty, yet I feel bound as a Choctaw, to give a distinct expression of my feelings on that interesting, (and to the Choctaws) all important subject.

We were hedged in by two evils, and we chose that which we thought least. Yet we could not recognize the right that the state of Mississippi had assumed to legislate for us. Although the legislature of the state were qualified to make laws for their own citizens, that did not qualify them to become law makers to a people who were so dissimilar in manners and customs as the Choctaws are to the Mississippians. Admitting that they understood the people, could they remove that mountain of prejudice that has ever obstructed the streams of justice, and prevented their salutary influence from reaching my devoted countrymen? We as Choctaws rather chose to suffer and be free, than live under the degrading influence of laws, where our voice could not be heard in their formation.

Much as the state of Mississippi has wronged us, I cannot find in my heart any other sentiment than an ardent wish for her prosperity and happiness.

I could cheerfully hope that those of another age and generation may not feel the effects of those oppressive measures that have been so illiberally dealt out to us; and that peace and happiness may be their reward. Amid the gloom . . . of the present separation, we are cheered with a hope that ere long we shall reach our destined home, and that nothing short of the basest acts of treachery will ever be able to wrest it from us, and that we may live free. Although your ancestors won freedom on the fields of danger and glory, our ancestors owned it as their birthright, and we have had to purchase it from you; as the vilest slaves buy their freedom.

Yet it is said that our present movements are our own voluntary acts— such is not the case. We found ourselves like a benighted stranger, following false guides, until he was surrounded on every side, with fire or water. The fire was certain destruction, and feeble hope was left him of escaping by water. A distant view of the opposite shore encourages the hope; to remain would be utter annihilation. Who would hesitate, or would say that his plunging into the water was his own voluntary act? Painful in the extreme is the mandate of our expulsion. We regret that it should proceed from the mouth of our professed friend, and for whom our blood was commingled with that of his bravest warriors, on the field of danger and death.

But such is the instability of professions. The man who said that he would plant a stake and draw a line around us, that never should be passed, was the first to say he could not guard the lines, and drew up the stake and wiped out all traces of the line. I will not conceal from you my fears, that the present grounds may be removed—I have my foreboding—who of us can tell after witnessing what has already been done, what the next force may be.

I ask you in the name of justice, for repose for myself and my injured people. Let us alone—we will not harm you, we want rest. We hope, in the name of justice, that another outrage may never be committed against us, and that we may for the future be cared for as children, and not driven about as beasts, which are benefitted by a change of pasture.

Taking an example from the American government, and knowing the happiness which its citizens enjoy, under the influence of mild republican institutions, it is the intention of our countrymen to form a government assimilated to that of our white breathern in the United States, as nearly as their condition will permit.

We know that in order to protect the rights and secure the liberties of the people, no government approximates so nearly to perfection as the one to which we have alluded. As east of the Mississippi we have been friends, so west we will cherish the same feelings with additional fervor; and although we may be removed to the desert, still we shall look with fine regard, upon those who have promised us their protection. Let that feeling be reciprocated.

Friends, my attachment to my native land is strong—that cord is now broken; and we must go forth as wanderers in a strange land! I must go—let me entreat you to regard us with feelings of kindness, and when the hand of oppression is stretched against us, let me hope that every part of the United States, filling the mountains and valleys, will echo and say stop, you have no power, we are the sovereign people, and our friends shall no more be disturbed. We ask you for nothing that is incompatible with your other duties.

We go forth sorrowful, knowing that wrong has been done. Will you extend to us your sympathizing regards until all traces of disagreeable oppositions are obliterated, and we again shall have confidence in the professions of our white brethren.

Here is the land of our progenitors, and here are their bones; they left them as a sacred deposit, and we have been compelled to venerate its trust; it is dear to us yet we cannot stay, my people are dear to me, with them I must go. Could I stay and forget them and leave them to struggle alone, unaided, unfriended, and forgotten by our great father? I should then be unworthy the name of a Choctaw, and be a disgrace to my blood. I must go with them; my destiny is cast among the Choctaw people. If they suffer, so will I; if they prosper, then I will rejoice. Let me again ask you to regard us with feelings of kindness.

Questions for Discussion

1. What similarities and differences are there between the situation of the Seneca and that of the Choctaw?
2. Does Harkins seem conciliatory in his letter? If so, why is he?

15.
Meriwether Lewis and William Clark
Diaries of the Lewis and Clark Expedition, 1805

In 1803 President Thomas Jefferson appointed Meriwether Lewis commander of an expedition to explore the territory west of the Mississippi River, newly acquired in the Louisiana Purchase. Lewis selected explorer William Clark to join him in his efforts to map the territory, catalog its plants and animal life, and establish relations with the Native Americans along the route. This expedition, which lasted from May 14, 1804, until September 23, 1806, began in St. Louis, made its way to the Pacific Ocean, and returned to St. Louis. The detailed diaries the explorers kept over the 8,000 miles they traveled are invaluable records of the land and its inhabitants.

These excerpts from both diaries, written at the crossing of the Great Divide, reflect Lewis and Clark's observations and their dealings with Native-American tribes, including Shoshone, Minnitares, and Mandans.

[Lewis] Saturday, August 17th 1805.

We made them [*the Indians*] sensible of their dependance on the will of our government for every species of merchandize as well for their defence & comfort; and apprized them of the strength of our government and its friendly dispositions towards them. we also gave them as a reason why we wished to pe[*ne*]trate the country as far as the ocean to the west of them

---

For a modern edition of the Lewis and Clark diaries, see Bernard DeVoto, ed. *The Journals of Lewis and Clark*. Boston: Houghton Mifflin, 1953. 202–215.

was to examine and find out a more direct way to bring merchandize to them. that as no trade could be carryed on with them before our return to our homes that it was mutually advantageous to them as well as to ourselves that they should render us such aids as they had in their power to furnish in order to haisten our voyage and of course our return home. that such were their horses to transport our baggage without which we could not subsist, and that a pilot to conduct us through the mountains was also necessary if we could not decend the river by water. but that we did not ask either their horses or their services without giving a satisfactory compensation in return. that at present we wished them to collect as many horses as were necessary to transport our baggage to their village on the Columbia where we would then trade with them at our leasure for such horses as they could spare us.

the chief thanked us for friendship towards himself and nation & declared his wish to serve us in every rispect. that he was sorry to find that it must yet be some time before they could be furnished with firearms but said they could live as they had done heretofore untill we brought them as we had promised. he said they had not horses enough with them at present to remove our baggage to their village over the mountain, but that he would return tomorrow and encourage his people to come over with their horses and that he would bring his own and assist us. this was complying with all we wished at present.

we next enquired who were chiefs among them. Cameahwait pointed out two others whom he said were Chiefs. we gave him a medal of the small size with the likeness of Mr. Jefferson the President of the U' States in releif on one side and clasp hands with a pipe and tomahawk in the other, to the other Chiefs we gave each a small medal which were struck in the Presidency of George Washing[ton] Esqr. we also gave small medals of the last description to two young men whom the 1st Chief informed us wer good young men and much rispected among them. we gave the 1st Chief an uniform coat shirt a pair of scarlet legings a carrot of tobacco and some small articles   to each of the others we gave a shi[r]t leging[s] handkerchief a knife some tobacco and a few small articles   we also distributed a good quantity paint mockerson awles knives beads looking-glasses &c among the other Indians and gave them a plentifull meal of lyed corn which was the first they had ever eaten in their lives. they were much pleased with it. every article about us appeared to excite astonishment in ther minds; the appearance of the men, their arms, the canoes, our manner of working them, the b[l]ack man york and the sagacity of my dog were equally objects of admiration. I also shot my air-gun which was so perfectly incomprehensible that they immediately denominated it the great medicine.

Capt. Clark and myself now concerted measures for our future operations, and it was mutually agreed that he should set out tomorrow morning

Lewis and Clark with their guide, Sacagawea, and their interpreter, an African-American slave named York. Though given minor places in the painting, Sacagawea and York played important roles in the expedition. *(Montana State Capitol Building)*

with eleven men furnished with axes and other necessary tools for making canoes, their arms accoutrements and as much of their baggage as they could carry. also to take the indians, C[h]arbono and the indian woman with him; that on his arrival at the Shoshone camp he was to leave Charbono and the Indian woman to haisten the return of the Indians with their horses to his place, and to proceede himself with the eleven men down the Columbia in order to examine the river and if he found it navigable and could obtain timber to set about making canoes immediately. In the mean time I was to bring the party and baggage to the Shoshone Camp, calculating that by the time I should reach that place that he would have sufficiently informed himself with rispect to the state of the river &c. as to determine us whether to prosicute our journey from thence by land or water. in the former case we should want all the horses which we could perchase and in the latter only to hire the Indians to transport our baggage to the place at which we made the canoes.

/////

[Clark] August 18th Sunday 1805

at 10 oClock I set out accompanied by the Indians except 3 the interpreter and wife, the fore part of the day worm, at 12 oClock it became hasey with a mist of rain   wind hard from the S.W. and cold which increased untill night   the rain Seased in about two hours. We proceeded on thro' a wide leavel vallie without wood except willows & Srubs for 15 miles and Encamped at a place the high lands approach within 200 yards in 2 points   the River here only 10 yards wide   Several Small Streams branching out on each Side below. all the Indians proceeded on except the 3 Chiefs & two young men.

[Lewis] Monday August 19th 1805

The Shoshonees may be estimated at about 100 warriors, and about three times that number [*in this band*] of women and children. they have more children among them than I expected to have seen among a people who procure subsistence with such difficulty. there are but few very old persons, nor did they appear to treat those with much tenderness or rispect. The man is the sole propryetor of his wives and daughters, and can barter or dispose of either as he thinks proper. a plurality of wives is common among them, but these are not generally sisters as with the Minnitares & Mandans but are purchased of different fathers. The father frequently disposes of his infant daughters in marriage to men who are grown or to men who have sons for whom they think proper to provide wives. the compensation given in such cases usually consists of horses or mules which the father receives at the time of contract and converts to his own uce. The girl remains with her parents untill she is considered to be about the age of 13 or 14 years. the female at this age is surrendered to her soveriegn lord and husband agreeably to contract, and with her is frequently restored by the father quite as much as he received in the first instance in payment for his daughter; but this is discretionary with the father. Sah-car-gar-we-ah had been thus disposed of before she was taken by the Minnetares, or had arrived to the years of puberty. the husband was yet living with this band. he was more than double her age and had two other wives. he claimed her as his wife but said that as she had had a child by another man, who was Charbono, that he did not want her.

They seldom correct their children particularly the boys who soon become masters of their own acts. they give as a reason that it cows and breaks the sperit of the boy to whip him, and that he never recovers his independence of mind after he is grown. They treat their women but with little rispect and compel them to perform every species of drudgery. they collect the wild fruits and roots, attend to the horses or assist in that duty, cook, dress the skins and make all their apparel, collect wood and make their fires, arrange and form their lodges, and when they travel pack the horses and take charge of all the baggage; in short the man dose little else except attend his horses hunt and fish. the man considers himself degraded if he is compelled to walk any distance; and if he is so unfortunately poor as only to possess two horses he rides the best himself and leaves the woman or women if he has more than one, to transport their baggage and children on the other, and to walk if the horse is unable to carry the additional weight of their persons. the chastity of their women is not held in high estimation, and the husband will for a trifle barter the companion of his bead for a night or longer if he conceives the reward adequate; tho' they are not so importunate that we should caress their women as the siouxs were. and some of their women appear to be held more sacred than in any nation we have seen. I have requested the men to give them no cause of jealousy by having connection with their women without their knowledge, which with them, strange as it may seem is considered as disgracefull to the husband as clandestine connections of a similar kind are among civilized nations. to prevent this mutual exchange of good officies altogether I know it impossible to effect, particularly on the part of our young men whom some months abstanence have made very polite to those tawney damsels. no evil has yet resulted and I hope will not from these connections. . . .

I was anxious to learn whether these people had the venerial [*venereal disease*], and made the enquiry through the interpreter and his wife; the information was that they sometimes had it but I could not learn their remedy; they most usually die with it's effects. this seems a strong proof that these disorders bothe ganaraehah and Louis Venerae are native disorders of America. tho' these people have suffered much by the small pox which is known to be imported and perhaps those other disorders might have been contracted from other indian tribes who by a round of communications might have obtained from the Europeans since it was introduced into that quarter of the globe. but so much detached on the other ha[n]d from all communication with the whites that I think it most probably that these disorders are original with them. . . .

/////

[Clark] August 20th Tuesday 1805
"So-So-Ne" The Snake Indians

Set out at half past 6 oClock and proceeded on (met maney parties of Indians) thro' a hilley Countrey to the Camp of the Indians on a branch of the Columbia River, before we entered this Camp a Serimonious hault was requested by the Chief and I smoked with all that Came around, for Several pipes we then proceeded on to the Camp & I was introduced into the only Lodge they had which was pitched in the Center for my party all the other Lodges made of bushes, after a few Indian Seremonies I informed the Indians that object of our journey our good intentions towards them by Consirn for the distressed Situation, what we had done for them in makeing a piece with the *Minitarras Mandans Rickara* &c. for them. and requested them all to take over their horses & assist Capt Lewis across &c. also informing them the object of my journey down the river, and requested a guide to accompany me, all of which was repeited by the Chief to the whole village.

Those pore people Could only raise a Sammon & a little dried Choke Cherries for us   half the men of the tribe with the Chief turned out to hunt the antilopes,   at 3 oClock after giveing a fiew Small articles as presents I set out accompanied by an old man as a Guide   I endevered to procure as much information from thos people as possible without much Suckcess they being but little acquainted or effecting to be So. I left one man to purchase a horse and overtake me and proceeded on thro a wide rich bottom on a beaten Roade 8 miles   Crossed the river and encamped on a Small run. I left our interpreter & his woman to accompany the Indians to Capt Lewis tomorrow the Day they informed me they would Set out.

Questions for Discussion

1. What were Lewis and Clark's assumptions about the Native Americans they encountered? How might their experiences have produced those assumptions?
2. In what ways were Lewis and Clark deceptive in their claims that their exploration would be mutually advantageous? Are there any signs that the Native Americans resisted Lewis and Clark's requests?
3. How do Lewis and Clark's perceptions of Native Americans compare with the Oregon Trail observation of Mary Louisa Black (p. 117)?

16.
Henry and Mary Lee
Diary and Letters from a Marriage, 1810–1814

By the early nineteenth century, attitudes toward marriage, child-raising, and the role of women were changing. Marriage, in earlier times arranged by parents for family or economic reasons, was coming to be regarded as a relationship based on mutual love and respect. In towns and cities, economic activity was no longer centered in the home, where husbands and wives had worked together. As work became separated from the household, wives in families that could afford it were increasingly expected to remain in the home rather than to work, and to make the home a refuge for husbands obliged to earn a living. At the same time, raising children took on a new importance, becoming the family's main preoccupation and the special responsibility of the wife. Family size declined during the nineteenth century, and more attention could be given to each child. Women were assured that though they might be confined to the home, the importance of raising children gave them all the status they could desire.

The letters and journals of Mary and Henry Lee from 1810 to 1814 give an insight into this evolving family pattern. The Lees were a socially prominent Boston couple. Suffering a financial reverse in 1811, Henry Lee was obliged to travel to India as a merchant in an attempt to regain his fortune. Trapped there by the War of 1812, he was unable to return to Boston until 1816. During his absence he wrote frequently to Mary, as she did to

Frances Rollins Morse, ed. *Henry and Mary Lee, Letters and Journals, With Other Family Letters, 1802–1860*. Boston: privately printed, 1926.

*him. In addition, Mary kept a journal in letter form of her
activities to be given to her husband upon his return. The selections here include letters from Mary to her sister Hannah before
Henry's financial difficulties, and selections from Henry's letters
and Mary's journal.*

Mary Lee to Hannah Lowell

Boston, August 13, 1810

. . . I have passed a most delightful day in tending my child; she has
been unusually pleasant, and I have enjoyed the true comfort of a *little*
baby. The close of the day is not so pleasant. My husband is at Nahant.
These temporary separations are very salutary, but they make me think
with horror of the long one I feared this summer. You know not how much
I dreaded it and what a struggle it was with me to give my consent. I was
spared then, but I have the terror continually of its becoming at some future period necessary. . . .

Boston, 27 February, 1811

. . . I hope you have, ere this, fixed upon some plan for your children
during your visit to London. I think it will certainly be best to leave them;
you cannot think of interrupting your studies by taking them with you. Sue,
perhaps, may spare the time from her books, etc., as you wish her heart to
be more richly cultivated than the head, and this cannot be under any one's
tuition so well as yours. A mother alone can do this, I believe. I shall quarrel
with you all if you do not say more of these little things. . . .

*[This letter describes both the death of Henry and Mary Lee's first
child and Henry's financial reverses.]*

25th May, 1811

. . . I think all my letters and those of others will convince you that,
although we have suffered, we have been supported, and are now, not only
tranquil, but oftentimes cheerful. Mr. Lee must have employment before
we can either of us feel at ease, and it is extremely difficult to say what that
employment had best be. I fear it must lead to a temporary separation. . . .
You who are parents can in some measure estimate how severely we have
again been tried. I suppose the loss we have sustained of a darling and only
child is more calculated to call forth the tender feelings than almost any
other, but you would find more alleviations than you would expect under

this affliction, particularly if as in our case the little creature did not suffer exquisitely or long. . . . Yet it is a very, very hard trial to *resign* them. It seems as if all my occupation was gone. I am convinced I ought not to allow this feeling, and you may be sure I will in time conquer it. I have still much to do for myself and others, and in employment will seek relief.

[A daughter Mary (called "Miss Molly" in the letters) was born to the Lees shortly before Henry's departure for India.]

Letter from India – Henry Lee
January 12, 1813

My respected and belov'd wife, —

I have made all the purchases and contracts which I shall venture upon until I hear of the removal of the Non-Intercourse Law which I expect daily to learn by arrival from America. You perhaps do not know that I have a partner in my business upon whose judgment I rely in all difficult cases. It is true the distance between us makes it sometimes difficult to profit by the prudence of my guide, but I apply the judicious advice I remember to have rec'd on all occasions where I can, and I am ever well satisfied when our opinions concur. Are you at loss to know who this sage adviser is? No other than yourself, my dear wife, from whom I have rec'd many wise counsels which I ought to have benefited by more than I have, as indeed I should if I had followed all of them. . . .

The letters you have written would do honour to any one. They gratify me now almost as much as when first rec'd—the affectionate concern you take in my welfare touches me most sensibly, and though I ought to lament your extreme sensibility upon this subject as a source of unhappiness, yet I cannot help loving you the better for it—but remember, my dear M., that your health is more precious to me than to yourself, because upon your existence I depend for all the happiness that I expect or wish for. Take care of it, then, for my sake. . . .

Good night, my dear wife and child, I embrace you both most cordially and pray that you may have abundance of health and happiness. Good night, dear wife.

Journal of Mary Lee

10th February [*1813*], evening.   I am quite alone and the temptation to write is too strong to be resisted: the day has been passed rather more to my satisfaction than usual and yet now I review it I cannot tell exactly why I feel better satisfied. . . . The first hours of the morning we passed quietly in our chamber: Molly was amusing us by her tricks without requiring scarce any attention. Betsey Cabot and Miss Dwight of Springfield came in and sat half an hour. . . . After the ladies left us we went out, called at Becca Gardner's to excuse ourselves for not going there yesterday afternoon as we partly engaged to do. . . . I then went to Hannah Jackson's where I met Miss Peabody, then to see Betsey Jackson, who is sick, and dined at our mother's . . . since dinner I have looked in at Charles's and Hannah Lowell's—the latter was dressing for a party at Mr. J. Lowell's. I have given you this detail to give you some idea of one of my visiting days— they are not usually as pleasantly passed as the more quiet ones in my own chamber, but today my friends all seemed to smile upon me, and I thought I cheered our father and mother a little, and this belief of course cheers me—indeed, all your family receive me as one of them, and though we sometimes differ a little in our opinions (or at least in our expressions, for I fancy it is more in words than anything), yet I believe on the whole they think well of me and feel interested in me. . . .

/////

28th Feb'y, Sunday evening. . . . Oh, my dear, dear husband, when we do meet I believe I shall hold you fast—for it appears to me that almost any labour, if together, would not be too hard for us. One great source of trouble to me now is that I am living a life of such corporeal ease. I think I should be better satisfied if I were obliged daily to make some efforts, either to gain or to avoid spending money—but my friends all think that I am spending as little as I can, and I suppose the pride of some of them would be sadly wounded if I were to do anything to gain—this is a pride I cannot conceive of. I know not why the wife should not work *a little* as well as the husband *labour so hard*, and did I feel a certainty that you would agree with me upon the subject, I should most certainly act upon the principle.

Wednesday evening, 3rd March, 1813. I am so much oppressed tonight with anxiety as to be almost unfit for any society, and must indulge myself a few minutes in writing. There is a N.E. storm raging without, attended with a thick snow and no moon—if your vessel is near the coast she must be in danger, but I am lost in such a variety of conjectures when I think of you that I know not what to fear the most, and endeavour not to be anxious about any particular thing—it will, however, sometimes force itself upon me. I have been employed, and very happily so, with the child all day, but now I cannot drive off unpleasant thoughts—I must try to, however, and will go down and endeavour to talk—this indulgence will not do; you would, I know, disapprove it . . . good night, I must commit you to the care of a good Providence, and pray that you may be preserved. . . .

The child-centered family, about 1824. *(Cheekwood Botanical Gardens and Fine Arts Center, Nashville)*

/////

Sunday, 1st of August, 1813.   Miss Molly has fairly imposed upon me this morning, or rather to tell the simple truth, I have been weak enough to indulge her whims so much that I have scarce done anything but attend upon her: now she is asleep and I shall indulge myself in scribbling a little to you. . . .

/////

Wednesday evening, September 1st, 1813.   . . . I think you will notice throughout these pages an air of importance given to trifles which will amuse you, my dear husband: let it not render me insignificant in your eyes, my beloved Hal—if it does I am sure I shall deeply regret having solaced myself by writing them: the fact is, when one is placed in a situation removed from care and responsibility, trifles gain importance, and I so much desire to feel as if I was of *consequence* to someone that if the child has the finger-ache, or nurse looks pale, I immediately think I cannot possibly leave them and thus gain my point. I shall soon have to give up even this ideal importance, for Molly is getting to an age that will suffer from too much attention. The darling has been quite unwell for four days. I have had some moments of apprehension but they were wholly unnecessary, I believe—when I see an appearance of disease without anything very positive I shall always in future be alarmed—this was so much the case with our other darling. I had not an idea of her danger till very late and then it was excited by the appearance of those around me rather than observation of the child. I cannot be sufficiently thankful that I have James to guide me. You can scarcely conceive how much she [*Molly*] talks of you. I have lately hit upon a method to make her feel her dependence upon you, and am very much pleased with the success of it. I had noticed that she understood the use of money, and one day when she wanted some for cracker, or cakey as she calls it, I gave it to her and then asked if she knew who gave it to her. She, of course, answered—mama—I told her "yes, but who do you think gives it to mama?" This puzzled her and I told her "papa"—then enumerated the clothes, etc., purchased for her and me—she was highly delighted, and now never mentions buying anything without recollecting, and saying "papa buy."

/////

28th October, 1813.   . . . The Indigo consigned to Patrick has sold at a very handsome advance; he was rallying about it last night, and said that one speculation had afforded you more than all he had done for ever so long. . . . As for the property consigned *to me*, I cannot give a very good account of my stewardship: it must be acknowledged we women are not capable of such accurate calculations as you mercantile men. I have sold all my goods but the handkerchiefs, and I fear they will sell so badly as to make my sales average very badly. They are in Tuckerman's shop.

/////

Wednesday evg., April 13th. [*1814*]   . . . I have had the child with me all day and she has been more than usually troublesome, and I fear I must acknowledge what I thought I never should, that she is more fretful with me than with any one—and yet I am the only one who ever has inflicted any punishment upon her, and I think I do not spare her. There must be some radical defect in my management or this would not be so. My mother says, and I begin to fear I must believe her, that the fault is in allowing her to see the power she has over me (she argues from human nature), and when that is too much discovered it is almost impossible to exercise authority with any effect. . . . One of my greatest mortifications is that as our child advances she is more and more difficult to govern, and if I do not soon acquire more firmness, both of body and mind, I shall have to fly from her to conceal my weakness.

/////

12th August, 1814. . . . Do, my beloved husband, return to me and give me the delightful occupation of attending to you, and feeling my presence *at home* of some importance.

Oh when shall I have this happiness! . . .

/////

6th October. . . . I have been alone for the last week, or rather Harriet is absent. I cannot feel *alone* while our child is with me. I really feel that I was peculiarly blessed to have the little creature sent at the moment she was—the attentions almost necessary for the preservation of an infant's life were exactly the best thing for me during the first months of your absence, and as she advances she necessarily leads me to more intellectual exertion than I should otherwise be called to, and I am often, I assure you, in so torpid a state, that nothing but necessity could arouse me to exertion of any kind. I hope she will keep me from actual stagnation till you return. . . .

Questions for Discussion

1. How would you describe Henry and Mary Lee's relationship to each other? What is Mary Lee's relationship to their child "Miss Molly"?
2. How does Mary Lee see her role in the family, and the roles of women in general?
3. Compare the experiences of Mary Paul (p. 137) and Mary Lee. Why are they so different?

17.
Mary Louisa Black
Diary of the Oregon and Overland Trail, 1865

By 1865, when John and Mary Louisa Black decided to leave their home in Mexico, Missouri, to join the westward movement, thousands had already traveled west along the Oregon Trail. On May 5, 1865, they set out with their two small children, Tilla and Clifton, and a helper, "Wat," for Jackson County, Oregon, where they planned to establish a farm under the provisions of the Homestead Act. Before leaving, the Blacks had sold their farm in Missouri and freed their slaves. The family traveled in two wagons, one pulled by mules, the other by a team of mares, in a train of 109, and brought along several head of horses and cattle. They reached the home of Mary Louisa's uncle, Josiah Hannah, in the Willamette Valley on the seventeenth of October. In January 1866 they moved into a cabin near the Rogue River, where they lived for the next forty years.

Mary Louisa, thirty years old, was sick during most of the journey with an illness similar to cholera. On reaching her destination, like many diarists, she apparently stopped writing.

June 20 We camped last night near a spring but not much grass. We travelled about 8 mile before breakfast, came to grass and water and some wood by carrying some distance.

June 21 Traveled most of the time today through grass knee high.

Diary of Mary Louisa Black. Webb Research Group, 1989. Pacific Northwest Books Co. Medford, OR. Copyright John M. & Marguerite Black.

Crossing the Great Plains. *(Library of Congress)*

/////

June 23   Last night the cattle were stamping from 10 o'clock till day. We encamped together. Saw some wigwams. Kirk [*leader of the train*] circled [*the train's wagons to be ready if we had*] to fight.

/////

June 25 Sunday morning.   We camped last night near Cashlapoo. About 1/2 mile from the main company. I hear some talk of staying here till noon, & have preaching. The grass is short. . . . We have plenty of wood so far on this stream: Willow & Cottonwood. The ranches occupy the best grass. I hear the order to gear up. One week's time has made quite a difference in the looks of the mountains. We can desern timber on the black hills [*northwest of Fort Collins*].

June 26   The Arapahoos, about 20, came into camp yesterday evening, exhibiting all the characteristics of natives excepting they had long hair filled with ornaments, that is 3 of the number. I suppose 2 to be chiefs & one other squaws. Nooned 26th at the foot of the Black Hills. . . . They are passing on I think from their whooping they are crossing the Cashlapoo which seams to merge from the Black Hills to the left. . . . Passed a sawmill and several nice cabins. . . .

June 27 . . . Some of the teams belonging to Coopers train stampeed, running against the hindmost wagon of our train, smashing one wheel. They took back a wheel and brought up the wagon & divided the load.

28 About 10 o'clock A.M.   Every one is busy. John is having his horses shod, while a great many are helping to repair the broken wagon. I was quite sick this morning with diareah. I took a full does of Laudanum [*tincture of opium*] this morning and some quinine about 8 & I feel some better & have just finished cutting out a pair of drawers for myself. The women have finished their washing. . . . A horseman came forward just now to halt the train, another stampee [*stampede*]. Some of the mule teamsters would not lock coming down a long hill they ran by some ox teams causing them to stampee, that's the first report. . . . The stampee commenced before they came to the hill & they ran down running agint the hind wheel of a hack occupying a place near the front of the right wing. It was occasioned by a matress falling from the hind hounds of a wagonn.

29th   We camped in the mountains again. I am still sick this morning. . . . The hills on this side are grey colored rocks with pines scattered over them. The stage passed this mo [*morning*]. Nooned on the road side. Made a fire under a large pine to boil some tea. Soon after we halted, a soldier came riding up for the Dr. of our train to go back to the next station to take an arrow out of a man's back. [*The man*] lives at the station and has been hunting for them for a number of years. It was done rite in the rear of our train by some Arapahos who shook hands with him, pretending friendly, and when he turned to leave they shot him. The arrow passed through his lung the Dr. says. The same [*Indians*] that visited our camp Sunday eve are the authors of the mischief, near as we can learn. The hunter knew them.

30th Noon   . . . We have just crossed the Laramere [*Laramie*] river [*in Colorado*] on a bridge, for 50 cts a wagon. . . . Not much grass in sight. The mosquetoes are so bad on the stock. Our horses took the river just below the camp. The young sorrel could not swim, but they all got across and clambered up an almost perpendicular bank on the other side. Mr. Helby's mule, tied head & foot attempted to follow, and was drowned.

/////

July 2   . . . We have been travailing over some of the roughest rockeyest road I ever saw. We noon near a ranch which had been vamoosed this morning fore we met them. They reported 100 Indians seen in this vicinity & that they had killed 2 emigrants. There was a large bank of snow in a revine to the left of the road in sight of our own noon camp. . . . We are encamped tonight on a nice mountain stream at a respectful distance from Kirk, Cooper & Dodson. Indians is [*what they*] chat [*about*].

3 Noon.,   Kirks train corelled together once more. Just passed the remains of a burned ranch, lately done, passed a calf laying near the road with the legs cut off, showing the Indians had taken a hastey fee [*feed*] from it. . . . It is about 25 mile to Fort Halek [*Wyoming*]. It is near the place we are corelled that a large train has had a fight lately with Indians. A shield with a fresh scalp tied to it was found near the place, and a chiefs head dress and some of the trinkets they wear round their neck. Some of Cooper's train found them. The shield consist of raw hide taken from the face of a buffalo streched over a hoop about the size of the top of a large woden bucket. There is considerable excitement in camp. We met 2 stages with heavy guard this morning. . . .

4th of July.   No alarms during the night. John still [*ill and*] complaining. All hands endeavoring to get an early start. . . . We passed the remains of a wagon that had been plundered and burned. part of one wheel was left and some of the cooking vessels. And a good many small pine boxes. Coming on a short distance was some cloths and feathers scattered over the ground apparently the contents of a feather bed. . . .

July 5   We camped last night within 3 mile of [*Fort*] Hallack, where we are now halted in the place, aranging as I thought to pay tole. . . . All the ranches are deserted excepting those at the tole bridges where they always keep a guard to collect. Sure enough we had to pay 50 cts for crossing 3 little pole bridges. The travlers give the soldiers here a bad name. A great many of them have Indian wives. The stage that corelled with us night before last, lost their team last night. The [*stage*] station near which we have camped say the Indians tried to run off their stock today. They think they are in a large body in the mountains near here. It is the opinion of some that they are trying to move south. It is reported at the Ft. that the Indians killed one of the Sheren boys & scalped him. He is buried at the Ft. . . .

July 5th   After candle light. Today has been a busy day. Mrs. McClure gave birth [*to*] two twins, one lived until 12 oclock A.M. The other but a few minutes. They were buried at the ranch.

/////

11th of July   . . . We are halted on a high mountain, a wagon having broken down and they are removing the load. . . . Emaline had a very high fever all day yesterday. She thinks she is some better today. I am so much pressed with work I have no time to write. Tilla has the flux [*form of diarrhea*] too & requires a goodeal of attention. . . . I tried to fish some but having no success. I washed some of the babes clothes. The train is going to separate . . . on account of the scarcety of grass. We remain with the main portion.

/////

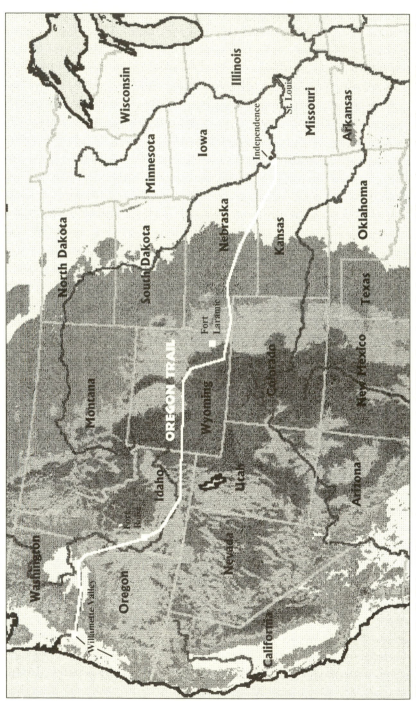

The Oregon Trail. This perilous pioneer route extended 2000 miles, from Independence, Missouri, on the Missouri River to the Columbia River and the Willamette Valley. (Present-day states outlined)

[Crosses Continental Divide]

14th   Our road today has been very rough & dusty. No grass. . . . Got some by going about a mile & a half from the road. But we hauled water for cooking. No wood but sage brush. But that is as good as [*buffalo*] chips [*for a fire*].

/////

16th Sunday.   I rose this morning with the sun as John went out last night with the horses. I gathered sage brush & made out my yeast biscuit & put them on to cook & Emaline finished the balance. It is now ready. Silas is on the sick list this morning.

17th   . . . We are now traveling down Bitter Creek. . . . We came near the creek and camped near Rock station. The houses have been built of rock for some time. I am not well at all. I think it is the water that phisics me.

18th   . . . Tilla fretted with the ear ache nearly all night, which was very cold and windy and drizzling.

/////

21st   I have been too sick to write any for 2 days. I have the flux now. . . . We have been travailing through a rough barrain country. . . . No good water yet. But we will soon get to snow water. . . . Last night we had to feed our horses grain we had been saving for an emergency. . . .

22nd   We are at Green River [*50 miles east of Fort Bridger*]. . . . We will soon commence crossing. . . . It is about 3 oclock P.M. Nearly all the train is across. Have [*been*] cross[*ing*] since 12 oclock, 1 wagon at a time. . . . $1.50 pr wagon with 4 head of stock. . . . I am some better today but was very sick last night. Green River will do to drink.

23rd Sunday.   They found good grazing for the horses but most too short for cattle about 1 1/2 miles from camp. I got out yesterday evening and helped about supper. Still had flux at night. . . . They had to go down some steep places to get grass. . . . Just room for the horses to go single file. We are drinking Green River water, which looks green.

/////

30th   . . . We are encamped on a grassy place and plenty of water. Sold our old feather bed for a sack of flower. . . . Silas's babe is rite sick.

31st   Old Mr. Evens a consumptive, going to the mountains for his health, died last night and was buried about 9 oclock this morning. . . .

August 1st   We halted all day yesterday on account of old Mr. Turpin being too sick to be moved. We are travailing in Wasatch or Bear mountains over a very rough road. . . .

Aug. 2   Last night ice froze 1/8 of an inch. . . . The Snake Indians came in to barter fish & antelope hides for bread, coffee.

3rd   . . . John made a hair line yesterday and caught some fine fish, the largest was about 15 inch long speckled. . . .

4th   . . . We paid $2 tole today. . . . We are near the line between Idaho and Utah, irrigated from the mountains . . . The [*people*] are Mormons.

/////

6th Sunday morning.   I have browned and ground my coffee. The Indians were around begging & picking up the scraps. . . .

/////

12th   We are laying up to-day in consequence of our tiresome travail yesterday. I . . . swaped a large tin of peaches for as many beans and cooked half of them for dinner. . . .

13th Sunday.   Mrs. Turpin complained terably last night. . . . We are detaining again on her account. There is several sick in the train. We are using spring water.

/////

16th   . . . I was rite sick during the night with diareah. . . . The sun shone so hot. Our road has been very steep and rocky, and very dusty. Almost insufferable. . . .

/////

20th   Came to a ranch about 10 and stoped long enough to water the teams. They say 17 miles to grass. We came to the ferry about noon. Got our dinner and was soon crossing the Snake River in a row boat. We had to come down a very steep side mountain road. The wagon I was in came very near running off. . . .

21st.   This morning is still and [*we are*] making rapid progress. The wagons & horses are over & they are swimming the cattle. . . . The bluffs are almost perpendicular, there hight is beyond my estimation. 10 Oclock A.M. The order is to get dinner and start. The [*men*] could not make [*the cattle*] swim the river. They are going to bring them on the boat. The cattle crowded up on the boat and sunk it and came near drownding some of the men. They had their boots and clothing on. The [*cattle*] all went to the other bank. The [*men*] were till night getting them over.

/////

23d   We stopped at noon long enough to rest the stock. . . . Dean is stopping a short distance above & Eaton went up there to rest his sick family. His oldest child is not expected to live. Himself and wife both sick.

/////

27th   . . . I am trying to write home, but I have so little time. I make slow progress. I have bread cooked for dinner. I will employ all the leasure that gives me. . . .

28th   . . . Nooning after a five mile drive, at a place where they had raised some vegetables by irrigation. I bought 2 lbs of potatoes for 30 cts and cooked them for dinner. They were small & I think had been dug for some time. . . .

/////

[Arrival in Oregon]

Sept. 4th   We have crossed the Snake again & waiting for the balance of the wagons to come over. They make quick trips and drive two wagons with 4 horses on at a time. . . . Tilla is very sick with diahrea & the road today has been rough. We are now in Oregon.

Sept. 5th   Tilla was very sick in the night. I gave her a dose of worm medicine. . . . We camped near Burnt river and got good bunch grass by going a mile up the Mt.

6th   . . . We halted today on account of Mr. Durhams little sons being very sick. I have been washing all day. I never saw nicer water for the purpose. . . .

/////

9th   So cold this morning I can hardly write, heavy frost and ice. We meet large pack trains. Met 11 yesterday.

10th   . . . We are nooning on the summit of the Blue Mounts. We have been coming up all the fore noon. The horses are very tired. Drizzling all the time too. . . . Tilla is very sick.

/////

16th   During a halt at a ranch I avail myself of an opportunity to write. It looks more like living than anything I have seen. Plenty of grain stacks. Pigs in a pen, near where we are stopped, and fatning [*fattening*] hogs and hens singing around and plenty of little chicks, all black with white topping. . . .

/////

18 Monday noon. I finished a letter home yesterday which occupied all the leisure I could get. We came to a spring about 1 oclock & stayed till this morning. John was quite sick when we stopped. took opium & slept all evening. Emaline and 2 of her children on the sick list. I have my hands full with sickness and stubbornness. I am almost at a loss to know what to do. But resolved to do my duty.

/////

27th Morning. We came to a very steep side Mt. road. [*Mr. Black and another man were taking Silas back to be with his ill wife, Emaline*] . . . those that were left tried to get the wagons up, with the assistance of some men traveling in a light 2 horse vehicle. The third drive, our wagon got nearly to the top of a short steep turn in the road and stopped. The wagon commenced running back, I called to the inexperienced foreigner to hold the wheel but he kept beating the horses til they became unmanageable, and the wagon turned off the road. . . . The man that was driving behind jumped down from his seat hollering for those within to get out, and just got to the hind wheel in time to save the wagon. I made all the haste I could to get the children out. It then took all hands to get the wagon back on the road.

/////

29th Knights. Where we stopped because I was not able to travail. I am not able to walk about & all the rest are sick. Sent for doctor for Mr. Black as he is worse than ever last night.

Nov. 3 Left Knights. landed at Uncle Josiah Hannah's 17th [*October; in Rogue Valley, Jackson County Oregon*].

/////

January 10th, 1866 Moved home, to a little cabin about one and half miles above Uncle Joes. Close to the river.

Questions for Discussion

1. What kinds of obstacles did this group encounter on its westward journey?
2. What are the clues that the water may have caused much of the illness?
3. Compare Mary L. Black's impressions of Native Americans with those of Lewis and Clark. What might account for the apparent increase in violence against whites since the time of Lewis and Clark?

18.
Abraham Kohn
An Immigrant Peddler's Diary, 1842–1843

On June 15, 1842, at the age of twenty-three, Abraham Kohn and his brother Moses left their native Bavaria to join brother Juda in America and seek their fortunes. Following a ten-day journey across Germany, often by foot, they arrived at Bremen, where they sailed in steerage to New York. Because jobs were scarce, the three brothers became itinerant peddlers in New England, selling their wares from house to house, from village to village.

Kohn's diary, translated from German, is a record of the struggle and disillusionment of a young German-Jewish immigrant whose religious faith, language and customs differed sharply from those he encountered in that first year in his adopted country.

By 1844 Kohn had settled in Chicago and opened his own business. He became a prominent citizen (elected city clerk of Chicago in 1860), a leading member of Chicago's Jewish community, an abolitionist, and an ardent supporter of Abraham Lincoln.

3. [*September 1842*]   At 8 o'clock on Saturday morning we saw the American coast. The rich green colors, the trees we have missed for so long [*on the ocean voyage*], the beautiful buildings along the shore, the many busy freighters and boats and coastal steamers which passed us—all of these impressed us in a way which I cannot describe.

Abraham Vossen. "A Jewish Peddler's Diary." *American Jewish Archives*. 3 (June 1950): 81–111.

At nine we saw from afar the city of New York, and at eleven we anchored some two hours' distance from the city, where we were kept in quarantine. I was allowed to go by boat to the islands which extend in front of New York, but only after I had been examined by a doctor and found well. From there we took a steamboat to the city itself. I enjoyed my first sight of the city immensely, but as I proceeded through the crowded streets on my way to see my brother [*Juda*], I felt somewhat uncomfortable. The frantic hurry of the people, the hundreds of cabs, wagons, and carts—the noise is indescribable. Even one who has seen Germany's largest cities can hardly believe his eyes and ears. . . .

Brother Moses was still on board ship, planning to enter the city on Monday night.

4. [*September 1842*]   Sunday, [*Jewish*] New Year's Day. On the eve of the New Year I found myself with a new career before me. What kind of career? "I don't know" [*original in English*]—the American's customary reply to every difficult question. . . .

/////

7–29 [*September 1842*]   . . . with a bundle on my back I had to go out into the country, peddling various articles. This, then, is the vaunted luck of the immigrants from Bavaria! O misguided fools, led astray by avarice and cupidity! You have left your friends and acquaintances, your relatives and your parents, your home and your fatherland, your language and your customs, your faith and your religion—only to sell your wares in the wild places of America, in isolated farmhouses and tiny hamlets. . . .

There is woe—threefold woe—in this fortune which appears so glamorous to those in Europe. Dreaming of such a fortune leads a man to depart from his home. But when he awakens from his dreams, he finds himself in the cold and icy night, treading his lonely way in America. . . .

. . . leading such a life, none of us [*Jewish peddlers*] is able to observe the smallest commandment. Thousands of peddlers wander about America; young, strong men, they waste their strength by carrying heavy loads in the summer's heat; they lose their health in the icy cold of winter. And thus they forget completely their Creator. They no longer put on the phylacteries [*a small leather box containing parchment inscribed with scriptures and worn during weekday morning prayers*]; they pray neither on working day nor on the Sabbath. In truth, they have given up their religion for the pack which is on their backs. Is such a life not slavery rather than liberty? Is this condition not misery rather than happiness? . . .

Today, Sunday, October 16th [*1842*],   we are here in North Bridgewater, and I am not so downcast as I was two weeks ago. The devil has settled 20,000 shoemakers here, who do not have a cent of money. Suppose, after all, I were a soldier in Bavaria; that would have been a bad lot. I will accept three years in America instead. But I could not stand it any longer.

The interior of Castle Garden, the immigrant depot in New York City. *(Museum of the City of New York)*

As far as the language is concerned, I am getting along pretty well. But I don't like to be alone. The Americans are funny people. Although they sit together by the dozen in taverns, they turn their backs to each other, and no one talks to anybody else. Is this supposed to be the custom of a republic? I don't like it. Is this supposed to be the fashion of the nineteenth century? I don't like it either. "Wait a little! There will be more things you won't like." Thus I can hear my brother talking. . . .

Today, the 30th of October [*1842*], we are here in Northborough, and I feel happier than I have for a fortnight. Moses is in New York, and we will meet him, God willing, at Worcester on Tuesday. The sky is clear and cloudless, and nature is so lovely and romantic, the air so fresh and wholesome, that I praise God, who has created this beautiful country.

Yet, at the same time, I regret that the people here are so cold and that their watchword seems to be "Help yourself; that's the best help" [*quote written in English*]. I cannot believe that a man who adapts himself to the language, customs, and character of America can ever quite forget his home in the European countries. Having been here so short a time, I should be very arrogant if I were to set down at this time my judgments on America. The whole country, however, with its extensive domestic and foreign trade, its railroads, canals and factories, looks to me like an adolescent youth. He is a part of society, talking like a man and pretending to be a man. Yet he is truly only a boy. That is America! Although she appears to know everything, her knowledge of religion, history, and human nature is, in truth, very elementary. . . . American history is composed of Independence and Washington; that is all! . . .

It seems impossible that this nation can remain a republic for many years. Millions and millions of dollars go each year to Europe, but only for the purchase of luxuries. Athens and Rome fell at the very moment of their flowering, for though commerce, art, and science had reached their highest level, luxury—vases of gold and silver, garments of purple and silk—caused their downfall. The merchant who seeks to expand too rapidly in his first years, whose expenses are not balanced by his income, is bound to become a bankrupt. America consumes too much, produces too little. Her inhabitants are lazy and too much accustomed to providing for their own comforts to create a land which will provide for their real and spiritual needs. . . .

/////

On Monday morning, December 5th, we set out for Groton in a sleigh and at night stayed with an old farmer. . . . It was a very satisfactory business day, and we took in about fifteen dollars. On Tuesday we continued through much snow, via Pepperell, to Hollis, in New Hampshire. Towards evening the good Moses managed to overthrow the sleigh, and me along with it, into the snow. I am sure that, should I ever come this way in future years, I shall always be able to recognize the spot where I lay in a snowdrift.

After spending Wednesday in Milford, we traveled beyond on Thursday and Friday, spending Saturday at Amherst and Sunday at the home of Mr. Kendall in Mount Vernon. Business, thanks be to God is satisfactory, and this week we took in more than forty-five dollars. We rode horseback for pleasure on Sunday.

Things will yet go well.
The world is round and must keep turning
Things will yet go well.

So goes an old German song which I once heard an actor sing in Furth in a play, which one, I don't remember.

On Monday the 12th to Lyndeborough; Tuesday to Wilton; Wednesday to Mason Village; Thursday, New Ipswich; Friday, Ashburnham. On Saturday we came to Westminster, where we stayed over Sunday, the 18th of December. It was extremely cold this week, and there was more snow than we had ever seen in our lives. At some places the snow was three to four feet deep, and we could hardly get through with the sleigh. How often we thanked God that we did not have to carry our wares on our backs in this cold. To tramp with a heavy pack from house to house in this weather would be terrible.

O youth of Bavaria, if you long for freedom, if you dream of life here, beware, for you shall rue the hour you embarked for a country and a life far different from what you dream of. This land—and particularly this calling—offers harsh, cold air, great masses of snow, and people who are credulous, filled with silly pride, cold toward foreigners and toward all who do not speak the language perfectly. And, though "money is beauty, scarce everywhere," yet there is still plenty of it in the country. The Whig government, the new bankruptcy law, the high tariff bill—all combine to create a scarcity of ready cash the like of which I have never seen nor the oldest inhabitants of the land ever experienced. . . .

/////

Monday, January 2nd, we went to Holden Factory; Tuesday, Hubbardston; Wednesday, Templeton; Thursday, Winchester; Friday, Rindge; Saturday, Jaffrey; Sunday, Peterborough; Monday, Hancock; Tuesday, Antrium; and, on Wednesday, the 11th, Nelson.

The weather is very bad and the sleigh sinks two feet into the snow. Money is scarce, but, God be thanked, sleeping quarters have been good. There is much work for little profit, yet God in heaven may send better times that all our drudgery will not have been in vain. . . .

Dear, good mother, how often I recall your letters, your advice against going to America: "Stay at home; you can win success as well in Germany." But I would not listen; I had to come to America. I was drawn by fate and here I am, living a life that is wandering and uncertain. . . .

We long to send a letter home which will bring joy and happiness, but, dear God, shall we lie like the Bavarians? This I should not like, yet they at home would be upset by the truth. It seems wisest to let them continue with golden hopes, and, for the time being, not to write at all. You alone, dear mother, may judge, should you read this journal at some future time, whether we have done right or wrong.

/////

On Tuesday morning [*January 17th*] at ten I left Worcester, it being my turn to travel alone for seven weeks. A thousand thanks to God. I felt far stronger than when I first left my brothers in Boston. Now I have become more accustomed to the language, the business, and the American way of life. . . .

On Monday, January 30th, I went from Phillipston to Athol, satisfied at night with my day's work. . . .

It is hard, very hard indeed, to make a living this way. Sweat runs down my body in great drops and my back seems to be breaking, but I cannot stop; I must go on and on, however far my way lies. . . .

Times are bad; everywhere there is no money. This increases the hardship of life so that I am sometimes tempted to return to New York and to start all over again. However, I must have patience. God will help. On Sunday every farmer urges me to attend church, and this week in Williamsburg, at each house where I tried to sell my wares, I was told to go to church.

God in Heaven, Father of our ancestors, Thou who has protected the little band of Jews unto this day, Thou knowest my thoughts. Thou alone knowest of my grief when, on the Sabbath's eve, I must retire to my lodging and on Saturday morning carry my pack on my back, profaning the holy day. . . . By the God of Israel I swear that if I can't make my living in any other way in this blessed land of freedom and equality, I will return to my mother, brothers, and sisters, and God will help me and give me His aid and blessing in all my ways.

The open field is my temple where I pray. Our Father in heaven will hear me there. "In every place where thou shalt mention my name I shall come to thee and bless thee." This comforts me and lends me strength and courage and endurance for my sufferings. And in only two more weeks I shall find something different.

/////

For more than three months I have not been in the mood to continue my diary or to write anything at all. In the middle of March I had hoped to get rid of my peddler's existence. But I was forced to take up my pack again and from February 26th to March 11th I journey towards Worcester, where I was to meet my dear brothers. . . .

/////

A year ago today I left Furth. Thou, God, guidest our destinies. I cannot say whether America has misled me or whether I misled myself. How quickly this year has passed! But how many sad and bitter hours has it brought me! In Furth ten years did not bring the worries and troubles that a single year has brought me in this land. Yet Thou, Father of all, who has brought me across the ocean and directed my steps up till today, wilt grant me Thy further aid. With confidence in Thy Fatherly goodness I continue my way of life. Thou alone knowest my goal. May I find contentment and a life of peace, united in well-being with my dear mother and with my brothers and sisters!

On Thursday [*June 22nd*] Juda and I . . . took the train to Natick and walked from there to Weston, Wayland, Lincoln, Concord, Carlisle,

Billerica, Wilmington, Reading, Middleton, and Topsfield, where we had a hard time finding a night's lodging. We next went on to Hamilton, Essex, Rockport and Gloucester. Here we had a magnificent view of the Atlantic coast and of the sea, filled with fishermen, schooners, and small boats. In the morning we went sailing in a boat and out into the open sea for fishing. But we did not enjoy it very much and soon sought the land again.

What else is there in life besides constant fishing? One man fishes this way, the other that way; this one fishes the small streams, that one the ocean. And when they tire of fishing, Death, the great Fisherman, comes to all of them alike and they, like the fish themselves, are caught. O tragic fishery!

How many experiences do you give, O America, to the young man who carries on his life of fishing! How many stones are caught in the nets which are set for fish! How often is an empty net pulled from the dark, unfathomable depths when a full net is expected!

Yet the fisherman says, "Patience." Patience, dear God—send me an abundance of it! Although there is still no sign of it, the net should, at some time, be full. [*Here the diary ends.*]

Questions for Discussion

1. What made the life of an immigrant peddler—and particularly this German-Jewish immigrant—such a difficult one? How do Abraham Kohn's experiences in the eastern United States compare with those of the two Norwegian immigrants in rural Minnesota described in the following selection?
2. How accurate are Kohn's views of American society?
3. At the end of Kohn's diary, he relates a fishing expedition with his brother. What is the significance of this final metaphorical soliloquy?

19.
Jens Gronbek and
Syver Christopherson
Norwegian Immigrants Write
Home, 1867 and 1869

These letters are by Norwegian immigrants who settled in Minnesota. Jens Gronbek writes enthusiastically about the United States and his job on a farm. He describes the many opportunities for hardworking immigrants, particularly in farming, and encourages his brother-in-law to consider joining him. Syver Christopherson, on the other hand, relates the shortage of jobs, the meager pay and the problems he experiences in finding work. The glowing reports others wrote home, he notes, are exaggerated, if not altogether false.

From Jens Gronbek, Rice County Minnesota to
Christian Heltzen (Gronbek's brother-in-law), Lesja, Norway.

September 1867.

Dear Christian,

Thank you for your welcome letter, which was both unexpected and remarkable. . . . You ask that I report to you concerning conditions here. This I will do by way of addition to what I have written to you before.

America is a naturally rich land, endowed with virtually everything, except to a dull-witted European who is disappointed not to find money in the streets or who expects to get things without moving his arms. Spring

Carlton C. Qualey. Translator and Editor. "Three America Letters to Lesja." *Norwegian-American Studies.* 27. (1977): 41–54.

An idealized drawing of emigrants on a mid-nineteenth-century ship. *(National Park Service: Statue of Liberty National Monument)*

work has been delayed by heavy rains this year. I think we sowed wheat in the middle of May. Now we have harvested and, thanks to God, it is good. The quantity is about average.

There are many thousand acres of available land here—government, school, and railroad land—although it is increasingly in the West. As for government or homestead land, one can take a quarter section or 160 acres free, except for payment of a registration fee of $14 per quarter, and this is almost all arable land. An acre is 4 1/2 Norwegian *maal*. Schools and railroad companies have received large grants of land for their support, and they sell for 6 shillings American or 75 shillings Norwegian per acre. This land you can use as you wish and can sell when you will, and therefore it is most sought. On homesteads, you are obligated to establish a residence, build a house, and start cultivation. You must live on the claim for six months of each year, and you may not sell it for five years, during which time it is free of taxes or further payments. It is this policy, of course, that makes the American government so generous and good for immigrants. . . .

Do you know what, my dear Christian? If you find farming in Norway unrewarding and your earnings at sea are poor, I advise you, as your friend and brother-in-law, to abandon everything, and—if you can raise $600—

to come to Minnesota. Do not believe that all is lies and fables in reports that in one year in America all will be well, for I can testify that it is true, despite the fact that, last fall when I came, I thought for a time I would starve. . . .

I have now worked for a Norwegian farmer since Christmas and will remain here until October. I have it very good here. Five meals each day of the best food in the world, so that I fear I have become choosy. You can best understand the food here when I say that the cost of board for a week is $5 and for individual meals $1 to $1.80.

Now, dear Christian, if you consider selling and emigrating across the Atlantic Ocean, please write me. Do not be worried about the voyage, either for your wife or for the children. Neither should you be alarmed about Indians or other trolls in America, for the former are now chased away, and the Yankees, that is Americans, are as kind a folk toward a stranger as I can imagine. . . .

. . . Nearly all newcomers want to return to the homeland until they have become American citizens, and then hardly anyone wants to return.

. . . Greet all friends and family.

From Syver Christopherson, Waseca, Minnesota to P.H. Kolstad, Lesja, Norway.

[Christopherson sold his farm in Norway to emigrate.]

October 3, 1869.

I have had in mind writing to you for some time, but have delayed in hopes of hearing from home in response to two letters I have written since coming to America, both without reply. Either your letters or mine have gone astray. I hope that you will send me a full report from home.

First, I will report on how things have gone with me since I came here. On my arrival in Christiania, I met several acquaintances who advised me to buy my ticket to Oconto [*Wisconsin on the north side of Green Bay*], known for its work opportunities. So I went there—it took six weeks from the time I left home. I got a job at $30 a month with free board. Wages ranged from $20 to $30 depending on the work. At the sawmill where I worked, there were many acquaintances. . . . With so many people there who knew me, I could not imagine that there would be any difficulty in securing payment of wages.

After two months or so I had earned about $70, but there was great difficulty in getting my money; it was almost impossible for newcomers who did not know the language. So I quit, for I could not work for promises and good faith. On my departure, I got only $10 of my wages, the remainder to be paid after the mill shut down in the fall. Whether or not I get anything then I know not. Even though several others have had the same experiences, I cannot understand how these Lesja people could have written, as they did, a much-too-favorable account despite conditions far different at best. I fear that every corner of America is infected with the same illness.

A month ago I left Oconto and came here [*Waseca*] where I now work on the railroad. Wages are $2 per day and I pay $3.50 weekly for board. The work is unusually heavy and strenuous, and there has been a lot of rain since I came, and so conditions have been difficult. Wages are paid as of the 15th of the month; there remain always 15 days unpaid. This is to hold workers on the job. I still have not received payment since I arrived here. . . . I am not sure how long I will be in this place, and I do not know if there will be work this winter. I plan to stay on as long as there is a job to be had. It is very difficult to work in the winter and wages are poor.

I can report little concerning general conditions, as I have been in America too short a time. However, I have traveled through a good part of the country and have talked with many Norwegians who have been here both a short and a long time. Some have thrived quite well, but even so I cannot understand where those who write so glowingly get their information. It is only a tenth part correct and I hear loud complaints from acquaintances and friends who have been fooled. In any case, Minnesota is a very cold and severe area. Even though it is only September, the weather at night has been so cold that there has been frost and rime, and added to this there is a penetrating wind. Nevertheless, over 100,000 acres have been settled this past summer. There is plenty of prairie land to be had but no woodland. What is one to do for wood to burn and to build with? To settle on such land seems to be impossible. Most people do not take this into consideration until too late.

I know all too well that there are many in Lesja who are quite well circumstanced but who have America notions. If they had seen what I have seen, they would regard these notions as wind and wine. I can truthfully advise you that if one in his situation in Norway used the same time and effort as must be devoted here, his situation would be quite different. I have heard the same from solid farmers who have been in this country for a longer time than I. Otherwise, America is in many respects attractive, if one does not dwell overly on either the bright or the dark.

. . . I am in good health, thank God, but as to any definite arrangement for my family, I cannot say until I have been able to accumulate some money. In addition, I must have a place for them to live. It is now very difficult to find a house to rent, and that is understandable when one thinks of the hundreds of thousands who are streaming into this area each year, most of them poor and without anything.

. . . I must break off this letter. You and the family are greeted most cordially by your friend, Syver Christopherson.

Questions for Discussion

1. How do you account for the difference in attitude between Gronbek and Christopherson? How do these attitudes compare with that of Abraham Kohn?
2. How do these three immigrant experiences compare with those of modern immigration?

20.
Mary Paul

Letters from the Lowell Mills and a Utopian Community, 1845–1855

Mary Paul probably would not have considered herself an adventurous spirit, but before her marriage in 1857, her search for a better life had led her to take part in two of the most significant developments of the early and mid-nineteenth century. She was both a worker in the factory system that was transforming the American economy and a participant in the movement for social reform.

Mary Paul was born in Vermont, and her wanderings took her to much of New England and as far south as New Jersey. Her close ties to her family, and particularly to her father, Bela, are evident in these letters. As a girl of fifteen she worked as a domestic, but she soon moved to Lowell, Massachusetts, home of the famous Lowell mills, to seek employment in the textile factories there. The Lowell mills employed girls and young women from the farms, attempting to provide them with a more or less sheltered environment as well as employment. It was widely held that women, or at least "ladies," should not earn their own living, and the regulations of the Lowell boarding houses were designed to assure the young women and their families that factory work was a respectable occupation. The regulations at the early mills also had another purpose—to impose industrial discipline on women whose farming background had attuned them to more natural rhythms than those of the factory.

Thomas Dublin, ed. *Farm to Factory: Women's Letters, 1830–1860*. New York: Columbia University Press, 1981. Reprinted by permission.

Young women working in a New England textile mill, about 1850. *(International Museum of Photography, George Eastman House)*

> *Tiring of this life, Mary Paul was attracted to a commune of the type inspired by the French reformer, Charles Fourier, whose disciples established several model communities in the United States in the 1840s and 1850s. A prominent feature of the ongoing romantic reform movement, most communes suffered an early death. Mary Paul's North American Phalanx was one of these.*

> *[The first letter was written while Mary Paul was a domestic with a farming family.]*

[*Woodstock, Vt.*] Saturday, Sept. 13th 1845

Dear Father

I received your letter this afternoon by Wm Griffith. You wished me to write if I had seen Mr. Angell. I have neither written to him nor seen him nor has he written to me. I began to write but I could not write what I wanted to. I think if I could see him I could convince him of his error if he would let me talk.

I am very glad you sent my shoes. They fit very well indeed they [*are*] large enough.

I want you to consent to let me go to Lowell if you can. I think it would be much better for me than to stay about here. I could earn more to begin with than I can any where about here. I am in need of clothes which I cannot get if I stay about here and for that reason I want to go to Lowell or some other place. We all think that if I could go with some steady girl that I might do well. I want you to think of it and make up your mind. Mercy Jane Griffith is going to start in four or five weeks. Aunt Miller and Aunt Sarah think it would be a good chance for me to go if you would consent—which I want you to do if possible. I want to see you and talk with you about it.

Aunt Sarah gains slowly.

Mary

/////

[By the time Mary Paul wrote this letter she had found work in the Lowell mills.]

Lowell Dec 21st 1845

Dear Father,

I received your letter on Thursday the 14th with much pleasure. I am well which is one comfort. My health and life are spared while others are cut off. Last Thursday one girl fell down and broke her neck which caused instant death. She was going in or coming out of the mill and slipped down it being very icy. The same day a man was killed by the car [*the railroad cars next to the factory*]. Another had nearly all of her ribs broken. Another was nearly killed by falling down and having a bale of cotton fall on him. Last Tuesday we were paid. In all I had six dollars sixty cents paid $4.68 for board. With the rest I got me a pair of rubbers and a pair of 50.cts shoes. Next payment I am to have a dollar a week beside my board. We have not had much snow the deepest being not more than 4 inches. It has been very warm for winter. Perhaps you would like something about our regulations about going in and coming out of the mill. At 5 o'clock the bell rings for the folks to get up and get breakfast. At half past six it rings for the girls to get up and at seven they are called into the mill. At half past twelve we have dinner are called back at one and stay till half past seven. I get along very well with my work. I can doff [*remove full bobbins of yarn and replace them with empty ones*] as fast as any girl in our room. The usual time for learning is six months but I think I shall have frames before I shall have been in three as I get along so fast. I think that the factory is the best place for me and if any girl wants employment I advise them to come to Lowell. Tell Harriet that though she does not hear from me she is not forgotten. I have little time to devote to writing that I cannot write all I want to. There are half a dozen letters which I ought to write today but I have not time.

Tell Harriet I send my love to her and all of the girls. Give my love to Mrs. Clement. Tell Henry this will answer for him and you too for this time.

This from

Mary S Paul

/////

Lowell April 12 1846

Dear Father

I received your letter with much pleasure but was sorry to hear you had been lame. I had waited for a long time to hear from you but no letter came last Sunday so I thought I would write again which I did and was going to send it to the [*post*] office Monday but at noon I received a letter from William and so I did not send it at all. Last Friday I received a letter from you. You wanted to know what I am doing. I am at work in a spinning room and tending four sides of warp which is one girls work. The overseer tells me that he never had a girl get along better than I do and that he will do the best he can by me. I stand it well, though they tell me that I am growing very poor. I was paid nine shillings [*about $1.50*] a week last payment [*exclusive of room and board*] and am to have more this one though we have been out considerable for backwater [*flooding that blocked the waterwheel providing the mill's power*] which will take off a good deal. The Agent promises to pay us nearly as much as we should have made but I do not think that he will. The payment was up last night and we are to be paid this week. I have a very good boarding place have enough to eat and that which is good enough. The girls are all kind and obliging. The girls that I room with are all from Vermont and good girls too. Now I will tell you about our rules at the boarding house. We have none in particular except that we have to go to bed about 10. o'clock. At half past four in the morning the bell rings for us to get up and at five for us to go into the mill. At seven we are called out to breakfast are allowed half an hour between bells and the same at noon till the first of May when we have three quarters [*of an hour*] until the first of September. We have dinner at half past 12 and supper at seven. If Julius should go to Boston tell him to come this way and see me. He must come to the Lawrence Counting room and call for me. He can ask someone to show him where the Lawrence is. I hope he will not fail to go. . . .

Yours affectionately,

Mary S Paul

/////

[Between the following letter and the last, Mary Paul had left Lowell and then returned.]

Lowell Nov 5th 1848

Dear Father,

Doubtless you have been looking for a letter from me all the week past. I would have written but wished to find whether I should be able to stand it—to do the work that I am now doing. I was unable to get my old place in the cloth room on the Suffolk or on any other corporation. . . . So I went to my old overseer on the Tremont Cor[*poration*]. I had no idea that he would want one, but he *did*, and I went to work last Tuesday—warping— the same work I used to do.

It is *very* hard indeed and sometimes I think I shall not be able to endure it. I never worked so hard in my life but perhaps I shall get used to it. I shall try to do so for there is no other work I can do unless I spin, and that I shall not undertake on any account. I presume you have heard before this that the wages are to be reduced on the 20th of this month. It is *true* and there seems to be a good deal of excitement on the subject but I cannot tell what will be the consequence. . . . The companies claim they are losing immense sums every *day* and therefore are obliged to lessen the wages, but this seems perfectly absurd to me for they are constantly making *repairs* and it seems to me that this would not be if there were really any danger of their being obliged to *stop* the mills.

It is very difficult for anyone to get into the mill on any corporation. All seem to be very full of help. I expect to be paid about two dollars a week [*exclusive of room and board*] but it will be dearly earned. I cannot tell how it is but never since I have worked in the mill have I been so tired as I have for the last week but it may be owing to the long rest I have had for the last six months. . . . But enough of this. The Whigs of Lowell had a great time on the night of the 3rd. They had an immense procession of men on foot bearing *torches* and *banners* got up for the occasion. The houses were illuminated (Whigs houses) and by the way I should think the whole of *Lowell* were Whigs. I went out to see the illuminations and they truly did look splendid. The Merrimack house was illuminated from attic to cellar. Every pane of glass in the house had a half candle to it and there were many others lighted in the same way. One entire block of the Merrimack Cor[*poration*] with the exception of one tenement which doubtless was occupied by a free soiler[1] who would not illuminate on any account whatever.

(Monday Eve) I have been to work today and think I shall manage to get along with the work. I am not so tired as I was last week. I have not yet found out what wages I shall get but presume they will be about $2.00 per week exclusive of board. I think of nothing further to write excepting I wish

---

[1] Free soilers opposed the extension of slavery to the territories.

you to prevail on *Henry* to write me, also tell *Olive* to write and *Eveline*
when she comes. . . .

Write soon. Yours affectionately,
Mary S Paul

/////

Brattleboro Nov. 27, 1853

Dear father,

I think I will write you a few words tonight as you may be wishing to
hear from me. . . .

I have a plan for myself which I am going to lay before you and to see
what you think of it. When I was in Manchester last spring my friend Carrie
and her husband were talking of going to New Jersey to live and proposed
that I should go with them. They have decided to go and are going in a few
weeks, maybe as soon as Jan. though they may not go until April or May.
I have been thinking of it all summer and have told them I will go if you do
not object. I can hardly get *my own* consent to go any farther away from
you, though I know that in reality a few miles cannot make much difference.
The name of the town is Atlantic . . . about 40 miles from New York City.
The people among whom they are going are Associationists. The name will
give you something of an idea of their principles. There [*are*] about 125
persons in all that live there, and the association is called the "North American Phalanx."[2] I presume that you may have heard of it. You have if you
read the "Tribune." The editor Mr "Greely" is an Associationist and a
shareholder in the "Phalanx," but he does not live there. The advantage
that will arise from my going there will be that I can get better pay without
working as hard as at any other place. The price for work there being 9 cts
an hour and the number of hours for a days work, *ten* besides I should not
be confined to one kind of work but could do almost anything, could have
the privilege of doing anything that is done there—*Housework* if I choose
and that without degrading myself, which is more than I could do anywhere
else. That is, in the opinion of most people, a very foolish and wrong idea
by the way, but one that has so much weight with girls, that they would
live on 25 cts per week at sewing, or school teaching rather than work at
housework. I would do it myself although I think it foolish. This all comes
from the way servants are *treated*, and I cannot see why girls should be
blamed after all, for not wishing to "work out" as it is called. At the "Phalanx" it is different. All work there, and all are paid alike. Both men and
women have the same pay for the same work. There is no such word as

---

[2]Phalanxes were the name given to the communities inspired by the French reformer
Charles Fourier. Fourier's disciples often called themselves Associationists.

TIME TABLE OF THE LOWELL MILLS,

Arranged to make the working time throughout the year average 11 hours per day.

TO TAKE EFFECT SEPTEMBER 21st., 1853.

The Standard time being that of the meridian of Lowell, as shown by the Regulator Clock of AMOS SANBORN, Post Office Corner, Central Street.

From March 20th to September 19th, inclusive.

COMMENCE WORK, at 6.30 A. M.　LEAVE OFF WORK, at 6.30 P. M., except on Saturday Evenings.
BREAKFAST at 6 A. M.　DINNER, at 12 M.　Commence Work, after dinner, 12.45 P. M.

From September 20th to March 19th, inclusive.

COMMENCE WORK at 7.00 A. M.　LEAVE OFF WORK, at 7.00 P. M., except on Saturday Evenings.
BREAKFAST at 6.30 A. M.　DINNER, at 12.30 P.M.　Commence Work, after dinner, 1.15 P. M.

BELLS.

From March 20th to September 19th, inclusive.

Morning Bells.	Dinner Bells.	Evening Bells.
First bell,...........4.30 A. M.	Ring out,.............12.00 M.	Ring out,...........6.30 P. M.
Second, 5.30 A. M. ; Third, 6.20.	Ring in,...........12 35 P. M.	Except on Saturday Evenings.

From September 20th to March 19th, inclusive.

Morning Bells.	Dinner Bells.	Evening Bells.
First bell,...........5.00 A. M.	Ring out,...........12.30 P. M.	Ring out at...........7.00 P. M.
Second, 6.00 A. M. ; Third, 6.50.	Ring in,.............1.05 P. M.	Except on Saturday Evenings.

SATURDAY EVENING BELLS.

During APRIL, MAY, JUNE, JULY, and AUGUST, Ring Out, at 6.00 P. M.
The remaining Saturday Evenings in the year, ring out as follows :

SEPTEMBER.	NOVEMBER.	JANUARY.
First Saturday, ring out 6.00 P. M.	Third Saturday ring out 4.00 P. M.	Third Saturday, ring out 4.25 P. M.
Second " " 5.45 "	Fourth " " 3.55 "	Fourth " " 4.35 "
Third " " 5.30 "		
Fourth " " 5.20 "	DECEMBER.	FEBRUARY.
OCTOBER.	First Saturday, ring out 3.50 P. M.	First Saturday, ring out 4.45 P. M.
First Saturday, ring out 5.05 P. M.	Second " " 3.55 "	Second " " 4.55 "
Second " " 4.55 "	Third " " 3.55 "	Third " " 5.00 "
Third " " 4.45 "	Fourth " " 4.00 "	Fourth " " 5.10 "
Fourth " " 4.35 "	Fifth " " 4.00 "	
Fifth " " 4.25 "		MARCH.
NOVEMBER.	JANUARY.	First Saturday, ring out 5.25 P. M.
First Saturday, ring out 4.15 P. M.	First Saturday, ring out 4.10 P. M.	Second " " 5.30 "
Second " " 4.05 "	Second " " 4.15 "	Third " " 5.35 "
		Fourth " " 5.45 "

YARD GATES will be opened at the first stroke of the bells for entering or leaving the Mills.

SPEED GATES commence hoisting three minutes before commencing work.

Penhallow, Printer, Wyman's Exchange, 28 Merrimack St.

Timetable of the Lowell mills. *(Museum of American Textile History)* aristocracy unless there is real (not pretended) superiority, that will make itself felt, if not acknowledged, everywhere. The members can live as cheaply as they choose and pay only for what they eat, and no profit on that, most of the provision being raised on the grounds. One can join them with or without funds, and can leave at any time they choose. Frank has been there this Fall and was very much pleased with what he saw there and thought that it would be the best thing for Carrie and me to do with ourselves. A woman gets much better pay there than elsewhere, though it is not so with a man, though he is not meanly paid by any means. There is more equality in such things according to the work not the sex. You know that men often get more than double the pay for doing the same work that women do. . . . Another advantage from living there is this, the members can have privileges of *Education* free of expense to themselves alone, the extent of this education must of course depend on the *means* of the society. If I could see you I could give you a better idea. That I can possibly do by writing, but you will know something by this, enough to form an opinion perhaps and I wish you to let me know what you think of my plans. . . . I hope sometime to be able to do something for you sometime and sometimes feel ashamed that I have not before this. I am not one of the *smart* kind, and never had a passion for laying up money. . . . One thing more, I have never had good pay. I am getting along slowly on coats, and shall do better as I get used to the business. I can work at my trade if I wish at the Phalanx. . . .

Affectionately yours,
Mary S Paul

/////

North American Phalanx, N.J.
Sunday morn May 7th 1854

Dear father

I feel that you must be anxious to hear from me, and so will write a few lines that you may know I am here safe and well. . . .

By the way it is spring here, peach trees are out of blossom, cherry & apple trees are in full glory. As far as I can see from the window, at which I am writing, nothing but immense orchards of peach, cherries, & apple trees present themselves to view. I never saw *orchards* before, but I have got a long way from my story. I'll go back. We arrived here a good deal *wet* & were kindly received, had been expected for a long time they told us. . . . Our things which should have been here with us did not come until Monday afterward, and then not all of them. We have been very busy all the week putting things to rights. Have not done much work beside our own. I have worked about two hours each day for the Phalanx, three quarters in sweeping, one and a quarter in the dining hall, clearing & laying the tables.

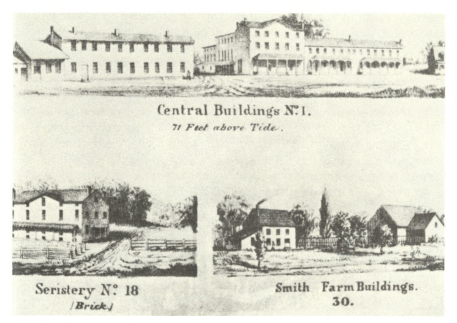

Central Buildings N.º I.
71 Feet above Tide.

Seristery N.º 18
[Brick]

Smith Farm Buildings.
30.

The North American Phalanx in 1855. *(New York State Historical Association)*

Tomorrow I am going to begin sewing which will add three hours each day to my work. On ironing days I shall iron one, two, or three days just as I like. I must prepare to go to my dinner now. We have one hour, from 12 to 1, for dinner, breakfast from 5 1/2 to 7, teas from 6 1/2 to 7 1/2. After dinner from one till quarter past two I do my work in the dining hall. Three o'clock, I have come back to finish my letter. I cannot tell you anything definite now about matters and things because I dont know about them myself. I shall write you again as soon as I can & then I will tell you more about ways here. The place is very pleasant and the people remarkably kind. Upon the whole I think that I may like it very well after I get used to the strange ways. . . .

Yours truly,
Mary S Paul

/////

Phalanx New Jersey March 3 [*18*]55

My dear father

I have been wishing to write to you for some time but was prevented by the state of affairs here, at least I did not wish to write until I had something definite to say respecting my prospects here. . . . I think I wrote you early in the winter that the loss of the mill [*to a fire*] involved the

Association in difficulties from which it would be hard to extricate it. The fear seemed to pass away and many seemed to think the foundations were too firm to be shaken even by an enormous debt, but it seems we were wrong for this Association is most certainly in the very last stage. . . . I do not know how long I can stay here but will not leave until I am obliged to. The life here has many attractions & advantages which no other life can have, and as imperfect as it is I have already seen enough to convince me that the Association is the true life. And although all the attempts that have ever yet been made toward it have been failures, inasmuch as they have passed away (but they have all left their mark) my faith in the principles is as strong as ever, stronger if possible. There is a better day coming for the world. "We may not live to see the day but the Earth shall glisten in the ray of the good time coming." Don't be worried about me father, for I am certainly more comfortable here than I could be anywhere else. I suppose when I leave here I shall have to take up sewing again as that seems to be the only thing open to me. I flatter myself that I had fairly escaped from the confinement of the needle, but I shall have to return to it after all. Well I expect it will all be for the best. . . . Give my love to everybody that cares for me and accept the same for yourself from

Your affectionate daughter
Mary S Paul

Questions for Discussion

1. What was life like at the Lowell mills? Why did Mary Paul go there, and why did she leave?
2. Does life at the North American Phalanx appeal to you? How would you compare it with life at the mills? Why did Mary Paul prefer it?

21.
Massachusetts Congregationalist Clergy
Pastoral Letter Opposing Women's Rights, 1837

This document expresses the Congregationalist clergy's reaction to the speeches of Sarah and Angelina Grimké in favor of abolitionism. The letter indicates the degree of authority felt and exercised by the clergy at that time, and their concern over the public role of women who were making speeches at antislavery conventions held in New England and New York. This letter inspired the Grimké sisters—see the next selection in this anthology—to speak out also about their views on women.

. . . We invite your attention to the dangers which at present seem to threaten the female character with wide-spread and permanent injury.

The appropriate duties and influence of woman are clearly stated in the New Testament. Those duties and that influence are unobtrusive and private, but the source of mighty power. When the mild, dependent, softening influence of woman upon the sternness of man's opinions is fully exercised, society feels the effects of it in a thousand forms. The power of woman is in her dependence, flowing from the consciousness of that weakness which God has given her for her protection, and which keeps her in those departments of life that form the character of individuals and of the nation. There are social influences which females use in promoting piety and the great objects of Christian benevolence which we cannot too highly

Extract from a Pastoral Letter of "the General Association of Massachusetts Congregational (Orthodox) to the Churches under their care"—1837. *History of Woman Suffrage*, Vol 1. Elizabeth Cady Stanton, Susan B. Anthony, and Matilda Joslyn Gage, eds. New York: Fowler and Wells, 1881.

commend. We appreciate the unostentatious prayers and efforts of woman in advancing the cause of religion at home and abroad; in Sabbath-schools; in leading religious inquirers to the pastors for instruction; and in all such associated effort as becomes the modesty of her sex; and earnestly hope that she may abound more and more in these labors of piety and love.

But when she assumes the place and tone of man as a public reformer, our care and protection of her seem unnecessary; we put ourselves in self-defence against her; she yields the power which God has given her for protection, and her character becomes unnatural. If the vine, whose strength and beauty is to lean upon the trellis-work and half conceal its clusters, thinks to assume the independence and the overshadowing nature of the elm, it will not only cease to bear fruit, but fall in shame and dishonor into the dust. We cannot, therefore, but regret the mistaken conduct of those who encourage females to bear an obtrusive and ostentatious part in measures of reform, and countenance any of that sex who so far forget themselves as to itinerate in the character of public lecturers and teachers. — We especially deplore the intimate acquaintance and promiscuous conversation of females with regard to things "which ought not to be named"; by which that modesty and delicacy which is the charm of domestic life, and which constitutes the true influence of woman in society, is consumed, and the way opened, as we apprehend, for degeneracy and ruin. We say these things, not to discourage proper influences against sin, but to secure such reformation as we believe is Scriptural, and will be permanent.

Questions for Discussion

1. What do these members of the clergy fear will be the effects of women's reform activities?
2. What assumptions are made regarding women's nature and proper role? Compare the attitudes of these clergy members with those of Mary Lee, Mary Paul, and the Grimké sisters.

22.
Sarah and Angelina Grimké
Letters on Abolitionism and Women's Rights, 1837

Sarah (1792–1873) and Angelina (1805–1879) Grimké grew up in a slaveholding family in Charleston, South Carolina. Both became Quakers and were active in the abolitionist cause. Encouraged by William Lloyd Garrison, they began publicly to denounce the evils of slavery, speaking at female antislavery societies in New York and New England in 1836 and 1837. As they drew larger and larger audiences, they aroused the concern of many clergy who believed that women's influence should be confined to their homes. The sisters, however, were convinced that women could not carry out their moral duty at home while remaining silent about the moral issue of slavery. Thus their initial concern for the antislavery cause developed into an equally strong one for women's rights. They asserted their kinship with female slaves, and refused to acknowledge any religious basis for male domination.

Although addressed to individuals, these letters had an instructional purpose and were intended for publication. Sarah's appeared in the New England Spectator, *and Angelina's letters were published in* The Emancipator *and* The Liberator.

Sarah Grimké, *Letters on the Equality of the Sexes and the Condition of Women*. Boston, 1838. In Alice Rossi, ed., *The Feminist Papers*. (New York: Columbia University Press, 1973), 311–315.

Letter from Sarah Grimké to Mary Parker, President of the Boston Female Anti-Slavery Society

Brookline, 1837

. . . During the early part of my life, my lot was cast among the butterflies of the *fashionable* world; and of this class of women, I am constrained to say, both from experience and observation, that their education is miserably deficient; that they are taught to regard marriage as the one thing needful, the only avenue to distinction; hence to attract the notice and win the attention of men, by their external charms is the chief business of fashionable girls. They seldom think that men will be allured by intellectual acquirements, because they find, that where any mental superiority exists, a woman is generally shunned and regarded as stepping out of her "appropriate sphere," which, in their view, is to dress, to dance, to set out to the best possible advantage her person, to read the novels which inundate the press, and which do more to destroy her character as a rational creature, than any thing else. Fashionable women regard themselves, and are regarded by men as pretty toys or as mere instruments of pleasure; and the vacuity of mind, the heartlessness, the frivolity which is the necessary result of this false and debasing estimate of women, can only be fully understood by those who have mingled in the folly and wickedness of fashionable life . . .

There is another and much more numerous class in this country, who are withdrawn by education or circumstances from the circle of fashionable amusements, but who are brought up with the dangerous and absurd idea, that *marriage* is a kind of preferment; and that to be able to keep their husband's house, and render his situation comfortable, is the end of her being. Much that she does and says and thinks is done in reference to this situation; and to be married is too often held up to the view of girls as the sine qua non of human happiness and human existence. For this purpose more than for any other, I verily believe the majority of girls are trained. This is demonstrated by the imperfect education which is bestowed upon them, and the little pains taken to cultivate their minds, after they leave school, by the little time allowed them for reading, and by the idea being constantly inculcated, that although all household concerns should be attended to with scrupulous punctuality at particular seasons, the improvement of their intellectual capacities is only a secondary consideration, and may serve as an occupation to fill up the odds and ends of time. In most families, it is considered a matter of far more consequence to call a girl off from making a pie, or a pudding, than to interrupt her whilst engaged in her studies. This mode of training necessarily exalts, in their view, the animal above the intellectual and spiritual nature, and teaches women to regard themselves as a kind of machinery, necessary to keep the do-

Angelina and Sarah Grimké. *(New York Public Library)*

mestic engine in order, but of little value as the *intelligent* companions of men . . . .

There is another class of women in this country, to whom I cannot refer, without feelings of the deepest shame and sorrow. I allude to our female slaves. Our southern cities are overwhelmed beneath a tide of pollution; the virtue of female slaves is wholly at the mercy of irresponsible tyrants, and women are bought and sold in our slave markets, to gratify the brutal lust of those who bear the name of Christians. In our slave States, if amid all her degradation and ignorance, a woman desires to preserve her virtue unsullied, she is either bribed or whipped into compliance, or if she dares resist her seducer, her life by the laws of some of the slave States may be, and has actually been sacrificed to the fury of disappointed passion. Where such laws do not exist, the power which is necessarily vested in the master over his property, leaves the defenceless slave entirely at his mercy and the sufferings of some females on this account, both physical and mental, are intense. Mr. Gholson, in the House of Delegates of Virginia, in 1832, said, "He really had been under the impression that he owned his slaves. He had lately purchased four women and ten children, in whom he thought he had obtained a great bargain; for he supposed they were his own property, *as were his brood mares.*". . . Nor does the colored woman suffer alone: the moral purity of the white woman is deeply contaminated. In the daily habit of seeing the virtue of her enslaved sister sacrificed without hesitancy or remorse, she looks upon the crimes of seduction and illicit intercourse without horror, and although not personally involved in the guilt, she loses that value for innocence in her own, as well as the other sex, which is one of the strongest safeguards to virtue. . . . In addition to all this, the female slaves suffer every species of degradation and cruelty, which the most wanton barbarity can inflict; they are indecently divested of their clothing, sometimes tied up and severely whipped, sometimes prostrated on the earth, while their naked bodies are torn by the scorpion lash. . . . Can any American woman look at these scenes of shocking licentiousness and cruelty, and fold her hands in apathy, and say, "I have nothing to do with slavery"? *She cannot and be guiltless.*

Letter from Angelina Grimké to Catherine Beecher

Catherine Beecher was a sister of Harriet Beecher Stowe, author of Uncle Tom's Cabin, *and daughter of Lyman Beecher, a noted Presbyterian and Congregationalist pastor in New York and New England and president of Lane Seminary, site of an important series of antislavery debates. Lyman Beecher was opposed to slavery, but, like his daughter, Catherine, supported gradualism against the radicalism of the abolitionists. Catherine was a pioneer of women's education, but declared that women's influence be confined to the "domestic and social circle."*

In a series of letters, Angelina Grimké took issue with Catherine Beecher's position on abolitionism as well as her ideas about women's proper place and their rights as citizens.

East Boylston, Mass. *10th mo. 2d,* 1837

. . . The investigation of the rights of the slave has led me to a better understanding of my own. I have found the Anti-Slavery cause to be the high school of morals in our land—the school in which *human rights* are more fully investigated, and better understood and taught, than in any other. Here a great fundamental principle is uplifted and illuminated, and from this central light, rays innumerable stream all around. Human beings have *rights*, because they are *moral* beings: the rights of *all* men grow out of their moral nature; and as all men have the same moral nature, they have essentially the same rights. These rights may be wrested from the slave, but they cannot be alienated: his title to himself is as perfect *now*, as is that of Lyman Beecher [*Rev. Beecher, Catherine's father*]: it is stamped

Angelina E. Grimké, *Letters to Catherine E. Beecher, In Reply to an Essay on Slavery and Abolitionism, Addressed to A.E. Grimké*, Revised by the Author. (Boston: Isaac Knapp, 1838; Reprint edition, Arno Press and the *New York Times*, 1969), 110–113. Reprinted by permission.

on his moral being, and is, like it, imperishable. Now if rights are founded in the nature of our moral being, then the *mere circumstance of sex* does not give to man higher rights and responsibilities, than to woman. To suppose that it does, would be to deny the self-evident truth, that the 'physical constitution is the mere instrument of the moral nature.' . . . My doctrine then is, that whatever it is morally right for man to do, it is morally right for woman to do. Our duties originate, not from difference of sex, but from the diversity of our relations in life, the various gifts and talents committed to our care, and the different eras in which we live.

This regulation of duty by mere circumstance of sex, rather than by the fundamental principle of moral being, has led to all that multifarious train of evils flowing out of the anti-Christian doctrine of masculine and feminine virtues. . . . Woman, instead of being regarded as the equal of man, has uniformly been looked down upon as his inferior, a mere gift to fill up the measure of his happiness. In 'the poetry of romantic gallantry,' it is true, she has been called 'the last *best* gift of God to man' . . . Where is the scripture warrant for this 'rhetorical flourish, this splendid absurdity?' Let us examine the account of her creation. 'And the rib which the Lord God had taken from man, made he a woman, and brought her unto the man.' Not as a gift—for Adam immediately recognized her *as a part of himself*—('this is now bone of my bone, and flesh of my flesh')—a companion and equal, not one hair's breadth beneath him in the majesty and glory of her moral being; not placed under his authority as a *subject*, but by his side, on the same platform of human rights, under the government of God only. This idea of woman's being 'the last best gift of God to man,' however pretty it may sound to the ears of those who love to discourse upon 'the poetry of romantic gallantry, and the generous promptings of chivalry,' has nevertheless been the means of sinking her from an *end* into a mere *means*—of turning her into an *appendage* to man, instead of recognizing her as a *part of man*—of destroying her individuality, and rights, and responsibilities, and merging her moral being in that of man. Instead of *Jehovah* being *her* king, *her* lawgiver, and *her* judge, she has been taken out of the exalted scale of existence in which He placed her, and subjected to the despotic control of man. . . . I recognize no rights but *human* rights— I know nothing of men's rights and women's rights; for in Christ Jesus, there is neither male nor female. It is my solemn conviction, that, until this principle of equality is recognized and embodied in practice, the church can do nothing effectual for the permanent reformation of the world. . . . Now, I believe it is woman's right to have a voice in all the laws and regulations by which she is to be *governed*, whether in Church or State; and that the present arrangements of society, on these points are *a violation of human rights, a rank usurpation of power*, a violent seizure and confiscation of what is sacredly and inalienably hers—thus inflicting upon woman outrageous wrongs, working mischief incalculable in the social circle, and in its influence on the world producing only evil, and that continually. *If* Ecclesiastical and Civil governments are ordained of God, *then* I contend that woman has just as much right to sit in solemn council in Conventions, conferences, Associations and General Assemblies, as men—just as much right to it upon the throne of England, or in the Presidential chair of the United States. . . .

Thy Friend,   A.E.GRIMKÉ

Questions for Discussion

1. What, according to Sarah Grimké, is wrong with the condition of American women?
2. On what principles or assumptions does Angelina Grimké base her argument for equality between male and female? How does her rhetoric (for example, her focus on rights) reflect the rhetoric of the Revolution?
3. How do Angelina's religious convictions influence her thinking about women's proper place?
4. What connections do the Grimké sisters make between the abolitionist cause and the issue of women's equality? How do their ideas compare with those of Abigail Adams (p. 90) and Mary Lee (p. 109)?

Part 4

Slavery, Civil War, and Reconstruction

During the early nineteenth century, slavery was gradually abolished in the North, while at the same time the cotton gin fastened the institution ever more firmly on the South. By 1830 what is now known as the Old South had emerged: a region that depended on slavery for the production of rice, sugar, tobacco and, above all, cotton. No longer did the South hesitantly defend slavery as a necessary evil; slavery was now pronounced a good. Though the majority of white Southern families did not own slaves, many hoped to do so, and others supported slavery as a method of racial control. By the 1830s criticism of the "peculiar institution" had largely disappeared from the South.

The North, too, was largely agricultural, but its products were primarily for home consumption, not export. The North, moreover, was changing at an ever-increasing rate to a commercial and industrial economy. Thus North and South disagreed on economic policy, especially the tariff. More important was the disagreement over slavery. Racist attitudes prevailed in the North as well as in the South although, while few would have called themselves abolitionists, many in the North regarded slavery as morally wrong. The question of the expansion of slavery to the territories gave an immediate, practical turn to the issue, since both North and South believed that their economic systems could not coexist in the same area. When Lincoln was elected in 1860 on a promise to end the expansion of slavery, Southern states began to secede from the Union.

In the Civil War that followed over 600,000 died, one for every ten white Southerners who were held in the Union, and one for every six slaves who were freed. With the war, the Old South disappeared, and few even in the North could remain unaffected by the carnage on the battlefield.

Rather than studying slavery simply as a question of the conditions imposed by owners, historians have recently given more attention to the lives that slaves were able to create for themselves within the harsh confines of the institution. In doing so, scholars have turned to sources long neglected, such as slave letters. Recent scholarship emphasizes the vitality of slave culture and family relationships. The selections here from George Pleasant Hobbs and others are letters between family members, and illustrate important aspects of slave life.

The nature of the relationship between slave and master has been the subject of considerable debate. Some historians regard slave owners as ambitious capitalist entrepreneurs who impersonally treated their slaves as they would any other commodity. Others, while recognizing the cruelty inherent in the relationship, see slave owners as men and women with pre-capitalist, paternalistic values who at least recognized the humanity of their slaves and attempted to establish a system of mutual obligation between slave and master. Selections from the diary of Bennet Barrow, a slave owner, illustrate the complexities of this issue.

The recent emphasis in historical writing on the experience of the average person has been reflected in the study of the Civil War. The war as seen through the eyes of the ordinary soldier may look somewhat different from the war experienced by the generals and strategists. We include selections from the diaries of two soldiers, Hamlin Coe from the North and Charles Blackford from the South. Both men had to deal with the dreariness of everyday army life, the terror of battle, and the larger question of the causes for which they fought. African-American soldiers had particular concerns of their own, as the letters of G. H. Freeman and others indicate. On the home front, life went on as normally as possible. But no community, however far removed from battle, remained untouched. The letters of Hannah Aldrich, living in the frontier area of southwestern Wisconsin, reflect the impact of the war at home and uncertainty about whether the goals justified the costs of the war.

When the Civil War ended, the nation was faced with the tasks of uniting North and South and at the same time providing a decent place in American society for the former slaves. Ultimately the two goals proved incompatible, and the rights of African Americans were sacrificed in the process of national reconciliation. The final selection from the diary of Laura Towne, a Northerner who went South to teach the former slaves, provides a unique perspective on this development.

23.
George Pleasant Hobbs, Elizabeth Hobbs, Sargry Brown, Emily Russell, Marie Perkins, James Phillips, Harriet Newby, and Louisa Alexander
Letters from Slaves, 1833–1863

Slave letters are valuable but traditionally overlooked sources of slave expression. Along with slave autobiographies and interviews, they provide direct entry into the experience of the slaves. Autobiographies, however, were often written for political purposes, and besides, the memory of the writer may have faded. Interviews were often conducted years after the end of slavery, and the interviewers' own biases could affect what the former slaves chose to tell. Letters do not share these difficulties. Letters written to family members are particularly revealing, for unlike letters to masters, which could not be candid, or letters to former masters, which were often intended as abolitionist propaganda, these could express honest ideas and emotions.

Hobbs Family Letters

Shelbyville [*Tennessee*]
Sept. 6, 1833

Mrs. Agnes Hobbs,
    Dear Wife: My dear biloved wife I am more than glad to meet with opportunity writee thes few lines to you by my Mistress who ar now about

---

John Blassingame, ed. *Slave Testimony*. Baton Rouge: Louisiana State University Press, 1977. Reprinted by permission.

starterng to virginia, and sevl others of my old friends are with her; in compeney Mrs Ann Rus the wife of master Thos Rus and Dan Woodiard and his family and I am very sorry that I havn the chance to go with them as I feele Determid to see you If life last again. I am now here and out at this pleace so I am not abble to get of at this time. I am write well and hearty and all the rest of masters family. I heard this eveng by Mistress that ar just from theree all sends love to you and all my old frends. I am a living in a town called Shelbyville and I have wrote a greate many letters since Ive beene here and almost been reeady to my selfe that its out of the question to write any more at tall: my dear wife I dont feeld no whys like giving out writing to you as yet and I hope when you get this letter that you be Inncougege to write me a letter. I am well satisfied at my living at this place I am a making money for my own benefit and I hope that its to yours also If I live to see Nexet year I shall have my own time from master by giving him 100 and twenty Dollars a year and I thinke I shall be doing good bisness at that and heve something more thean all that. I hope with gods helpe that I may be abble to rejoys with you on the earth and In heaven lets meet when will I am detemind to nuver stope praying, not in this earth and I hope to prase god. In glory there weel meet to part no more forever. So my dear wife I hope to meet you in paradase to prase god forever. . . . I want Elizabeth to be a good girl and not thinke that because I am bound so fare that gods not abble to open the way. . . .

George Pleasant Hobbs

/////

Hillsboro, [*North Carolina*], April 20, 1838

My Dear Mother: — I have been intending to write to you for a long time, but numerous things have prevented, and for that reason you must excuse me.

I thought very hard of you for not writing to me, but I hope that you will answer this letter as soon as you receive it, and tell me how you like Marsfield, and if you have seen any of my old acquaintances, or if you yet know any of the brick-house people who I think so much of. I want to hear of the family at home very much, indeed, I really believe you and all the family have forgotten me, if not I certainly should have heard from some of you since you left Boynton; if it was only a line, nevertheless I love you all very dearly, and shall, although I may never see you again, nor do I ever expect to. Miss Anna is going to Petersburgh next winter, but she does not intend to take me; what reason she has for leaving me I cannot tell. I have often wished that I lived where I knew I never could see you, for then I would not have my hopes raised, and to be disappointed in this manner, however, it is said that a bad beginning makes a good ending, but I hardly

A slave family. *(Library of Congress)*

expect to see that happy day at this place. Give my love to all the family, both white and black. I was very much obliged to you for the presents you sent me last summer, though it is quite late in the day to be thanking for them. Tell Aunt Bella that I was very much obliged to her for her present; I have been so particular with it that I have only worn it once.

There have been six weddings since October, the most respectable one was about a fortnight ago; I was asked to be the first attendant, but, as usual with all my expectations, I was disappointed, for on the wedding day I felt more like being locked up in a three-cornered box than attending a wedding. About a week before Christmas I was bridesmaid for Ann Nash; when the night came I was in quite a trouble; I did not know whether my frock was clean or dirty; I only had a week's notice, and the body and sleeves to make, and only one hour every night to work on it, so you can see with these troubles to overcome my chance was rather slim. I must now close, although I could fill ten pages with my griefs and misfortunes; no tongue could express them as I feel; don't forget me though; and answer my letters soon. I will write you again and would write more now, but Miss Anna says it is time I had finished. Tell Miss Elizabeth that I wish she would make haste and get married, for mistress says that I belong to her when she gets married.

I wish you would send me a pretty frock for this summer; if you will send it to Mrs. Robertson's Miss Bet will send it to me.

Farewell, darling mother.

Your affectionate daughter,

Elizabeth Hobbs

[Elizabeth Hobbs was able to buy her freedom and became a successful seamstress in St. Louis.]

/////

Sargry Brown to Moses Brown

Richmond, Virginia, october 27 1840

Dear Husband—

this is the third letter that I have written to you, and have not received any from you; and dont no the reason that I have not received any from you. I think very hard of it. the trader has been here three times to Look at me. I wish that you would try to see if you can get any one to buy me up there. If you dont come down here this Sunday, prhaps you wont see me any more. give my love to them all, and tell them all that perhaps I shan't see you any more, give my love to your mother in particular, and to mamy wines and to aunt betsy, and all the children; tell Jane and Mother they must come down a fortnight before Christmas. I wish to see you all, but I expect I never shall see you all—never no more.

I remain your Dear and affectionate Wife,

Sargry Brown

/////

Emily Russell to Nancy Cartwright

Alexandria [*Virginia*] Jan. 22, 1850

My dear mother—I take this opportunity of writing you a few lines to inform you that I am in Bruin's jail and aunt Sally and all her children, and aunt Hagar and all her children, and grandmother is almost crazy.

My dear mother will you please come on as soon as you can? I expect to go away very shortly. Oh, mother! come now and see your distressed and heartbroken daughter once more. Mother! my dear mother! do not forsake me; for I feel desolate

Please come now.

Your daughter,
Emily Russell

[Joseph Bruin was a slave trader. Despite efforts to buy and free her, Emily Russell was sold and died on the journey south.]

/////

Marie Perkins to Richard Perkins

Charlottesville [*Virginia*] Oct. 8, 1852

Dear Husband I write you a letter to let you know of my distress my master has sold Albert to a trader on Monday court day and myself and other child is for sale also and I want you let [*me*] hear from you very soon before next cort if you can I don't know when I don't want you to wait till Chrismas I want you to tell Dr. Hamilton your master if either will buy me they can attend to it now and then I can go afterwards

I don't want a trader to get me they asked me I had got any person to buy me and I told them no they told me to the court house too they never put me up A man buy the name of brady bought albert and is gone I don't know whare they say he lives in scottsville my things is in several places some is in stanton and if I would be sold I don't know what will become of them I don't expect to meet with the luck to get that way till I am quite heart sick nothing more I am and ever will be your kind wife

Marie Perkins

/////

James Phillips to Mary Phillips

[James Phillips had escaped from Virginia in 1838. Arrested in Pennsylvania in 1852, he was taken back to Virginia.]

Richmond [*Virginia*] June 10, 1852

Dear Wife—I will now write to you to inform you where I am and my health. I am well, and I am in hope when you receive this, it may find you well also. I am now in a trader's hands, by the name of Mr. Branton, and he is agoing to start South with a lot of negroes in August. I do not like this country at all, and had almost rather die than to go South. Tell all of the people that if they can do anything for me, now is the time to do it. I can be bought for $900. Do pray, try and get Brant and Mr. Byers and Mr. Weaver to send or come on to buy me, and if they will only buy me back, I will be a faithful man to them so long as I live. Show Mr. Brant and Mr. Weaver this letter, and tell them to come on as soon as they possibly can to buy me. My master is willing to sell me to any gentleman who will be so kind as to come on to buy me. They have got poor James Phillips here with leg irons on to keep him from getting away, an do pray gentlemen, do not feel any hesitation at all, but come on as soon as you can and buy me. Feel for me now or never. If any of you will be so kind as to come on to buy me, inquire for Cochron's Jail. I can be found there, and my master is always at the Mail himself. My master gave me full consent to have this letter written, so do not feel any hesitation to come on and see about poor James Phillips. Dear wife, show it to these men as soon as you get it, and let them write back immediately what they intend to do. Direct your letter to my master William A. Branton, Richmond, Va. Try and do something for me as soon as you can, for I want to get back very bad indeed. Do not think anything at all of the price who will buy me, in a short time. I have nothing more to write, only I wish I may be bought and carried back to Harrisburg in a short time. My best love to you, my wife. You may depend I am almost dying to see you and my children. You must do all you can for your husband.

Your husband,
James Phillips

/////

Harriet Newby to Dangerfield Newby

[Dangerfield Newby was a free African American. His wife Harriet and their seven children were slaves in Virginia, and feared being sold farther south.]

Brentville [*Virginia*], April 11th, 1859

Dear Husband

I must now write you apology for not writing you before this, but I know you will excuse me when I tell you Mrs. Gennings has been very sick. She has a baby—a little girl, ben a grate sufferer: her breast raised, and

Dangerfield Newby. *(Library of Congress)*

she has had it lanced, and I have had to stay with her day and night; so you know I had no time to write, but she is now better, and one of her own servent is now sick. I am well: that is of the grates importance to you. I have no news to write you, only the children are all well. I want to see you very much, but am looking forward to the promest time of your coming. Oh, Dear Dangerfield, com this fall without fail, monny or no monney, I want to see you so much. That is one bright hope I have before me. Nothing more at present, but remain

Your affectionate wife,
Harriet Newby

P.S. Write soon, if you please.

Brentville [*Virginia*], April 22nd, 1859

Dear Husband:

I received your letter to-day, and it gives much pleasure to here from you, but was sorry to [*hear*] of your sikeness; hope you may be well when you receive this. I wrote to you several weeks ago, and directed my letter to Bridge Port, but I fear you did not receive it, as you said nothing about it in yours. You must give my love to Brother Babial, and tell him I would like to see him very much. I wrote in my last letter that Miss Virginia had a baby—a little girl. I had to narse her day and night. Dear Dangerfield, you cannot imagine how much I want to see you. Com as soon as you can, for nothing would give more pleasure than to see you. It is the grates Comfort I have in thinking of the promist time when you will be here. Oh, that bless hour when I shall see you once more. My baby commenced to crall to-day; it is very delicate. Nothing more at present, but remain

Your affectionate wife
Harriet Newby

P.S. Write soon.

Brentville [*Virginia*], August 16, 1859

Dear Husband:

Your kind letter came duly to hand, and it gave me much pleasure to here from you, and especely to here you are better off [*with*] your rhumatism, and hope when I here from you again, you may be entirely well. I want you to buy me as soon as possible, for if you do not get me somebody else will. The servents are very disagreeable: they do all they can to set my mistress against me. Dear Husband you [*know*] not the trouble I see; the last two years has ben like a trouble dream to me. It is said Master is in want of monney. If so, I know not what time he may sell me, an then all my bright hops of the futer are blasted, for their has ben one bright hope to cheer me in all my troubles, that is to be with you, for if I thought I shoul never see you this earth would have no charmes for me. Do all you can for me, witch I have no doubt you will. I want to see you so much. The children are all well. The baby can not walk yet [*at*] all. It can step around everything by holding on. It is very much like Agnes. I must bring my letter to a Close, as I have no newes to write. You mus write soon and say when you think you can come.

Your affectionate wife,
Harriet Newby

[Dangerfield Newby participated in John Brown's raid on Harpers Ferry, Virginia, in October, 1859. He was the first raider killed in the attack.]

/////

Louisa Alexander to Archer Alexander

Naylor's Store [*Missouri*], Nov. 16, 1863

My Dear Husband,—I received your letter yesterday, and lost no time in asking Mr. Jim if he would sell me, and what he would take for me. He flew at me, and said I would never get free only at the point of the Baynot, and there was no use in my ever speaking to him any more about it. I don't see how I can ever get away except you get soldiers to take me from the house, as he is watching me night and day. If I can get away I will, but the people here are all afraid to take me away. He is always abusing Lincoln, and calls him an old Rascoll. He is the greatest rebel under heaven. It is a sin to have him loose. He says if he had hold of Lincoln, he would chop him up into mincemeat. I had good courage all along until now, but I am almost heart-broken. Answer this letter as soon as possible.

I am your affectionate wife,
Louisa Alexander

[Archer Alexander was able to arrange Louisa Alexander's escape, along with that of their daughter.]

Questions for Discussion

1. What concerns seem to be uppermost in the minds of the slaves represented in these letters?
2. What do the letters reveal about the conditions of slavery as the slaves perceived them?
3. What do the letters reveal about the slave family?

24.
Bennet Barrow
A Plantation Diary, 1837–1845

Bennet Barrow (1811–1854) was a Louisiana cotton planter. His father had established the family in the area around the turn of the century. Bennet Barrow, who inherited much of his father's estate, did not represent old wealth, but was an established, respected member of his community, living the life of a well-to-do planter. He was not the sort of newly-rich planter whom historians have often regarded as particularly given to the abuse of slaves. Indeed, he appears to have been seen as treating his slaves better than did many other slave owners in the area.

October 1837
7 Cloudy fresh wind from the North. Stormed ceased at noon— George drowned in L. Creek in the field found him this morning, a verry great loss. one of the best negroes I ever saw, or knew. to his family as a White person, one fourth of Cotten blown out at least. Corn verry much blown down.

/////

December 1837
26 Cloudy cool negros went to Town
28 Pleasant day sent 3 of Mr. Turnbulls boys off, for smoking cegars in my front yard—with a note to him—and never to put their foot on the place again
29 Pleasant. negros preparing for a dinner

Edwin Davis Adams. *Plantation Life in the Florida Parishes of Louisiana, 1836–1845 as Reflected in the Diary of Bennet H. Barrow.* New York: AMS Press, 1943. Reprinted by permission.

Bennet Barrow. *(Columbia University Press)*

31 Cloudy pleasant. Negros seemed to enjoy Christmas verry much ran two of Uncle Bats negros off last night—for making a disturbance—no pass—broke my sword Cane over one of their skulls

/////

January 1838

14 Appearance of rain—pressed 7 B. last Sunday—pressing to day at Gibsons—Will ship on Tuesday next 66 B.[*Bales of cotton*] in 381 in No. 50 to Gin -On selling from 5 to 11 1/2 cts.—The times are seriously hard—all most impossible to raise one dollar, and that in shin plasters—great Excitement in Congress, Northern States medling with slavery—first they com'ced by petition—now by openly speaking of the sin of Slavery in the southern states—on the floor of congress—must eventually cause a separation of the Union

/////

23 White Frost pleasant day—during my stay at Mr. Joors [*Bennett Barrow's brother-in-law*] last week my House servants Jane Lavenia & E. jim broke into my storeroom—and helped themselves verry liberally to every thing—Center—Anica—& Peter had some of the good drink "as they say"—I Whiped the three first worse than ever Whiped any one before

24 Showery day. Finished Ginning yesterday started 15 ploughs for oats near 150 Bales—putting up stalles for work horses—My house boy

E. Jim the meanest, dirtiest boy I ever had about me—women and trash gang cleaning up

/////

October 1838

11 Clear cold morning. Frost Gave the negros shoes last night hands picked worse to day by dinner than they have done this year. Owens excepted, 146 Bales shiped—205 out last night

12 Clear verry cold morning—hands picked worse yesterday than they have done this year. lowest avreage 157—picked in the morning—in the bottom on I. creek—rotten open long time—the same this morning—Whiped near half the hands to day for picking badly & trashy Tom Beauf came up and put his Basket down at the scales and it is the last I've seen of him—will Whip him more than I ever Whip one, I think he deserves more—the second time he has done so this year—light Frost yesterday and today

/////

26 Clear pleasant weather—Cotten picks verry trashy—Whiped 8 or 10 for weight to day—those that pick least weights generally most trash

27 Clear warm—picking Gns [*a reference to another piece of property Barrow owned*]—Dennis ran off yesterday—& after I had Whiped him—hands picked verry light weight by dinner—complaint picking in Rank & Rotten Cotten—4 sick—have out 270 Bales or upward of 400. certain 250 or upwards by 1st of November. Will [*be*] at least 30 Bales ahead of last year

28 Cloudy cool wind from the North. Misty—Ruffins overseer was over here this evening and informed me that his Home place hands avreaged 353 never heard any thing to Eaquel it—Trashy as could be—my hands picked verry trashy . . .

/////

May 1839

21 Clear verry warm—Finished hilling Cotten—Darcas & Fanny are the greatest shirks of any negroes I have—laid up twicet a month—Went to Town—man tried for whipping a negro to Death. trial will continue till to morrow—deserves death—Cleared!

/////

July 1839

21 Few clouds verry warm Gave G. Jerry Sam Wash & Bartley Bagging skirts to wear—instead of shirt and pants [*Note the unusual form of punishment. Also see July 5, 1840.*]

Barrow's plantation house. *(Library of Congress)*

/////

25 Morning clear verry warm Fine grass & Tie Vines verry thick— Appointed overseer of the roade—swamp roade—I hope the time will come When every Overseer in the country will be compelled to addopt some other mode of making a living—they are a perfect nuisance cause dissatisfaction among the negroes—being more possessed of more brutal feelings—I make better crops than those Who Employ them

/////

October 1839

6 Cold morning. & strong wind from the N.West—never felt a more pleasant day than yesterday—pure bracing wind from the North—went driving yesterday—& never was so put to a stump in my life Mr. jno.E. Barrow (a young Tennessee scamp) invites the two Mr. Howels over to join us men possessed of no feeling of the gentleman—I thought this bad Enough—but Mr. Riddel must invite T Purnells Molatto boy with him & when at dinner handed him some thing to Eat Which was sufficient invitation for him to join &c. respect for Riddell kept me from giving him H— Respect for no one shall prevent my doing my duty in such a case again— so goes this world—made the hunt as *little* uninteresting *as I could*

8 Cloudy & verry warm—windy—& from the East. A Harralson died yesterday I shall loose by him $1300. His family will be dependent on a negro woman I have a mortgage on—as a matter of course—cannot take her—&c. Com'enced hawling Cotten this morning. rainy evening.

/////

April 1840

16   Damp Foggy morning   The ground works verry heavy, ploughing verry heavy during ther winter & at this time, Cotten improving verry muchy & corn looks well   half leg high in new ground   10 inches in old Land, My Hands appear determined to make a crop, if work can do it, never saw hands Work as Well. have never said a word to them—feeling an interest, they look a head & see What is to be done—I doubt if Jacks equal can be found to work, at any work you put him at, "rascally"&c. I am well paid for my trouble in teaching my small gang to Hoe, never saw such hoe hands as they are, two year ago took two on a row—now Eaquel to a woman, am directing them to make a slow & sure lick in one place & to cut the full width of the hoe every time—unless reminded of it they would stand & make 4 or 5 licks in one place, tire themselves & do no work, have several grown ones that work harder & do less work than any in the field. had the best colt Foaled this morning I ever had—Nancy Miller & Jos Bell—stoped 5 ploughs to scrape cotten—15 running.

/////

July 1840

4   Clear Beautifull day. Wish the prospects of every one were as bright, as this memorable day, preparations for great doings at Couces to day   Barn dance &c. will not go   having been started by a few Loco Focos [*a reformist wing of the Democratic Party*] Who have the impudence to call themselves democrats, such men as the Howells figure Largely, Political Excitement is such that the greater the sycophant the more notice does he get. old Capt Howells breed are a head of any thing in these diggins, Killed more negroes by their cruelty, & find them dead in the stocks, and yet A G Howell calls himself a big man, Married Dawsons niece. Dawson being a man that never looks for merit   When appointing aids &c. Thinks it is not Democratic, Democracy of the present day means serve your party right or wrong your party, they are the zelous supporters of Martin Van Buren, and all under the name of Democracy, All this corruption has grown out of the conduct of Genl. Jackson, Federal acts done every day by the V[*an*] B[*uren*] party yet they are Democrats

5   Few clouds, warm   negroes appeared quit Lively last night, and the Jack [*a donkey*] rigged out this evening with red flanel on his ears & a Feather in them & sheet on, "in the Quarter." every negro up. Made Alfred and Betsy ride him round the Quarter dismont and take a kiss, for quarreling, Jack & Lize   Frank & Fanncy the same [*Note the unusual form of punishment; compare July 21, 1839.*]

/////

July 1841

18 . . . Received a note from Ruffin stating that several of my negroes were implicated in an intended insurection on the 1st of August next. It seems from What he writes me, it was to have taken place Last March— mine are O Fill O Ben   Jack Dennis & Demps—will go to Robert J.B. to have them examined &c. six negroes were found guilty in the first degree, it appears they were to meet at jno. Towles Gate and at Mr. Turnbulls inheritance place, Leaders one of Robert J. Barrow one Bennet J.B. one of Towles one of C. Perceys One W.J. Forts & one of D. Turnbulls, none of mine were implicated farther than one of Robert J.B boys said he heard the names of the above mentioned &c. intend having an examination of the Whole plantation & the neighbourhood

19 Clear Verry Hot—Examined Mrs Stirlings negroes Courtneys & my own yesterday found none of them concerned in the Expected insurection, Went to Judge Wades this morning, found several of his men concerned it. Dave Bonner the most & he was the Leder, Sent to Jail for trial.

20 Clear Verry warm. Thermometer Lower this morning than it has been in 3 weeks, fine shower

21 Cloudy Verry warm—Examined Robt H. Barrows negroes yesterday. one or two deeply concerned. Sit last night for negroes on the road, good many runaways about.

22 Clear Verry warm, Examined Ruffins negros yesterday they pretended more ignorance than any Negros I've met with—one of his Old Pete deeply concerned

23 Clear verry warm—Examined A. Barrows & Mrs. Joors negros couldent find any thing of importance, Cotten shedding Forms small bolls & Leaves for want of rain

27 Cloudy. Verry warm, Negros all Cleared. But will be tried by the Planters themselves &c. Working roads women spinning, making scaffolds

28 Clear verry warm—rece'd a Letter from the Committee on Perceys creek requesting information in regard to the negros rising Excitement &c. pulling Fodder, running scrapers twicet in a row next to the cotten

///////

August 1841

16 Cloudy warm—Several of my negros in returning off of the road Saturday night came through Ruffins Quarter. he having the measles forbid their Returning that way, had them staked down all yesterday, several of them had killed a hog, found the right ones, gave them al a severe Whipping, Ginney Jerry has been sherking about ever since Began to pick cotten. after Whipping him yesterday told him if he ever dodged about from me again would certainly shoot him. this morning at Breakfast time Charles came & told me that Jerry was about to run off. took my Gun found him in the Bayou behind the Quarter, shot him in his thigh—&c raining all around.

/////

June 1842
15   Clear quit cool since last evening, never saw my corn worse burnt than the new ground in places, hoeing lane place new ground splendidly branched & formed bolled &c. Ginney jerry has not been seen since Monday morning, ran off and for What can't imagine—Came up Sunday for a dose of oil, has been for 8 or 10 days getting timber no one to watch him his old habits returned "of shirking," will shoot to kill him if an opportunity offers—otherwise will sell him, am satisfied will always run away unless constantly watched—has not been touched this year, nor have I said a word to him, pray for a shot at him

/////

April 1844
19   Cloudy disagreeable morning—threatning rain—Mr. Turnbulls negros are cutting up a great many shines—16 ran off & have defied him— are well armed killed two of his dogs while in pursuit of them—all this grows out of his having them preached to for 4 or 5 years past—greatest piece of foolishness any one every guilty of no true Christianity among the Church going Whites—& how Expect to Preach morality among a set of ignorant beings—proper discipline may improve them and make them better—so Long as the same course & interest is kept up

/////

April 1845
20   Emily [*Bennet Barrow's wife*] quite unwell very Low spirits seems to think of Death in fact thinks she is not to survive this year out . . . Had I only taken the advice of Emily would never have been in debt Who could have been more happy than we Emilys feelings and situation at this time makes me reflect on the past and think there are many things neglected that might have been done. & ought to have been, for our mutual happiness—human nature to postpone for to morrow What could be done to day . . . I acted for the Best and so far have never injured any human being to my knowledge, But will try and take care of my own the remainder of my life—shall quit fox hunting—and study amusements with my wife & children, God speed an end to all my troubles, hope in a short time to be able to start some Where with all the family for health pleasure & happiness—20 April 1845—B.H. Barrow—sick and worn out from yesterdays folly—will try and rest a while—Cloudy, warm—heavy rain yesterday

[Emily Barrow died on August 2, 1845.]

Questions for Discussion

1. What does Barrow's diary tell you about his character and values? What does he mean by the statement that he has "never injured any human being to my knowledge"?
2. How would you characterize Barrow's attitudes and behavior toward his slaves? How did he attempt to get his slaves to work efficiently?
3. Can you tell anything from the diary about the attitudes and feelings of Barrow's slaves?

25.
Hamlin Alexander Coe
Diary of a Union Soldier, 1862–1865

In August 1862, at the age of twenty-two, Hamlin Coe (1840–1899) enlisted in the Michigan Volunteer Infantry. For the next three years he served in the Union army and recorded, in several pocket-sized notebooks, "a correct statement" of his "observations and actions while a soldier in the U.S. Army." His grandson, David Coe, discovered the diaries in 1966 in a trunk at his father's home.

Included in the diaries are descriptions of the long, arduous marches from one battlefield to another, Coe's capture by the Confederate army, and his bouts with pneumonia and typhoid fever, ailments that killed more Union and Confederate soldiers than did the battles.

In his first entry, on September 14, 1862, Coe pledged to "commence a diary of things and scenes as they transpire and meet my view while I am soldiering," a pledge he kept throughout his military service.

November 13, 1862   At early dawn we were upon the march. We have traveled eighteen miles over a good road and through a splendid country, halting at Nicholasville, Kentucky. . . . We are now in the very heart of Kentucky, and I wish I could always live in as pretty a country as this. If

Hamlin Alexander Coe. *Mine Eyes Have Seen the Glory: Combat Diaries of Union Sergeant Hamlin Alexander Coe.* Teaneck: Fairleigh Dickinson Press, 1975. Reprinted by permission.

Hamlin Coe. *(Fairleigh Dickinson Press)*

there were free labor here and free institutions of learning, the state could not be excelled. But here they pay from $20 to $30 per quarter for schooling, and hire negro labor for $50 to $100 per year; and the inhabitants tell me their labor is dear at that, for they have to stand over the eternal nigger with a club to make him do anything. I have stood the march today better than any day since we started. We have pitched tents and carried straw about two hundred rods for our beds. I shall sleep well tonight.

/////

December 5, 1862   Early upon the morning of November 15, I was taken with a severe chill. A high fever followed, and from that time to the present date I have been perfectly insane. Upon inquiring into my case, I find I have been having the pneumonia and typhoid fever. I have had the best of care (for a Hospital) by both surgeons and nurses. I find I am very weak and emaciated, but if I am careful it will be alright with me in a few days. . . .

/////

January 1, 1863 . . . I have been wandering about all day, and more than once my mind has wandered homeward, and I have been reminded of the pleasures and pastimes of one year ago. How I wish I could enjoy this bright moonlight night as I did then. In its stead, I am in the town of Nicholasville, Kentucky, among entire strangers . . . but I have been awake to the transactions of the day. I will relate them briefly. Early this morning the streets were thronged with vehicles of every kind and a great many on horseback. About ten o'clock the public sale of horses commenced, lasting until noon. After dinner commenced the hiring out of negroes. They are hired for from $50 to $125 per year and are to be clothed and given medical attendance in the bargain. I noticed some that I thought were tough bargains. There were some private sales of negroes, but nothing that attracted attention in that line. I have had a good dinner at Mr. Bronaugh's and helped the steward draw rations for the hospital. Since supper I have been writing home and reading the news of the day. Thus ends the New Year. As a holiday it is but little thought of by Kentuckians.

/////

February 2, 1863 We lay at the wharf all day awaiting orders. About three o'clock the expected message came, and we were soon streaming down the Ohio. It being very cold, I could not be out on deck to make any observations, so I returned to the cabin, concluding that the comforts of a good fire were preferable to the cold wind upon the hurricane deck. . . .

February 4, 1863 I did not sleep much last night, the old boat trembled and squeaked so. About two o'clock we came to the mouth of the Cumberland River. The boat hauled up to the landing for coal. I went down and helped them load. At this place the Colonel received a dispatch stating that they were fighting at Fort Donaldson and urging this regiment forward with all haste; but nine gunboats and fourteen transports have gone up the river already. I think the contest will be decided before we can reach the Fort. . . .

About sundown we hove in sight of Fort Donaldson. All we could see of it in passing by were the earthworks and trenches. As we passed by it was ascertained that the fight had ceased and that it was a complete victory for our side. The forces engaged were about six hundred on our side and about six thousand of the enemy.

About a mile above the Fort we came upon the fleet, and ran to shore. The boys all started for the battlefield, but I feel too poorly to run around tonight. There are all sorts of rumors afloat concerning the fight, but I cannot credit all. I hear everyone is frantic with joy over the victory.

/////

February 7, 1863   . . . Towards night the city of Nashville hove in view, but the banks were so high and so thickly built with storehouses that I could see but little of the city. Passing up above the bridges (the railroad bridge is in ruins) the boat moved to the landing where we shall stay the night.

/////

February 21, 1863   Early this morning we struck tents. Taking the macadamized road to the South, we traveled about nine miles and camped at a little place called Brentwood. It is simply a way station upon the railroad. The face of the country is level and extensively cultivated.

February 22, 1863   Company E is upon picket [*guard*] duty today. It is cold and windy, so much so that when sitting around the fire we could freeze upon one side and roast on the other; but we went to work and built a hovel (such as we used to build for the sheep at home) which was quite comfortable. We had little to eat, but plenty of good water to drink, which distilled through the rocks.

February 23, 1863   Before coming off picket this morning, Jim, Delos, and I went in advance of the post to get some straw to take to camp. While there, an old darky came along with some dried peaches, and we made him shell out. He was rather reluctant about it. About ten o'clock we were relieved and went to camp and have spent the remainder of the day in rest and hunting gray-backs [*lice*], but as before, I have found none. . . .

/////

March 5, 1863   We met the rebs again. The artillery duel commenced at nine o'clock A.M. and by eleven o'clock the fight became general. We fought until three o'clock P.M. when overpowered by numbers and completely surrounded by three lines of battle, we were obliged to surrender. We were then marched to Columbia under guard, a distance of eighteen miles. Darned if I'm not tired, but I hope a night's sleep will make me alright.

> *[At the time of this engagement, Coe's regiment was in Tennessee preparing to join General Rosecrans's force prior to what became the Battle of Chickamauga. Coe's capture spared him from participating in that bloody Union defeat.]*

/////

March 22, 1863   Early this morning we arrived at Richmond and were marched to Libby prison where the boys, as well as myself, were glad to seek a resting place. Many of the boys sank down upon the floor (unable to support themselves longer) from exhaustion and hunger. As we passed up the stairs, they gave us some blankets. About every third man got one.

Libby prison, Richmond, Virginia, where Coe was held in 1863. *(Museum of Fine Arts, Boston)*

About ten o'clock A.M. and five o'clock P.M., we received about three ounces of bread and the same of stinking meat, which is all we have had to eat. Do they mean to starve us? But I guess it is best for us to eat but little.

During this journey we have suffered greatly from incessant rain or snow, our clothes wet most of the time, and while upon the train outward bound from Lynchburg we were banked up in the snow and remained there forty-eight hours without anything to eat, but we had plenty of good dry rails to burn and thus kept warm. Our provisions upon the whole route have consisted of rotten and maggoty bacon and corn bread. The bread was made from meal that had not been sifted, mixed with water, a little grease from the stinking bacon and no salt and baked in an old iron bakette or upon a board in front of the fire. The Rebels claimed they were giving us half rations, but I have received at no time as much for three days as we did within our own lines for a single meal. . . .

There are none but the toughest of men that can keep alive with such usage; but the Guards (Mississippi) divided their rations with us. They appear to be gentlemen in every respect. Their officers too were gentlemen and courteous. They allow us a great many privileges we did not expect to receive at their hands.

The country we have passed through is anything but prosperous. Everything seems to be going to destruction; buildings and fences upon whole plantations burned and torn down. No crops growing, no stock to graze upon the now green and growing grass. The inhabitants tell me that they do not know where their next year's supply of meat and bread is coming from for their individual wants, to say nothing of supplying their army. They say they have no cattle, no hogs, no horses, and that they have been stripped of everything that would be of any use to their army. God knows they must have something to live upon in this rocky region. I have found several people in the South who will take U.S. greenbacks for their commodities before they will their own money.

[Coe was taken to Annapolis, where on April 18th he contracted typhoid fever and was hospitalized. In late June he was released and ultimately furloughed; in October he returned to the front. The following entries were written from his post of provost marshal in McMinnville, Tennessee.]

November 16, 1863 . . . I was surprised on first doing Provo duty to find that the chewing of snuff was a very common habit among the ladies of Tennessee. I would not believe it at first, but every day I see them parading the streets with their little sticks in their mouths. I will not speak disrespectfully of them, however, for who knows—but what I shall place my affections on one of these birds and become one among them, and, too, my feelings of hatred of them arise more from shame than hatred, so I will rather take a lesson from them. I notice, too, they have another very common habit that I thank God I have not yet formed, that is drinking strong drink. I find Applejack whiskey is a great treat among the ladies of Tennessee. . . . To tell the truth, Southern society in a moral and social point of view is *beneath* that of the Negro.

/////

January 11, 1864 . . . There was a company of the Corp. d'Afrique came in town today under arms. I was quite surprised to see their efficiency in drill and soldierly appearance. It is evident they are to become a standing arm of the service.

January 12, 1864 The only excitement I have seen today and the only thing talked about upon the street is the Negro company of soldiers. It does me good to see the old master look upon his slave with fear when he gets a musket in his hands. After seeing the negro drill and go through the Manual of Arms, the master turns upon his heel, convinced for the first time in his life that the darky has an intellect, which can be cultivated and, when cultivated, is bound to shine.

January 13, 1864 . . . There was a little stir tonight among the soldiers, occasioned by the return of the negro company. It seems they were out in the country recruiting when a young man was heard to say he wished every negro soldier and officer would be captured before they could return to McMinnville, whereupon they arrested him and brought him to town. The assistant Provost Marshal, after scaring him pretty well, made him go before the negro company and (upon bended knees) ask their forgiveness. It caused a general shout.

/////

[In April 1864 Coe and his company left McMinnville, Tennessee, and began the daily march southward.]

April 19, 1864   We are encamped in an old Rebel earthwork at the northern base of Whiteside Mountain, the summit of which is cleared of timber, and the stars and stripes are floating from the forts that are built thereon.

Deserted rebel works appear on every hand, but they are poor excuses and, I am told, were taken easily. . . . The landmarks of the retreating enemy appear everywhere. There are carcasses of dead horses and mules, sometimes dozens together and as often as one every five rods, showing the cost of our efforts in this quarter.

Thousands of soldiers are buried by the way. A small spring of the best of water graces our camp tonight. The boys generally are well.

/////

May 3, 1864   . . . We are encamped tonight near the field hospital of the battlefield of Chickamauga. Many trees eighteen inches in diameter were actually cut down with balls, while the underbrush is seemingly mowed down with musketry.

Old clothing and all kinds of war implements lay scattered upon the ground. The most interesting thing I saw was a rebel's letter to his brother, also a rebel. I tried to get possession of it but failed. The worst sight I saw was the dead that had been buried, particularly upon the ground the rebels occupied. They buried their own men decently, putting a board and inscription at the head of each, but the Union forces they covered so slightly that their hands, feet, and their skulls are now uncovered and exposed to the open air. They burned a great many and their bones are now lying with the ashes about the ground. *This I saw* and examined for myself. We found one that was buried with leaves of the forest. One whose feet and legs were unburied was actually petrified; but enough. I shall always remember the scene and pray God I may never see another such.

May 6, 1864   . . . We are but six miles from our position yesterday. Coming to a sudden halt, the boys began to throw up breastworks across an open field at a gap in the mountains, where we expected to bag some Rebs that our cavalry was drawing on, but at this hour, four o'clock, the work has ceased, and we have established camp for the night. It surprised me to see how quickly the boys made their preparation for a fight. They would cut down a tree and carry it bodily to the works, and the next moment the bank of earth would complete the work. In the short space of twenty minutes the line of works was complete, over three miles in extent, and in one half hour more the whole Corps would have been entrenched. . . .

/////

[Coe was a member of General Thomas's Army of the Cumberland, one of three armies collectively under command of General Sherman. The engagement described here occurred as Sherman began his march into Georgia.]

May 13, 1864 . . . The firing commenced about four o'clock and it has been an incessant roar ever since. . . . Thus far our division has not been engaged, but we expect to every moment.

It is now sundown and the musketry is still firing. We are now lying in line of battle by division . . . and while I sit here writing what a scene is presented!

In front is the roar and din of battle. The boys about me are talking upon many subjects, and invariably they are making light of the strife before us, and I never saw the boys cooler or more steady.

Directly in our rear, regiment after regiment is passing double quick to their relative positions. To be brief, it is a wilderness of bayonets and sabers where we are now resting. Still farther in the rear are the ambulances carrying off the wounded. What part we shall be called upon to perform God only knows. Action is inevitable, and God protect the right. . . .

May 14, 1864 . . . Fortune has favored us in that we are being held in reserve thus far today, but our turn must come. It is now almost dark, and the battle still rages. The roar is as incessant as it was at noon. . . . I have heard and met the storm of battle before, but never so severe and long as today.

We were only too lucky to escape the storm, but the storm is not yet over, and we cannot lie in reserve through the whole of this great battle. . . .

May 15, 1864 Today we were led into the strife, and I hope I can forget the events of the day. By the guidance of Him who protects us all, I was saved to tell the tale.

Early in the morning we were moved to the left of our lines to support General Howard. At eleven o'clock we were ordered to charge the Rebel works upon the heights. The boys charged over a whole division that lay upon the ground in front of us and gained the first hill, the Rebs fleeing as we advanced. . . .

A good many of the boys were picked off by sharpshooters. The regiment lost one hundred one in all. Although our regiment was broken and in disorder, they charged like tigers. I was with the guard of colors. There were ten of us when we charged, and only three came off the field. I brought the old flag off the field torn and riddled with balls. The boys cheered the rags when I brought them off, and we had a grand greeting. . . .

/////

May 18, 1864 . . . We were marched beyond reason today, and hundreds of the boys were tired out and lay by the roadside. I kept up but I am the tiredest man that ever lived. When will this running fight ever cease? Hundreds of men are suffering more from marching than from fighting. God speed the time when this strife will cease. . . .

/////

[Coe describes the Battle of Peachtree Creek, just outside Atlanta.]

July 20, 1864 This is another eventful day long to be remembered by the heroes of the day. . . . At three o'clock it was announced along the line that the Rebs were charging upon us. They came down upon us in seven lines of battle, threatening the 3rd Division with destruction. No commanding officers seemed to be present. Our gallant Colonel Coburn ordered his brigade forward, swinging in to the left, which saved the whole division from retreat. By this time the roar of battle was loud and constant. In our turn we charged the Rebels, driving them back in confusion. Coming up to our former skirmish line, we halted and the battle was kept up until night, when the work of fortifying commenced. We worked all night, and a tireder and lamer set of men I never saw. I never suffered so from heat before. My clothes were as wet as though I had been in water. Our loss was comparatively light. Three men from my company were wounded, which is about the average, but the Rebels suffered dreadfully. In front of our regiment the boys have buried nearly two hundred, and thousands have been wounded. I noticed several places where the blood has run in streams down the hillside, and go where you will, there are pools of blood. It is a sickening and horrid sight such as I never wish to see again, though tomorrow may renew the strife. . . .

/////

March 20, 1865 This day has been celebrated by the negroes of the city. A large number paraded the streets with music, badges and banners. On the latter were several mottoes. Among them were, "We Ask Not for Social but for Political Equality," "We Can Forget and Forgive the Past," etc. The crowd went to a grove in the suburbs to have their dinner and speaking, and the morning papers speak very highly of the affair. I only saw the procession pass through the street, and, to give my opinion, the nigger is getting mighty saucy, but I give them credit for good organization and order. . . .

/////

April 3, 1865   The Freeman's Legislature of Tennessee met at the state house early this morning and were drawing great crowds of people. When the glorious news of the fall of Richmond and Petersburg came, the state house was almost instantly deserted, and the people gathered in squads upon the streets to read the extras. Thousands of flags were flung to the breeze, a salute of artillery and musketry was fired, and the people were intoxicated with the good news.

/////

April 11, 1865   It continues raining. The telegraph bore to us the glorious news of the surrender of Lee's Army, and there is great rejoicing among the citizens. The soldiers make but a few demonstrations of their joy, though it is intense.

/////

April 15, 1865   At early dawn troops began to move in different directions, and citizens began to assemble upon the sidewalks to celebrate the day. All was going off lively, and anticipations were running high for a grand time, when, with the speed of lightning, the news of the assassination of the President and the Secretary of State came upon us. The report was not credited at first, and all went forward gaily, but dispatch after dispatch finally forced it upon the minds of the people, and for a short time everything seemed to be spellbound. Not a word was spoken, not a command was given, not a person moved. At last the spell was broken. Flags were lowered to half-mast. The column of troops moved off with reversed arms and drooping march to the time of the dead march or funeral music. From this moment every countenance wore a look of sorrow. Even the merry youth of eight or nine summers wore a sad and mournful countenance as he carried his little draped flag in his hand. . . . The procession dispersed, and citizens returned to their homes. . . . The streets were again thronged at a late hour to hear and read the extras that had been published, and here again a new scene occurred. . . . Every man that rejoiced over the news was doomed to death on the spot. Some were shot, others bayonetted, others mauled to death. At this writing I learn of six or seven that have thus met their doom. . . . For my part I have been silent and kept my temper, though it has been a hard blow, and it has been hard work to restrain my feelings. . . .

/////

May 19, 1865 I settled with the U.S. in full, receiving $195.70 as my due at the Pay Department in the City of Nashville. . . . I can hardly realize that I am a citizen, but, nevertheless, I am and must assume the position of one. It will not be until I can reach home in safety that I can realize the fact, where I hope my friends will help me to reclaim my position in society and throw off the habits of a soldier. . . .

Questions for Discussion

1. What does Coe's diary reveal about the military life of this Union soldier? What is his attitude toward combat?
2. What are Coe's attitudes toward Confederate soldiers and civilians? Toward African Americans? Do those attitudes seem to change? If so, in what ways?

26.
Charles Minor Blackford
Letters from a Confederate Soldier, 1861–1865

Charles Minor Blackford (1833–1903), a lawyer by profession, enlisted in the Confederate army on June 2, 1861, and served during the entire war. Accompanying him was John Scott, his "free negro" servant who saw to his needs throughout the war. In the course of his military career Blackford was promoted to captain and later acted as judge advocate in his regiment. He fought in significant battles with such military leaders as Robert E. Lee and Stonewall Jackson, about whom he writes in his letters.

Characterized by his grandson as "middle class," Blackford was nonetheless part of the social elite in Virginia. A pioneer in the building of Southern railroads, he amassed a fortune but was penniless at the close of the war. Following his discharge from the army, he returned home and resumed his law practice.

From 1861 until 1865, Blackford wrote letters, often daily, from the camps and battlefields to his wife, Susan Colston Blackford. They were, he noted, "a species of diary . . . thoughts and theories" that comprised a record of the war and a legacy for his children.

July 20, 1861 . . . Just as we crossed Bull Run I saw Edmund Fontaine, of Hanover, resting on a log by the roadside. I asked him what was the matter, and he said he was wounded and dying. He said it very cheerfully and did not look as if anything was the matter. As we came back we

Susan Leigh Blackford. *Letters from Lee's Army*. New York: Charles Scribner's Sons, 1947.

found him dead and some of his comrades about to remove the body. It was a great shock to me, as I had known him from boyhood. . . .

It was a day long to be remembered, and such a Sunday as men seldom spend. To all but a scattered few it was our first battle, and its sights and wonders were things of which we had read but scarcely believed or understood until seen and experienced. The rout of the enemy was complete but our generals showed much want of skill in not making the material advantages greater. The Federal army was equipped with every species of munition and property, while ours was wanting in everything. They were stricken with a panic; wherever the panic was increased by the sight of an armed rebel it discovered itself by the natural impulse to throw away arms and accoutrements and to abandon everything in the shape of cannon, caissons, wagons, ambulances and provisions that might impede their flight, yet they managed, despite their flight, to carry off much. They only lost some thirty-odd cannon for example, while with proper management on our part they would not have reached the Potomac with two whole batteries and so with other properties. . . .

During the evening [*a Southern expression for afternoon*] as I was riding over part of the field where there were many dead yankees lying who had been killed . . . I noticed an old doll-baby with only one leg lying by the side of a Federal soldier just as it dropped from his pocket when he fell writhing in the agony of death. It was obviously a memento of some little loved one at home which he had brought so far with him and had worn close to his heart on this day of danger and death. It was strange to see that emblem of childhood, that token of a father's love lying there amidst the dead and dying where the storm of war had so fiercely raged and where death had stalked in the might of its terrible majesty. I dismounted, picked it up and stuffed it back into the poor fellow's cold bosom that it might rest with him in the bloody grave which was to be forever unknown to those who loved and mourned him in his distant home.

The actual loss of the enemy I do not know but their dead extended for miles and their wounded filled every house and shed in the neighborhood. The wounded doubtless suffered much. Their own surgeons abandoned their field hospitals and joined the fleeing cohorts of the living, and our surgeons had all they could do to look after their own wounded, who of course were the first served. They received kind treatment however, and as soon as our surgeons were free they rendered all the aid in their power.

. . . Along the road and amidst abandoned cannon and wagons we found many a forsaken carriage and hack with half-eaten lunches and half-used baskets of champagne, and we received most laughable accounts from the citizens on the roadside of the scenes they saw and the sharp contrast between the proud and confident advance and the wild panic of the flight. The men of our company got many a spoil not known to the ordnance department or used by those who filled the ranks. . . .

Confederate volunteers, 1861. *(Valentine Museum, Richmond)*

October 28, 1861 . . . As soon as we reached Leesburg we found the
enemy had all gone back over on the other side of the river, but there was
a rumor they were preparing to cross at a ferry about twelve miles up the
river at "Speaks." I was at once ordered to take a small party and go up
there and see about it. I took four men, making a hard ride on an empty
stomach, through a most beautiful country, using my bay, which had come
up from Centreville. When near the ferry, at the infantry picket post, I
heard cannon fire and a bomb burst in the woods just ahead. We then
dismounted and crept up the hill just over the ferry where we had a good

view of the other side, the enemy firing all the time but the bombs bursting behind us. We crept up to the house at which they had been firing and then showed ourselves. Then, strange to say, they ceased firing and moved their battery off without even a salute. I had my field glasses and could see all they did with perfect ease. I found they had four guns and an encampment of about two regiments of infantry. They seemed much amused at us coming out so freely, but only looked at us through their glasses, sitting on a fence seeming to hold a consultation as to what it all meant.

We surveyed each other for about an hour, then both parties retired. . . .

/////

November 8, 1861 [*Manassas*]   I was much less interested in the bat- tlefield than I anticipated. Some of its horrors are still fresh. The earth having been washed off, many of the bodies were exposed entirely to view. Strange to say, they seemed to have just dried up without decay. It was the same way with the horses, none of which have either decayed or been devoured by buzzards, but have dried within their skins leaving the bones inside. . . .

November 16, 1861 [*Leesburg*]   . . . We are now comfortably camped about a mile from the town in an encampment with four other companies, over which Col. Jenifer has command. Everything here is very quiet. The pickets on the other side of the river are very friendly with our men, exchanging visits, papers and other courtesies. Some of our men went over a mile into Maryland and took dinner with some officers in the yankee camp. A very dangerous and improper thing to do, I think. . . . I suppose it is better this way than for the pickets to be firing constantly at each other. . . .

December 15, 1861   I spent this Sunday in the saddle. I was Officer of the Day on the picket line and had to inspect every post and have ridden since breakfast. I went alone and had no companions except in the picket posts and I enjoyed the quiet scenery very much. I rode for fifteen miles along the bluffs and I enjoyed the view very greatly. The river was as smooth as a lake, and all nature seemed reposing in a universal Sabbath. Nothing was stirring except occasionally a lazy sentinel on the Federal shore would come out of his tent, take a look at me on the bluff above him and then retire. . . .

General Hill is making various strategic moves tonight to deceive the enemy as to our numbers. He has been doing this sort of thing for several nights. Fires are kept burning in secluded woods, and bands play as if in a regiment. Old tents are pitched with no one to occupy, and everything is arranged that a casual observer, or an observer from the balloon the yan- kees daily send up, would estimate our force at double at what it is. . . .

July 13, 1862   . . . I am comfortably camped on the Mechanicsville Pike about a hundred yards from [*Stonewall*] Jackson's headquarters. . . .

. . . I was invited by Col. A.S. Pendleton, his adjutant, to go with General Jackson and his staff into town this morning. I was proud to be of such a distinguished party although a very small atom of it. We went first to the Governor's mansion and there, I suppose by appointment, we met General Lee. . . . Lee was elegantly dressed in full uniform, sword and sash, spotless boots, beautiful spurs and by far the most magnificent man I ever saw. The highest type of the Cavalier class to which by blood and rearing he belongs. Jackson, on the other hand was a typical Roundhead. He was poorly dressed, that is, he looked so though his clothes were made of good material. His cap was very indifferent and pulled down over one eye, much stained by weather and without insignia. His coat was closely buttoned up to his chin and had upon the collar the stars and wreath of a general. His shoulders were stooped and one shoulder was lower than the other, and his coat showed signs of much exposure to the weather. . . .

July 19, 1862   . . . Mr. Kean has lost seven of his negro men; gone over to the enemy. Everybody about here has lost some of their force. . . .

August 11, 1862 [*Slaughter Mountain*]   . . . I was at the point where troops were thrown into line of battle. Here . . . I saw what I had never seen before: men pinning strips of paper with their names, company and regiment to their coats so they could be identified if killed. . . .

After what seemed to me a long time the firing on my front and to the left of the road became very sharp and was nearing me rapidly, showing that our men were either being driven or were falling back . . . in an instant a regiment or two burst through into the spot where I was standing, all out of order and mixed up with a great number of yankees. I could not understand it; I could not tell whether our men had captured the yankees or the yankees had broken through our line. In an instant, however, I was put at rest, for Jackson, with one or two of his staff, came dashing across the road from our right in great haste and excitement. As he got amongst the disordered troops he drew his sword, then reached over and took his battleflag from my man, Bob Isbell, who was carrying it, and dropping his reins, waved it over his head and at the same time cried out in a loud voice, "Rally, men! Remember Winder! Where's my Stonewall Brigade? Forward, men, Forward!"

As he did so he dashed to the front, and our men followed with a yell and drove everything before them. It was a wonderful scene—one which men do not often see. Jackson usually is an indifferent and slouchy looking man but then, with the "Light of Battle" shedding its radiance over him his whole person was changed. His action as graceful as Lee's and his face was lit with the inspiration of heroism. The men would have followed him into the jaws of death itself; nothing could have stopped them and nothing did.

Even the old sorrel horse seemed endowed with the style and form of an Arabian.

Just as this scene was being enacted a very handsome and hatless yankee officer, not over twenty-one or two, whose head was covered with clusters of really golden curls and who had in his hand a broken sword, showing he had led the gallant charge which had broken our ranks, laid his hand on my knee as I sat on my horse and said with great emotion, "What officer is that, Captain?" And when I told him, fully appreciating the magnetism of the occasion, he seemed carried away with admiration. With a touch of nature that makes the whole world kin he waved his broken sword around his head and shouted, "Hurrah for General Jackson! Follow your General, Boys!" I leaned over, almost with tears in my eyes and said, "You are too good a fellow for me to make prisoner; take that path to the left and you can escape." He saluted me with his broken sword and disappeared in an instant. I hope he escaped. . . .

October 14, 1862   . . . my men have become much infested with vermin, derived largely from camping so often on camp grounds recently used by Federal and Confederate troops alternately. I find it impossible to keep them off me, but I am having a thorough scouring and washing and hope I will get the men in better condition. . . .

November 30, 1862 [*near Fredericksburg, Virginia*]   . . . My company is becoming smaller and smaller through sickness, wounds and lack of horses, chiefly the latter. It is, as you well know, difficult for a city company like ours to keep up in mounts. My men do not have farms, or relatives and neighbors with farms from whom they can draw when their horses get killed or disabled, but have to purchase their horses at prices even I hesitate to pay. I believe this is the only army in history where the men have to furnish their own horses and it is the main weakness of our cavalry. To me to lose a horse is to lose a man, as they cannot afford a remount and new recruits with horses of their own are almost nil. . . .

December 5, 1862 [*near Spotsylvania Courthouse*]   Never since I have been in the service have I ever been camped in such a stupid spot. We are twelve miles from the rest of the army, in a pine woods, and even out of the reach of a newspaper. As we have no men on picket we hear nothing even of the enemy. My coat is giving signs of dissolution which warns me I must be making arrangements for another: so have one made for me out of the cloth I sent you by Callahan. I do not want yellow cuffs or collar, but have it braided with gold lace, bars on the collar and knots on the sleeve, of the regulation style. Let the buttons be of the handsomest staff variety you can get. I burned quite a hole in my coat yesterday, and I am in daily dread my pantaloons will not stand much longer the strain of this cruel war. To be breechless in this weather and in the face of the enemy will not do.

June 20, 1863 [*Clarke County*]   I have nothing much to do. I carry an occasional message for the General or get some information, but, as a rule, I merely go along the road with the rest of the army. . . . I find it very hard to control a burning desire for revenge when I hear the piteous tale of wrongs which these people of Clarke have suffered at the hands of the yankee soldiers. It is scarcely fair, however, to call them yankees, for nine-tenths of them are foreigners sent as substitutes for the native-born patriots who thus would bleed vicariously for the Union. . . .

June 25, 1863   . . . The crossing of the [*Potomac*] river by our troops was very picturesque. General Lee was on the bank on the Maryland side surrounded by ladies who came down to see the sight and to admire him. The soldiers waded into the water without stopping to roll up their panta-loons and came over in good order as if on review, cheering at every step. One fellow, as he stepped on the Maryland shore, exclaimed: "Well, boys I've been seceding for two years and now I've got back into the Union again!" Another said to the crowd of ladies he thought were Union in their sentiments: "Here we are ladies, as rough and ragged as ever but back again to bother you."

The joy of the day was marred this evening by a military execution which took place in this division. I heard the death-march but fortunately did not hear the firing. It was not the victim of any trial of which I was judge-advocate, I am glad to say. . . .

June 26, 1863 [*Greencastle, Pennsylvania*]   I crossed "Mason's and Dixon's Line" to-day and am now some five or six miles within the bound-aries of the Keystone State, surrounded by enemies and black looks, Dutch-men and big barns. Night before last I slept on the sacred soil, last night in "My Maryland" and to-night I will sweetly slumber in the land of Penn and Protection. This is a very large change of venue for so large an army. . . . The people are greatly divided in sentiment, but far the greater part are Unionists. The minority, however, are very large and very enthusiastically Southern and very bold in expressing their sentiments. . . . So far as I have seen since crossing the Pennsylvania line, there is not much to indicate that we are in enemy's country. The people, of course, are not pleased to see us, but they are not demonstrative in their hatred or very shy in their treat-ment to us. As no maltreatment is permitted, and no pillage of other than their stock, they are so favorably disposed towards us that they almost seem friendly. Private property is respected and men are not allowed even to go into a yard to get water without permission of the owner. The orders even go so far, and they are strictly enforced, as to prohibit the burning of rails for firewood, a rule not enforced in Virginia and one I must say I think unnecessary here. Of course there will be some pillaging and even more violent robbery, for it is hard to strictly enforce any rule in so large an army, but such acts will be exceptional, as every possible means are taken to enforce General Lee's order, and the rule meets the approval of the army generally. . . .

July 3, 1863   I left Chambersburg yesterday at two o'clock in the morning and we made a march of twenty-three miles by twelve o'clock without a single straggler, I believe. On the road we heard that on the evening before (July 1) General Lee had met the enemy about two miles from Gettysburg and drove them back several miles, capturing some five thousand prisoners, without any serious loss on our part. Soon after we reached this place yesterday a very terrible battle began, which raged until nine, the particulars of which I have been unable to gather, except the two wings of the enemy were driven back with great loss, but their center stood firm. We captured some two thousand prisoners and, it is said, fifteen guns. All this, however, is but a rumor, and even at corps headquarters we know little. . . . The fight commenced again this morning about four o'clock and has been raging at intervals and in different quarters ever since, until now, at ten o'clock, as I write under the shade of a tree, a terrible cannonading is going on. General Longstreet is a little to my right, awaiting orders I suppose. His men are not yet engaged except the artillery. . . .

July 4, 1863   The battle [*of Gettysburg*] so increased in violence that I could no longer write. I knew it was a terrible battle but how terrible I did not know until it was over. The results of the day even now are not accurately known. . . . I can only speak of what I saw. . . . They vastly outnumbered us, and though our men made a charge which will be the theme of the poet, painter and historian of all ages, they could not maintain the enemy's lines much less capture them—The might of numbers will tell. Our loss of men and officers exceeds anything I have ever known. The loss is especially great among the officers, and those from Virginia particularly. . . .

July 18, 1863   . . . we have never been strong enough, or well enough provided with munitions to justify an invasion. The enemy has a better chance of invading us because of the information they derived from the negroes; but with these advantages, in Virginia at least, they have always been defeated. . . .

October 25, 1863   . . . The army is very badly generalled and the result is there is much demoralization and want of confidence. Bragg ought to be relieved or disaster is sure to result. The men have no faith. The difference between this army and Lee's is very striking. . . .

October 29, 1863   . . . The social conditions of the country in which we are camped are very strange. There are no gentlemen nor gentlemen's houses; the people all live in cabins with little cultivated patches of ground around them. As to patriotism there is none. Fully one-half went off with the yankee army when it retreated. The people down in these states are not as much enlisted on principle in this war as we in Virginia. They regard it as a war to protect their property in slaves and when they are lost take no further interest in it. In Virginia we are fighting for the right to govern ourselves in our own way and to perpetuate our own customs and institutions among our own people without outside interference. This feeling being universal no loss of property or temporary defeat affects our people and they remain true. In East Tennessee the people are about equally divided and there rages a real civil war, which causes great misery. . . .

January 18, 1864   . . . The question of supplies for the army is a serious one . . . but I think we are safe for two months. . . . We have to adopt the mode of foraging here that we did in Pennsylvania, sending a guard with every wagon train for its protection and to enforce the collection of supplies from unfriendly parties. The mountains are filled with deserters from both armies, who are banded together for the purpose of robbing trains of both sides as well as all citizens.

January 22, 1864   . . . My stock of reading matter is nearly finished. I have read Bourienne's Napoleon and am now deep in Napier's Peninsular Wars, the latter being also read by John Scott; very curious literature for a negro servant. . . .

June 7, 1864 [*Corps Headquarters, McKay's Farm*]   Should the yankees come you must stand your ground, hiding all your supplies and valuables, or send them away, if you know where to send them. You might have your pieces of bacon hid away in various parts of the house. Peggy should pack some away in her mattress as the yankees will, I suppose, respect her race, or at least not suspect the hiding place. . . .

March 24, 1865 [*Richmond, Virginia*]   . . . Our men are deserting quite freely. It looks very blue to them, and the fact that Sherman marched from Atlanta to Savannah without seeing an armed Confederate soldier is well calculated to make them despondent.

Questions for Discussion

1. What do Blackford's letters reveal about army life for this Confederate soldier?
2. What are Blackford's attitudes about the war? About the Union soldiers and civilians? About African Americans? Do those attitudes change? If so, in what ways?
3. How do Blackford's attitudes and experiences compare with those of Coe?

27.
G. H. Freeman, Spotswood Rice, "EDW," Charles Torrey Beman, "Fort Green," Cassius M. Clay Alexander, Garland H. White, and William Gibson

Letters from African-American Soldiers During the Civil War, 1864–1865

The letters here are divided into two sections: those written privately to officials or friends and those written for publication in the African-American newspapers of the North. Though African Americans had served in the military in every war fought by the United States, there was initial resistance to enlisting them in the Union army. Until the summer of 1862 Northern conservatives and border state slaveholders blocked enlistment of black soldiers. When given the opportunity to fight, African-American soldiers often performed heroically. The letters written to newspapers served as vehicles for soldiers to express political concerns about their treatment in the army and their hopes.

Private Letters

Near Petersburge [*Virginia*] August 19th 1864

Dear Madam   I receave A letter from You A few day Ago inquir in regard to the Fait of Your Son   I am sarry to have to inform You that thear

Edwin S. Redkey, ed. *A Grand Army of Black Men*. New York: Cambridge University Press, 1992, and Ira Berlin et al., eds. *Free At Last*. New York: The New Press, 1992. Reprinted by permission.

Company E, 4th U.S. Colored Infantry. *(Library of Congress)*

is no dobt of his Death   he Died A Brave Death in Trying to Save the
Colors of Rige[*ment*] in that Dreadful Battil   Billys Death was unevesally
[*mourned*] by all but by non greatter then by my self   ever sins we have bin
in the Army we have bin amoung the moust intimoat Friend   wen every
our Rige[*ment*] wen into Camp he sertan to be at my Tent and meney happy
moment we seen to gether Talking about Home and the Probability of our
Living to get Home to See each other Family and Friend   But Providence
has will other wise and You must Bow to His will   You and His Wife Sister
and all Have my deepust Simppathy and trust will be well all in this Trying
moment

    You Inquired about Mr Young   He wen to the Hospetol and I can not
give You eney other information in regard to Him

    Billys thing that You requested to inquired about I can git no informa
of us in the bustil of the Battil every thing was Lost

    Give my Respects to Samual Jackson and Family not forgetting Your
self and Family   I remain Your Friend

                                                      G.H. Freeman

/////

[Benton Barracks Hospital, St. Louis, Missouri, September 3,
1864. Spotswood Rice was an African-American soldier writing
to his children in captivity.]

    My Children   I take my pen in hand to rite you A few lines to let you
know that I have not forgot you and that I want to see you as bad as ever
now my Dear Children I want you to be contented with whatever may be

your lots be assured that I will have you if it cost me my life on the 28th of the mounth. 8 hundred White and 8 hundred blacke solders expects to start up the rivore to Glasgow and above there thats to be jeneraled by a jeneral that will give me both of you when they Come I expect to be with, them and expect to get you both in return. Dont be uneasy my children I expect to have you. If Diggs dont give you up this Government will and I feel confident that I will get you Your Miss Kaitty said that I tried to steal you But I'll let her know that god never intended for man to steal his own flesh and blood. If I had no confidence in God I could have confidence in her But as it is If I ever had any Confidence in her I have none now and never expect to have And I want her to remember if she meets me with ten thousand soldiers she [*will?*] meet her enemy I once [*thought*] that I had some respect for them but now my respects is worn out and have no sympathy for Slaveholders. And as for her cristianantty I expect the Devil has Such in hell You tell her from me that She is the frist Christian that I ever hard say that aman could Steal his own child especially out of human bondage

You can tell her that She can hold to you as long as she can I never would expect to ask her ain to let you come to me because I know that the devil has got her hot set againsts that that is write now my Dear children I am a going to close my letter to you Give my love to all enquiring friends tell them all that we are well and want to see them very much and Corra and Mary receive the greater part of it you sefves and dont think hard of us not sending you any thing I you father have a plenty for you when I see you Spott & Noah sends their love to both of you Oh! My Dear children how I do want to see you

[*Spotswood Rice*]

Letters to Newspapers

March 13, 1864

To the *Christian Recorder*
It is with pleasure that I now seat myself to inform you of our last battle . . .

The battle took place in a grove called Olustee, with the different regiments as follows: First there was the 8th U.S. [*Colored Infantry*]; they were cut up badly, and they were the first colored regiment in the battle. The next was the 54th Mass., which I belong to. . . . The firing was very warm, and it continued for about three hours and a half. The 54th was the last off the field. . . .

Now it seems strange to me that we do not receive the same pay and rations as the white soldiers. Do we not fill the same ranks? Do we not cover the same space of ground? Do we not take up the same length of ground in a grave-yard that others do? The ball does not miss the black man and strike the white, nor the white and strike the black. But sir, at that time there is no distinction made; they strike one as much as another. The black men have to go through the same hurling of musketry, and the same belching of cannonading as white soldiers do.

E.D.W. [*Private*]

[*In August 1864 African-American soldiers who had been free before the war began receiving equal pay. Units made up of former slaves did not receive full back pay until March 1865.*]

/////

June 20, 1864

To the *Weekly Anglo-African*
   . . . Since I last wrote, almost half of the 5th Massachusetts Cavalry have been in several engagements, and about thirty have been killed and wounded. The first notice I had of going into the engagement was about 1 o'clock, a.m., Wednesday, the 15th. We heard the bugle, and sprang to our arms, and, with two days rations, we started towards Petersburg, and when about four miles on our way toward that city, at a place called Beatty's House, we came in front of the rebels' works. Here we formed a line of battle, and started for the rebs' works. I was with some thirty of my Company. We had to pass through the woods; but we kept on, while the shell, grape and canister came around us cruelly. Our Major and Col. [*Henry F.*] Russell were wounded, and several men fell—to advance seemed almost impossible; but we rallied, and after a terrible charge, amidst pieces of barbarous iron, solid shot and shell, we drove the desperate greybacks from their fortifications, and gave three cheers for our victory. But few white troops were with us. Parts of the 1st, 4th, 6th and 22nd [*United States Colored Infantry*] were engaged.
   The colored troops here have received a great deal of praise. The sensations I had in the battle were, coolness and interest in the boys' fighting. They shouted, "Fort Pillow,"[1] and the rebs were shown no mercy.

[*Private Charles Torrey Beman*]

/////

August 21, 1864

To the *Christian Recorder*
   . . . I will say something about the prejudice in our own regiment when we returned from Olustee to Jacksonville. One of our captains was sick,

---

[1]At Fort Pillow in April 1864, Confederate troops shot prisoners, especially African Americans, who had surrendered.

and there was no doctor there excepting our hospital steward, who administered the medicines and effected a cure; he was a colored man, Dr. [*Theodore*] Becker, and a competent physician, and through the exertions of this recovered captain, there was a petition got up for his promotion. All the officers signed the petition but three, Captain [*Charles*] Briggs, and two lieutenants; they admitted he was a smart man and understood medicine, but he was a negro, and they did not want a negro Doctor, neither did they want negro officers. The Colonel, seeing so much prejudice among his officers, destroyed the document; therefore the negro is not yet acknowledged.

Notwithstanding all these grievances, we prefer the Union rather than the rebel government, and will sustain the Union if the United States will give us our rights. We will calmly submit to white officers, though some of them are no so well acquainted with military matters as our orderly sergeants, and some of the officers have gone so far to say that a negro stunk under their noses. This is not very pleasant, but we must give the officers of Company B of the 54th Massachusetts regiment, their just dues; they generally show us the respect due to soldiers, and scorn any attempt to treat us otherwise. . . .

"Fort Green" [*54th Massachusetts Infantry*]

/////

October, 1865

To the *Weekly Anglo-African*

I have never before attempted to pen a line for your columns, but in this case I am compelled to, because I have been waiting patiently to see if I could see anything in regard to our noble Regiment, and have seen nothing. We have fought and captured Blakesly's Fort. We were only ten days on the siege, and had nothing to eat but Parched Corn. But as luck would have it, I crept out of my hole at night and scared one of the Jonnys so bad that he left his rifle pit, gun and accouterments, also one corn dodger and about one pint of buttermilk, all of which I devoured with a will, and returned to my hole safe and sound. After sleeping the remainder of the night, about day I was awakened by our turtlebacks that were playing with the enemy's works. At that time I forgot myself and poked my head out of my hole, and came very near getting one of Jonny's cough pills. We had to keep our heads down all the time or else run the risk of getting shot. So me and my friend of whom I was speaking had it all that day, shooting at each other. Finally, he got hungry and cried out to me, "Say, Blacky, let's stop and eat some Dinner." I told him, "All right." By the time I thought he was done eating, I cried, "Hello, Reb." He answered, "What do you want?" I said, "Are you ready" "No, not yet," he said. Then I waited for a while.

I finally got tired and cried for a chew of tobacco. He then shot at me and said, "Chew that!" I thanked him kindly and commenced exchanging shots with him.

I must not take too much time in relating all the incidents, for Parched Corn takes the day also. We have accomplished all undertakings, and excel in the drill. We ask nothing now but to be mustered out.

[*Sergeant Cassius M. Clay Alexander*]

/////

April 12, 1865

To the *Christian Recorder*

I have just returned from the city of Richmond; my regiment was among the first that entered that city. I marched at the head of the column, and soon I found myself called upon by the officers and men of my regiment to make a speech, with which, of course, I readily complied. A vast multitude assembled on Broad Street, and I was aroused amid the shouts of ten thousand voices, and proclaimed for the first time in that city freedom to all mankind. After which the doors of all the slave pens were thrown open, and thousands came out shouting and praising God, and Father, or Master Abe, as they termed him. In this mighty consternation I became so overcome with tears that I could not stand up under the pressure of such fullness of joy in my own heart. I retired to gain strength, so I lost many important topics worthy of note.

Among the densely crowded concourse there were parents looking for children who had been sold south of this state in tribes, and husbands came for the same purpose; here and there one was singled out in the ranks, and an effort was made to approach the gallant and marching soldiers, who were too obedient to orders to break ranks.

We continued our march as far as Camp Lee, at the extreme end of Broad Street, running westwards. In camp the multitude followed, and everybody could participate in shaking the friendly but hard hands of the poor slaves. Among the many broken-hearted mothers looking for their children who had been sold to Georgia and elsewhere, was an aged woman, passing through the vast crowd of colored, inquiring for [*one*] by the name of Garland H. White, who had been sold from her when a small boy, and was bought by a lawyer named Robert Toombs, who lived in Georgia. Since the war has been going on she has seen Mr. Toombs in Richmond with troops from his state, and upon her asking him where his body-servant Garland was, he replied: "He ran off from me at Washington, and went to Canada. I have since learned that he is living somewhere in the State of Ohio." Some of the boys knowing that I lived in Ohio, soon found me and said, "Chaplain, here is a lady that wishes to see you." I quickly turned, following the soldier until coming to a group of colored ladies. I was questioned as follows:

"What is your name, sir?"

"My name is Garland H. White."

"What was your mother's name?"

"Nancy."

"Where was you born?"

"In Hanover County, in this State."

"Where was you sold from?"

"From this city."

"What was the name of the man who bought you?"

"Robert Toombs."

"Where did he live?"

"In the State of Georgia."

"Where did you leave him?"

"At Washington."

"Where did you go then?"

"To Canada."

"Where do you live now?"

"In Ohio."

"This is your mother, Garland, whom you are now talking to, who has spent twenty years of grief about her son."

I cannot express the joy I felt at this happy meeting of my mother and other friends. But suffice it to say that God is on the side of the righteous, and will in due time reward them. I have witnessed several such scenes among the other colored regiments. . . .

[*Chaplain Garland H. White*]

/////

May 18, 1865

To the *Christian Recorder*

It is the first time in the history of my life that one so humble as myself ever attempted to write anything for publication through the columns of your most worthy journal; and it is with great reluctance that I attempt it on the present occasion, owing to my short stay at home in Park Co[*unty*], Ind[*iana*], on a furlough, where I found many friends to rejoice over, and many disadvantages upon the part of the colored people to mourn over. It seems very strange to me that the people of Indiana are so very indifferent about removing from their statute books those Black Laws, which are a curse to them in the eyes of God and man, and above all things in life, the most grievous to be borne by any people.

Shall the history of the old 28th [*United States Colored Infantry*], which was raised in that State, stand upon the great record of the American army second to none? Shall these brave sons return home after periling their lives for several years in the storm of battle for the restoration of the Union and to vindicate the honor and dignity of that fair Western State which is classed among the best composing this great nation, but to be treated as slaves? Shall it be said by the nations of the earth that any portion of the United States treated her brave defenders thus? I hope never to see the day; yet it is fast approaching.

Have we no friends at home among the whites to look this great injustice in the face, and bid its sin-cursed waves forever leave? Have we no colored friends at home who feel tired of the burden and are willing to pray to the thinking public to lighten it? As for us, we have done our duty and are willing to do it whenever the State and country call us; but after responding, are you not willing to pay the laborer for his hire? It is to be seen in all past history that when men fought for their country and returned home, they always enjoyed the rights and privileges due to other citizens.

We ask to be made equal before the law; grant us this and we ask no more. Let the friends of freedom canvass the country on this subject. Let the sound go into all the earth. . . .

William Gibson, Corporal

Questions for Discussion

1. What issues are of most concern to the writers of these letters?
2. What do the soldiers think about the rebels? What do they think about their own officers?
3. How does combat as described in these letters differ from modern day warfare?
4. Compare Hamlin Coe's attitudes with those of the white officers described in these letters.

28.
Hannah Aldrich
Letters from the Home Front, 1861–1864

In 1856 Herman and Hannah Aldrich moved from Swanzey, New Hampshire, to the frontier of Wisconsin. There they lived during much of the Civil War on eighty acres in Sylvan, a community in northwestern Richland County. During those years, Hannah wrote more than a hundred letters to her family in Swanzey (especially to her mother and sisters, Maria and Emily) describing her life on the Wisconsin frontier. In 1864 the Aldriches gave up their effort to make a living in Wisconsin and returned to Swanzey, where Herman first worked in local factories and then started his own successful insurance business. Hannah saved the letters from Sylvan for over thirty years, and in 1899 gave them to her daughter, Emily. Besides offering a glimpse into the daily struggles of pioneer life, her letters and the replies from family members in Swanzey describe the effects of the Civil War even on remote communities.

Sylvan
June 2, 1861

My dear Emily:

. . . It is Sabbath day. We are all at home. Herman is quite unwell with a sick headache and feeling sort of lonesome while he is lying on the bed.

"Hannah's Letters: The Story of a Wisconsin Pioneer Family, 1856–1864: Part I," eds. Elizabeth Krynski and Kimberly Little, *Wisconsin Magazine of History* 74.3 (Spring, 1991): 163–195; Part II, eds. Krynski and Little, *Wisconsin Magazine of History* 74.4 (Summer, 1991): 272–296; and Part III, eds. Krynski and Little, *Wisconsin Magazine of History* 75.1 (Autumn, 1991): 39–62. Reprinted by permission.

I have seated myself at my writing desk to pen a few lines to you. You do not know how often my thoughts wander back over lakes and rivers, prairies, and woodland to my own native hills far, far away, and I often in imagination see all my friends whom I have left behind for a home in the "far distant west." Sometimes it seems hard to be so far from all our friends and to be deprived of so many of the privileges which you enjoy. . . .

The men here have all formed themselves into a military company, from the oldest grandfather to the boy of 17. Considerable excitement prevails in regard to the war, although we do not get the news very early. Some have enlisted and others would if they could leave. It makes me feel bad to think of it. I always had a horror of war. . . .

My paper is poor and somewhat dirty, too, but it is the last sheet and you must excuse it. I have not told you about having a log rolling a few weeks since; I had 16 men to cook for. Have had work folks considerable since, which makes my work harder. I begin to be quite impatient to have some milk and butter. Our cow has not come in yet, has been dry more than two months. Hard getting along without either. We have plenty good water in our cistern which seems good, I tell you; you that have always had water so plenty do not know how to prize it as we do. One of our neighbors had their house burned up two weeks ago and everything they had. They were gone to a Union meeting and from all circumstances it is thought by most people that it was set on fire by someone whom he had offended in a speech he made at a flag raising a few days before, but we do not know. We all have to lift hard to help them as they were poor. The man had quite a library and a set of surveyor's tools which will be hard for him to lose and which he will probably not get made up to him. No more at present. Write soon. Love to all who enquire.

Hannah

/////

Sylvan
October 28, 1861

Dear Emily:

Did you think I was never going to answer your kind letter written so long ago? It is now three weeks since we received it, but we have had so much to do it seemed we could never get time to write by daylight and as we have no lights it is pretty difficult to write evenings, but to-day I am going to take the time for I can wait no longer and I know you will be anxious to hear from us. . . .

. . . I have a good deal of sewing and knitting to do or shall have if we can manage to get the material which we must have in order to keep comfortable in cold weather. Herman can get no money on his last winter's wages so he will be obliged to take land sale certificates [*at a discount*] and lose 25 cts. on a dollar.[1] This is really too bad, but it will not do to suffer for clothes so we shall be obliged to do it. . . .

A great many of our neighbors and townsmen have gone to the war. O this dreadful war, I wish it could be over. It troubles me night and day. I have such awful dreams in the night and then when I read of battles it makes me so nervous I can hardly hold myself together. . . .

You spoke of your cheese and said Vermont cheese was worth only 4 cents a lb. How I wish I could get hold of some. I would pay more than that and set up nights to earn something to buy it. Herman has taken the school in our own district to commence the 18 of Nov. Has to teach for very low wages, but will be better than nothing if he can ever get his pay. I am willing to be contented with small wages and to get along with a very little if he can only remain at home, for I do not see how I could possibly get along and take care of my family if he were away. It takes so little to upset me, a little harder day's work or a little uncommon exposure making me sick. . . .

Hannah

/////

Swanzey, New Hampshire
January 7, 1862

[*Father Aldrich to Herman and Hannah*]:
    . . . If you knew how hard it is for me to write. I think of you. I assure you we have all our children near us but you. . . . It is pretty hard times for people to get a living hear [*sic*]. Poor people have to go to the War or starve. Things have come to a pretty pass. How terrible it is to have such a fighting spirit in the world. Tis not the spirit of the Savior . . . that the North should march down into the South. . . . To hear you say, Herman, that you would go if you could leave your family looks strange to me. Let those that want to go, but I hope none of my family will be guilty of going to this War. Let people come up to us; then we must defend ourselves. What this will amount to no one can tell. We must pray and hope for the best.

Now I will tell you what I would like to do. Sell all our land. Paul and Charley go out West and buy land, now it is cheap. [*Paul is Herman's*

---

[1]The Civil War was indirectly responsible for one of Herman's difficulties—getting paid for teaching. In the spring of 1861, the Wisconsin banking system collapsed since many of the banks had invested in Confederate bonds during the 1850s. Over the course of the Civil War, the value of the notes backed by those bonds plummeted.

A Midwestern pioneer farm in the 1850s. *(Clarke Historical Library, Central Michigan University)*

brother; Charley, his brother-in-law.] Don't you think so? Paul says he wishes he was back there. Says he shan't buy here. Says he is homesick. If we could get rid of our old farms we should come and see where you live. At any rate, have good courage, Herman, there is better times coming if not in this life in the life to come. Hannah, it makes me feel bad that you are so far from us and so poor that you can't write to us. I should have sent you money before this if I had it. I have spoken about it many times to your Father. He says if you want money you must say so. He has sent all you sent for. I feel most afraid to send money in a letter. . . .

/////

Swanzey, New Hampshire
June 29, 1862

[*Emily to Hannah*]:
. . . Don't over-do and get down again. Was glad to hear that you was gaining your health in any degree. Wish you lived a little nearer so I could step in and help you about your work, for you know that is the way the "old maid" do—go about doing good—but as it is impossible for me to go so far in my charities at present, I must content myself in cautioning you to take care of yourself. . . . Father is quite lame yet but goes without his staff most of the time. It is too much of a bother to look after it when he is about his work. . . .

There is considerable excitement here in regard to raising men for the war, every able-bodied man has been enrolled and there is considerable talk about drafting but I hardly think they will have to draft as two regiments are nearly full already.

Mowry has been enrolled and talks quite strong of enlisting. Jerusha worried night and day for fear he will enlist. O how much sorrow and anxiety is caused by this terrible, terrible war. When will it end. Charles Sebastian came home a few weeks ago. He was taken prisoner at the Battle of Bull Run [*July 21, 1861*] one year ago and has been a prisoner until now. He said there were 500 of them shut in one room and fed with horse and mule meat together with a little rice and water. He suffered considerable while there but is anxious to go into the army again. . . .

Emily

/////

[*Mother Thompson to Hannah (1862), sheet missing*]:
. . . . Is Herman teaching school this winter? I hope he will get his pay. Most all of our schools have female teachers so many have gone to war. Oh this terrible war, when will it end? I wish it was near an end as Father and Mowry are ploughing for next spring. . . .

Mother

Sylvan
January 19, 1863

My dear sisters Maria and Emily:
Now I am going to write to you both, for I have received letters from both of you since I wrote and some from mother too. Well, I will address my letter to you all, thanking you for your kind letters and begging you not to pattern after my example and neglecting to answer the same. You must know that with all my housework, making, mending, knitting, and tending baby, doing chores etc. while Herman and the boys are at school my time is pretty well taken up. I am up before light and very seldom go to bed till eleven o'clock. I find I am growing old fast. Tomorrow if I live I shall be 31 years old. It does not seem possible. It seems but a short time since I was a school girl, but so rapid time flies, fast carrying us on to our eternal home. My health is very good for me but I have to work so hard that I feel tired and worn out most of the time. . . .

We have killed three hogs. Laid up two for ourselves and are going to sell the other one. Pork is worth—well, I don't know. It was, last week, $3.75, I think. Hope the hog will come to enough to get the boys some clothes as they need them very much. I am wearing my last calico dress.

Do not know when I shall have another. Calico is 25 cts. a yard and every-thing else according. We went to a New Year's party at Mr. Wood's. There were between 40 and 50 there. Their youngest son had come home from the army. Was taken prisoner at the battle of Pittsburg landing [*Shiloh, April 6–7, 1862*] and had been in Georgia for a long time. They had heard nothing from him and supposed him to be dead.

The old gentleman said it was meet that he should rejoice and make merry with his friends for his son was dead and is alive again, was lost and is found. He had suffered everything but death while in the hands of the rebs. After a while he was paroled and finally exchanged. He was offered his discharge while at St. Louis on account of ill health, but would not accept it. He had regained his health in a great measure and was going the next week to join the army to try his fortunes once more among the brave boys who were fighting the battles of their country. . . .

. . . I have written in the biggest hurry so you will please excuse all mistakes and bad writing. Have written it all in less than an hour. Love to all enquiring friends. From

Hannah

Sylvan
April 12, 1863

Dear Sister:

We received your kind letter in due time, and I ought to have answered it before now, but my old excuse want of time has prevented my doing so. I have to do most of the writing as Herman does not have much time and he thinks I can write so much easier than he can that he puts it upon me. But there is nothing I have to do except *reading* letters from my friends that I take more pleasure in doing. . . .

I got me a calico dress a few weeks ago. had to pay 25 cts. Last night we heard calico had got up to 35 cts. Blue drilling 50 cts. and poor at that. I do not know what we are coming to. It seems now as if we could begin to live quite comfortable if the times were good, but if this war continues much longer we must with many others be in very destitute if not in a suffering condition for clothing. But if we can get clothes so [*as*] to not actually suffer I do not mean to complain, as there are so many poor families who are worse off than we are and so many mourning the loss of husbands and brothers in this wicked war.

Oh I do wish it could be over. It seems so wicked. I know that this wicked rebellion must be put down but it seems sometimes that the sacrifice is almost too great. We had a visit several days since from a young man in the Army of the Potomac, that used to live near neighbor. He has been through several battles but he'd never been hurt. He said they were in good spirits, eager to be led on. We sent the Sylvan boys some sugar by him. Thought it would seem good to them to get some Wisconsin sugar away in Virginia. Mr. Wood has lost his oldest son. He belonged to a Cavalry Regt. from Iowa. He died in the hospital of Chronic Diarrhea. The other one is at St. Louis.

We have gotten two of the cunningest little calves you ever saw, about one day's difference in their ages. The heifers are only two years ole. They give quite a mess of milk considering they get so little to eat. Everyone is way short of feed and we are in quite a hurry to have warm weather come so feed will start. Have to browse the cattle besides giving them some corn. Herman had his oxen wintered away from him too. Well Maria I see my sheet is getting full and I must stop, though it seems as if I have wrote nothing that I wanted to, but paper is so high I don't know but I must make it do for this time. Sometimes I think we shall have to leave off writing entirely. . . .

. . . I do not see any room to sign my name but "reckon" you will know who it is from without, if you had not forgotten that you had a sister.

Hannah

/////

Sylvan
March 15, 1864

Dear Mother and Sister Emily:
Your letters have been duly received and should have been answered before this but I am so busy now that I do not find time to write as often as I would like. You were quite right, Emily, in thinking a letter from home would be acceptable at any time and I was glad you for once broke the rules of etiquette and wrote to me before you got an answer from me. Now I am going to write only an apology this time, having no time and no ink, but just to let you hear from us so you won't feel uneasy about us.

We are very busy making sugar. Have made 140 lbs. Most people have hardly commenced. Hope to make some to sell to get the children clothes. I feel most discouraged sometimes, everything is so high, and goods are so poor. Can get nothing that will last any time at all. I expect Herman will be drafted and then I don't know what will become of us. There are about 40 enrolled and 12 to be drafted and he may be one of the number. I do not know what I could do here alone with the children the way my health is. If I could go out and work and carry on the place like some women there is here I could get along but I cannot do my work in the house as it ought to be. My health has not been so good through the winter as it was last summer. . . .

Please answer this scrawl and I will try and get some ink and write a good long letter soon.

Hannah

/////

Sylvan
September 26, 1864

Dear Sister:

It is a long long time since I received your last letter and since I have written to any of you. . . . We have been very much afflicted with sickness since that time, but thanks to a kindly Heavenly Father our circle is yet unbroken and we are once more restored to comfortable health. . . .

. . . But I do not mean to complain as long as our lives were all spared while so many of our friends and neighbors have been taken away. It has been a very sickly season. More deaths than has been since we came here and so many of our neighbors that went into the army have been killed or have died.

Truly our country and our town and neighborhood is clad in the robes of mourning for the loss of her brave sons, husbands and brothers that have fallen, a sacrifice to this cruel war. O will it ever close? Shall we ever hear the glad news of peace and see our brave soldiers return to their homes, those that are spared? Alas, how many will be left on southern soil never to return to loved ones that have long and anxiously waited their return?

I have long been expecting Herman would go, as there are but few men left to fill the quota. Some say he will be exempt on account of his teeth.[2] He would have gone long ago if he could have seen any way to leave us comfortably situated, but as it has been, he did not deem it his duty. . . .

Hannah

Questions for Discussion

1. What do you learn about the impact of the war on the community of Sylvan? How would you describe Hannah's attitude toward the war? What attitudes do her family in New Hampshire express?
2. Identify some of the economic effects of the war indicated in these letters.

---

[2]Bad teeth were one of the few things that could exempt men from the army. Soldiers needed strong teeth to tear cartridges and load their guns. They also needed the ability literally to bite a bullet during painful surgery with no anesthesia.

29.
Laura M. Towne

Diary and Letters from the Sea Islands During Reconstruction, 1862–1884

The Sea Islands of South Carolina, between Charleston and Savannah, were among the first Confederate areas to fall to the Union during the Civil War. On November 7, 1861, the Union navy reduced the fort on Hilton Head Island, and Northern soldiers soon occupied the Sea Islands. Immediately the question arose of what was to be done with the slaves on the islands, whose owners had fled. What was to be their status?

The government decided that volunteers from the North would organize production; the old plantations would now be under the supervision of Northern "superintendents." Representatives of Northern missionary societies would meanwhile provide schooling for the islands' inhabitants.

Laura M. Towne was one of these teachers. She arrived on the islands in April 1862, little realizing they would be her home for the rest of her life. Born in Pittsburgh in 1825, Laura Towne was a dedicated abolitionist. She had received some medical training, which was of great use to her on the islands, but her lifelong passion was for education. She founded the Penn School on St. Helena Island, and with her friend and fellow teacher, Ellen Murray, bought a house nearby. There she remained, witnessing and

Rupert Sargent Holland, ed. *Letters and Diary of Laura Towne*. New York: Negro Universities Press, 1969. Reprinted by permission.

participating in the dramatic events of the Reconstruction era on the islands — the former slaves' struggle for land and for political power, their growing independence of their white mentors, the postwar return of the old master class, and the political violence that accompanied the end of Reconstruction and the disfranchisement of African Americans.

Some of the remarks in Laura Towne's diary and letters grate upon modern sensibilities — she was not free of condescension, of the assumption that whites would naturally lead. Yet she showed a capacity for change. After 1862, for example, she makes no more references to "our people." Rather, she uses the term "the people," and there is at times something powerful about her evocation of those words. Laura Towne died in 1901, by then respected even by the white inhabitants of the islands, to whom she had been slow to accommodate.

April 17, 1862 . . . Besides soldiers the streets are full of the oddest negro children — dirty and ragged, but about the same as so many Irish in intelligence. . . . I think a rather too cautious spirit prevails — anti-slavery is to be kept in the background for fear of exciting the animosity of the army, and we are only here by military sufferance. But we have the odium of out-and-out abolitionists, why not take the credit? . . . I wish they would all say out loud quietly, respectfully, firmly, "We have come to do anti-slavery work, and we think it noble work and we mean to do it honestly." . . .

April 18, 1862 . . . There has been a little rebellion upon Mr. Philbrick's[1] plantation. . . . Two men, one upon each estate, refuse to work the four hours a day they are required to give to the cotton, but insist upon cultivating their own cornpatch only. They threaten, if unprovided with food, to break into the cornhouse. One man drew his knife upon his driver, but crouched as soon as Mr. Philbrick laid his hand upon his shoulder. . . .

April 21, 1862 . . . The number of little darkies tumbling around at all hours is marvelous. They swarm on the front porch and in the front hall. If a carriage stops it is instantly surrounded by a dozen or more wooly heads. They are all very civil, but full of mischief and fun. . . . The hands

---

[1] Edward Philbrick was one of the superintendents least trusted by the missionary teachers, who tended to believe that his methods were too reminiscent of slavery and that his goal was wealth rather than reform. In this case, however, Philbrick learned a valuable lesson. The workers forced him to abandon the old "gang" labor system that had been the norm under slavery. To this change Philbrick was to attribute much of his later success.

on the place are all obliged to work. All who can be are kept busy with the cotton, but there are some women and young girls unfit for the field, and they are made to do their share in housework and washing, so they may draw pay like the others. . . .

April 24, 1862 . . . The negroes take it hard that they must work at cotton again this year, especially as it must be to the neglect of their corn, upon which they have the sense to feel that their next winter's food depends. . . .

A stereotyped "shout." (*The New York Public Library. Astor, Tilden, and Lennox Foundations*)

April 27, 1862 . . . Tonight I have been to a "shout", which seems to me certainly the remains of some old idol worship. The negroes sing a kind of chorus—three standing apart to lead and clap—and then all the others go shuffling around in a circle following one another with not much regularity, turning round occasionally and bending the knees, and stamping so that the whole floor swings. I never saw anything so savage. They call it a religious ceremony, but it seems like a regular frolic to me, and instead of attending the shout, the better persons go to the "Praise House." This is always the cabin of the oldest person in the little village of negro houses, and they meet there to read and pray. . . .

/////

May 1, 1862 . . . Our young men say they have to decide suddenly upon such weighty questions that they are kept anxious and overworked. They have learned to settle questions in an offhand way. Mr. Pierce, in talking with the negroes, has to alter many a half-considered thing. It is very picturesque to see him in a negro village with such unclad and oddly clad groups around him, talking, reasoning, and getting such shrewd answers too. . . .

/////

May 13, 1862 . . . This is a sad time here. On Sunday afternoon Captain Stevens . . . who commands here . . . came here with a peremptory order from General Hunter for every able-bodied negro man of age for a soldier to be sent at once to Hilton Head. This piece of tyranny carried dismay into this household, and we were in great indignation to think of the alarm and grief this would cause the poor negroes on this place. We have got to calling them *our* people and loving them really—not so much individually as the collective whole—the people and *our* people. . . .

/////

July 20, 1862 This morning there was no white preacher. After church Father Tom and his bench of elders examined candidates for baptism and asked Ellen to record their names. We stayed. Each candidate, clothed in the oldest possible clothes and with a handkerchief made into a band and tied around the forehead, stood humbly before the bench. Father Tom, looking like Jupiter himself, grave, powerful, and awfully dignified, put the most posing questions, to which the candidates replied meekly and promptly. He asked the satisfactory candidates at last, "How do you pray?" Then the soft musical voices made the coaxing, entreating kind of prayer they use so much. A nod dismissed the applicant and another was called up. There were sixty or seventy to examine . . .

/////

January 1, 1863 [*The Emancipation Proclamation was signed on this date.*] We rejoiced at midnight with great pride and joy to think our country is at last free.

/////

February 24, 1863 Hurrah! Jubilee! Lands are to be set apart for the people so that they cannot be oppressed, or driven to work for speculators, or ejected from their homesteads.[2] . . .

/////

January 7, 1864 We have no milk, and at times no wood. There is nobody, not a single hand—not one man up and well enough to get these things. All the boys are getting sick also. It is a tight time. I am nearly ill too. Every morning I fold powders and every afternoon I take to the street and stop at every house, giving medicine at the door, but lately not going in as I used to, for they keep their rooms so dark I cannot see the patients, and if I order a window opened, I find it nailed up the next time I come. . . .

/////

February 7, 1864 . . . We are getting very much interested in the villagers, particularly in the minister, a certain black or brown man who is certain to make his mark in the world. He is very eloquent and ambitious and makes a great stir in the department by his public speaking. He lives near us and his sister teaches in the school here. He often comes in of an evening, and the other day he found out to his intense horror that I was a Unitarian. But, though he says he expected better things of me, and various other things like that, he is really wonderfully liberal, and, as he will probably fall in with the right kind of people by reason of his eloquence and genius, he will one day perhaps be a Unitarian himself. . . .

/////

Christmas, 1864 . . . Miss Lynch and a colored teacher from the North, Mr. Freeman, dined here and seemed well satisfied. They have just gone. I suppose it would seem strange to you to sit down with two colored people, but to us it is the most natural thing in the world. I actually forget these people are black, and it is only when I see them at a distance and

---

[2] Laura Towne was too optimistic in this entry, but while there would be obstacles placed in their way, many African Americans on the Sea Islands did eventually acquire their own land. In this they were more fortunate than most former slaves.

Laura Towne. *(Library of Congress)*

cannot recognize their features that I remember it. The conversation at dinner flowed just as naturally as if we were Northern whites. . . .

/////

[This letter is about the death of Abraham Lincoln.]

April 29, 1865 . . . It was a frightful blow at first. The people have refused to believe he was dead. Last Sunday the black minister of Frogmore said that if they knew the President were dead they would mourn for him, but they could not think that was the truth, and they would wait and see. We are going tomorrow to hear what further they say. One man came for clothing and seemed very indifferent about them—different from most of the people. I expressed some surprise. "Oh" he said, "I have lost a friend. I don't care much now about anything." "What friend," I asked, not really thinking for a moment. "They call him Sam," he said; "Uncle Sam, the best friend I ever had." Another asked me in a whisper if it were true that the "Government was dead." Rina says she can't sleep for thinking how sorry she is to lose "Pa Linkum." You know they call their elders in church—or the particular one who converted and received them in—their spiritual father, and he has the most absolute power over them. These fathers are addressed with fear and awe as "Pa Marcus," "Pa Demas," etc. One man said to me, "Lincoln died for we, Christ died for we, and me believe him de same mans." . . .

/////

June 13, 1865 . . . Our school does splendidly, though I say it. The children have read through a history of the United States and an easy physiology, and they know all the parts of speech, and can make sentences, being told to use a predicate, verb, and adverb, for instance. Ellen's class is writing compositions. We are going to have a grand school exhibition before we close, with dialogues, exercises in mathematics, in grammar, geography, spelling, reading, etc., etc. We are cramming for it. Young Gabriel Capus [*a white former plantation owner*] has come back to his place, which was one reserved for the people. He warns them to buy no more of his land, as he shall soon have possession of it again! He went to his people, told them he had no money and nothing to eat, and begged them to let him stay with them. Old Rina took him in, and he lives in her house, but he begins already to show airs. Hastings and Rina are greatly exercised upon this question of the return of the old masters. . . .

/////

February 23, 1866 . . . [*The agents appointed by the Northern military*] are often more pro-slavery than the rebels themselves, and only care to make the blacks work—being quite unconcerned about making the employers pay. Doing justice seems to mean, to them, seeing that the blacks don't break a contract and compelling them to submit cheerfully if the whites do. . . .

/////

March 3, 1867 . . . To-day the white folks of the island who, under General Bennett's influence, are getting too uppish (most of them being low sutlers and camp-followers) to associate with blacks, even in church, have determined to have a white church of their own. We received an invitation to attend this afternoon, and went. We had a good sermon from a Beaufort minister—Northern—and a great turnout of the beauty and fashion of the island—such as whiskey-selling Mr. S. and his wife, etc., etc. There were some nice people there, and altogether I did not know there were so many white folks on the island. Two Southern teachers were there, and *I* only fraternized enough to speak to them—or but one person besides myself that I know of. They were tawdrily dressed—one of them in a pink silk—and were in the war undoubted rebels. Indeed we hear that they whip the children in their school and make them call them "massa" and "missus," as in the old time. . . . I think this whole church plan a snobbish affair, and that there will probably be more rigid exclusion of blacks from equality and civility than in the most snobbish of Northern or Southern churches, for there is no hater of the negro like these speculating planters, but I am going to attend for a while and watch matters. Perhaps this snap judgment is not a just one. We shall go to the black church in the morning, where, of all the white people here, the Ruggles, Murrays, and I are the only attendants, and to this white place in the afternoon. . . .

/////

May 12, 1867 We have had to take our holiday—Saturday—for a mass meeting of Republican citizens! . . . The speakers were all black men, except for Mr. Hunn [*one of the original superintendents*]. The white men did not attend—they are going to have a *white* party, they say. One black man said he wanted no white men on their platform, but he was taken to task by all the other speakers, who disclaimed all such feelings. It was funny to hear the arguments from the other side—such as—

"What difference does skin make, my bredren. I would stand side by side a *white* man if he acted right. We musn't be prejudices against their color."

"If dere skins *is* white, they may have principle."

"Come my friends, we musn't judge a man according to his color, but according to his acts," etc., etc. . . .

June 1, 1867 The people are just now in a great state of excitement over their right to vote, and are busy forming a Republican Party on the island. Today in church Mr. Hunn announced another meeting next Saturday. "The females must stay at home?" asked Demas from the pulpit. "The females can come or go as they choose," said Mr. Hunn, "but the meeting is for men voters." Demas immediately announced that "the womens will stay at home and cut grass," that is, hoe the corn and cotton fields—clear them of grass. It is too funny to see how much more jealous the men are of one kind of liberty they have achieved than of the other! Political freedom they are rather shy and ignorant of; but domestic freedom—the right, just found, to have their own way in their families and rule their wives— that is an inestimable privilege. . . .

/////

May 29, 1870 . . . We have taken in a little child to live with us— perhaps to bring up. She is Miss Puss—about the worst little monkey that ever was. Topsy is nothing to her. . . . That poor child has been undergoing all sorts of ill treatment all winter from her father. She is a dwarf already, and he starved and beat her every day. She is one of the best scholars in my class; as bright as a dollar; always noticed by strangers for here intelligence, good reading, etc. . . . She often ran away to escape a beating, and almost lived in the woods. . . . Ellen and I concluded to take her for poultry minder at half a dollar a month and food, but not clothing. The father did not feel willing to let her come, but the mother would have it, so the next day as we went to school and saw her in a field eating blackberries, we hailed her and told her she was to come to Frogmore to live. You never

The Penn School. *(Library of Congress)*

saw such a delighted little creature. So far she is good as gold, but the time will come when we will have our trials. She has been my scholar for years. . . .

/////

October 28, 1877 . . . Our school is a delight. It rained one day last week, but through the pelting showers came nearly every blessed child. Some of them walk six miles and back, besides doing their task of cotton picking. Their steady eagerness to learn is just something amazing. To be deprived of a lesson is a severe punishment. "I got no reading today," or no writing, or no sums, is cause for bitter tears. This race is going to rise. It is biding its time.

/////

October 29, 1878 . . . Political times are simply frightful. Men are shot at, hounded down, trapped, and held till certain meetings are over, and intimidated in every possible way. It gets worse and worse as election approaches. . . .

November 6, 1878 On Saturday I went to a Republican meeting at the church. Robert Smalls [*an African-American state senator*] told of his mobbing at Gillisonville . . . Men and women were coming up the street to attend the meeting when eight hundred red-shirt men [*white political terrorists*], led by colonels, generals, and many leading men of the state, came dashing into town, giving the real "rebel yell," the newspaper said. Robert Smalls called it "whooping like Indians." They drew up, and as a body stood still, but every few minutes a squad of three or four would scour down street on their horses, and reaching out would "lick off the hats" of the colored men or slap the faces of the colored women coming to the meeting, whooping and yelling and scattering the people on all sides. This made the colored men so mad that they wanted to pitch right into a fight with the eight hundred, but Robert Smalls restrained them, telling them what folly it was. . . . He [*Smalls*] withdrew into the store with his forty men and drew them up all around it behind the counters. They had guns. He told them to aim at the door, and stand with finger on trigger, but on no account to shoot until the red-shirts broke in. Meantime . . . the outsiders began to try to break down the door. They called Smalls and told him they would set fire to the house and burn him up in it. They fired repeatedly through the windows and walls. . . . He would not come out, and the leaders led off part of the red-shirts and began to make speeches, leaving the store surrounded, however, for fear Smalls should escape.

The people who had come to the meeting meanwhile ran to raise the alarm in every direction, and in an incredible short time the most distant parts of the county heard that their truly beloved leader was trapped in a house surrounded by red-shirts, and that his life was in danger. Every colored man and women seized whatever was at hand—guns, axes, hoes, etc., and ran to the rescue. By six o'clock afternoon a thousand negroes were approaching the town, and the red-shirts thought it best to gallop away . . . Smalls thinks this attack was caused by Hampton [*Wade Hampton, Democratic governor of South Carolina*] saying there was but one man now he thought *ought* to be got out of the way, and that man was Robert Smalls. . . .

/////

July 9, 1884   . . . I had a very pleasant trip down, in the long freight train, which was just as fast as the passenger train, and two hours earlier. . . . That old plague, the North Penn conductor, came and talked to me a long time at Yemassee. He says the Reading has bought the Newtown, and is going to make a connection between Fern Rock and Bethaires which will cut off nine miles of the distance to New York. He said the whole race of niggers ought to be swept away, and I told him my business was with that race and that they would never be swept away, so he was disgusted and went away, leaving me to read in peace.

[This is the last entry in the diary.]

Questions for Discussion

1. In what ways do Laura Towne's opinions seem to change during her years on the islands? In what ways do they remain the same?
2. What can you learn from the diary about the attitudes and culture of the former slaves?
3. What appears to be the Southern white attitude toward African-American equality?